Air Fryer Cookbook

2100 days of tasty, healthy and wholesome recipes to prepare in less than 20 minutes. Including 60-days meal plan

Ethan Taylor Johnson

Copyright © 2024 by Ethan Taylor Johnson © 2024 by

Ethan Taylor Johnson. All right reserved.

No part of this book may be used or reproduced in any manner whatsoever without written permission except in the casa of brief quotations embodied in critical articles and reviews.

1.1 Introduction 13
1.2 Embracing the Air Fryer Revolution 13
1.2 Health Benefits & Nutritional Perks 13
1.3 Tips and Tricks for Air Fryer Mastery 14
2. The Basics of Air Frying 17
2.1 Essential Air Fryer Tools 17
2.2 Understanding Temperature and Timing 18
2.3 Ingredient Selection and Preparation 19
3. Breakfast Delights 22
3.1 Quick and Nutritious Morning Treats 22
3.1.1 Crispy Granola Clusters 22
3.1.2 Avocado Toast with a Twist 23
3.1.3 Banana Pancake Bites 24
3.1.4 Stuffed Breakfast Peppers 25
3.1.5 Crispy Breakfast Burritos 27
3.1.6 Fruit-Filled Morning Pastries 28
3.1.7 Healthy Veggie Frittata 29
3.2 Weekend Brunch Specials 31
3.2.1 Mediterranean Shakshuka with Feta and Fresh Herbs. ... 31
3.2.2 Crispy Chicken and Waffles with Maple Syrup Drizzle ... 32
3.2.3 Air Fryer Breakfast Burritos 34
3.2.4 Lemon Blueberry Scones with Vanilla Glaze 36
3.2.5 Spinach and Mushroom Quesadillas for Breakfast 37
3.2.6 Creamy Vanilla French Toast with Caramelized Bananas ... 39
3.2.7 BLT Sandwiches with the Garlic Aioli for Breakfast 41
3. Sweet Beginnings and Savory Egg Dishes 44
3.3.1 The Cinnamon Roll Pancakes that are Loaded with Cream Cheese Drizzle.
3.3.2 Moroccan-Spiced Vegetable Tagine 46
3.3.3 Stuffed Breakfast Peppers with Sausage and Cheese ... 48
3.3.4 Savory Spinach and Feta Quiche with a Flaky Crust 49
3.3.5 Cheddar and bacon breakfast burritos with chipotle mayo ... 51
3.3.6 Sweet Potato Hash with Poached Eggs and Avocado ... 52
3.3.7 Sausage and Veggie Breakfast Strata with Herbed Breadcrumbs ... 54
4. Appetizers and Snacks 56
4.1 Crispy Bites and Party Favorites 56
4.1.1 Crispy Baked Zucchini Fritters 56

- 4.1.2 Parmesan and Garlic Roasted Chickpeas 58
- 4.1.3 .Crispy Brussels Sprouts with Balsamic Glaze 59
- 4.1.4 Honey and Spicy Asian Chicken Wings 61
- 4.1.5 Loaded Potato Skins with Bacon and Cheddar 62
- 4.1.6 Crispy Coconut Shrimp with Mango Salsa 63
- 4.1.7 Stuffed Jalapeño Poppers with Cream Cheese 65

4. 2 Healthy Nibbles and Dips 67
- 4.2.1 Air Fryer Crunchy Kale Chips with Herbed Yogurt Dip 67
- 4.2.2 Spicy Edamame with Sesame-Ginger Dipping Sauce 68
- 4.2.3 Sweet Potato Hummus with Crispy Chickpea Toppers 70
- 4.2.4 Spicy Lemon-Pepper Zucchini Sticks 72
- 4.2.5 Roasted Beetroot and Garlic Dip with Multi-Seed Crackers 73
- 4.2.6 Cumin-Spiced Carrot Fries with Avocado Aioli 74
- 4.2.7 Smoked Paprika Cauliflower Bites with Blue Cheese Dip 76

4.3 Vegetarian Pleasers 78
- 4.3.1 Stuffed Portobello Mushrooms Air-Fried 78
- 4.3.2 Crispy Tofu and Veggie Spring Rolls 79
- 4.3.3 Curried Vegetable Samosas 80
- 4.3.4 Balsamic Glazed Brussels Sprouts 81
- 4.3.5 Mediterranean Stuffed Peppers 82
- 4.3.6 Garlic herb air fryer falafel 83
- 4.3.7 Cheesy Broccoli and Corn Fritters 84

5. Meat and Poultry Magic 86
5.1 Chicken and Turkey Creations 86
- 5.1.1 Herbed chicken and mushroom skewers 86
- 5.1.2 Crispy Turkey Cutlets with Lemon-Caper Sauce 87
- 5.1.3 Spicy Orange Glazed Chicken Wings 88
- 5.1.4 Garlic-Lemon Roasted Turkey Breast 90
- 5.1.5 Chicken Piccata with Capers 91
- 5.1.6 Maple-Dijon Turkey Meatballs 92
- 5.1.7 .Szechuan Pepper Chicken with Stir-Fried Vegetables 93

5.2 Beef and Pork Classics Reinvented 96
- 5.2.1 .Smokey BBQ Beef Brisket Sliders 96
- 5.2.2 Herb-Crusted Pork Tenderloin with Apple Chutney 97
- 5.2.3 Korean-Style Beef Bulgogi Wraps 99
- 5.2.4 Italian Stuffed Pork Loin with Balsamic Glaze 100

  5.2.5 Spiced Beef Kofta with Tzatziki 101

  5.2.6 Slow Cooked Pulled Pork with Tangy Coleslaw 103

  5.2.7 Balsamic Glazed Steak Rolls with Vegetables 104

5.3 Quick and Easy Meaty Morsels 106

  5.3.1 Honey-Mustard Glazed Ham Bites 106

  5.3.2 Mini Meatball Skewers with Tomato Sauce 107

  5.3.3 Quick BBQ Pork Riblets 108

  5.3.4 Chicken Satay with Peanut Sauce 109

  5.3.5 Spiced Lamb Kebabs with Yogurt Sauce 111

  5.3.6 Teriyaki Beef Strips with Sesame Seeds 112

  5.3.7 Buffalo Chicken Poppers with Blue Cheese Dip 113

6. Fish and Seafood Sensations 116

6.1 Light and Flavorful Fish Dishes 116

  6.1.1 Lemon-Herb Baked Cod with Zucchini 116

  6.1.2 Chili-Lime Tilapia with Mango Salsa 117

  6.1.3 Parmesan Crusted Halibut with Lemon Butter. 119

  6.1.4 - Ginger-Soy Glazed Salmon filets 120

  6.1.5 Herbed Tuna Steaks with Olive Tapenade 121

  6.1.6 Cajun-Spiced Catfish and Corn Relish 123

  6.1.7 Maple-Mustard Glazed Trout with Asparagus 125

6.2 Shrimp, Scallops and More 127

  6.2.1 Garlic Butter Shrimp with Herbed Couscous 127

  6.2.2 Seared Scallops with Creamy Polenta 128

  6.2.3 Spicy Cajun Shrimp Skewers 130

  6.2.4 Cajun-Spiced Catfish with Corn Relish 131

  6.2.5 Honey-Lime Tilapia with Zesty Quinoa 133

  6.2.6 Coconut-Coated Shrimp with Pineapple Salsa 134

  6.2.7 Garlic Lemon Scallops with Spinach 136

6.3 Seafood Snacks and Appetizers 138

  6.3.1 Crispy Calamari with Spicy Marinara 138

  6.3.2 Smoked Salmon and Cream Cheese Pinwheels 139

  6.3.3 Coconut Shrimp with Mango Salsa 141

  6.3.4 Crab-Stuffed Mushrooms 143

  6.3.5 Oysters Kilpatrick 144

  6.3.6 Zucchini and Corn Fritters with Spicy Aioli 145

  6.3.7 Garlic and Herb Mussels 147

7. Vegetarian and Vegan Varieties ... 148
7.1 Plant-Based Main Courses ... 148
- 7.1.1 Falafel Platter with Tahini Sauce ... 148
- 7.1.2 Spicy Sweet Potato and Black Bean Tacos ... 150
- 7.1.3 Grilled Portobello Mushroom Steaks ... 151
- 7.1.4 Vegan Shepherd's Pie with Lentils ... 152
- 7.1.5 Stuffed Bell Peppers with Quinoa and Black Beans ... 154
- 7.1.6 Ratatouille with Herbed Couscous ... 156
- 7.1.7 Moroccan-Spiced Vegetable Tagine: ... 157

7.2 Vegan Snacks and Sides ... 160
- 7.2.1 Air Fryer Avocado Fries ... 160
- 7.2.2 Air Fryer Vegan Cauliflower Buffalo Wings ... 161
- 7.2.3 Black Bean and Sweet Potato Taquitos: ... 164
- 7.2.4 Crispy chickpeas and roasted peppers bites: ... 165
- 7.2.5 Roasted Brussels Sprouts with Balsamic Glaze and Garlic: ... 167
- 7.2.6 Stuffed Mushrooms with Pesto and Pine Nuts ... 168
- 7.2.7 Vegan Mozzarella Sticks and Marinara Dip ... 169

7.3 Tofu and Tempeh Innovations ... 172
- 7.3.1 Smoky BBQ Tempeh Ribs: ... 172
- 7.3.2 Crispy Tofu Nuggets with Sweet Chili Sauce ... 173
- 7.3.3 Tempeh and Vegetable Stir-Fry with Peanut Sauce ... 175
- 7.3.4 Tofu Tikka Masala ... 177
- 7.3.5 Balsamic-Glazed Tempeh Steaks ... 179
- 7.3.6 Szechuan Tofu and Peppers with Peanuts ... 181
- 7.3.7 Teriyaki Tempeh and Pineapple Skewers ... 184

8. Sides and Salads ... 186
8.1. Vegetables and Potatoes Air Fryer ... 186
- 8.1.1 Herbed Root Vegetable Medley ... 186
- 8.1.2 Spicy Cajun Sweet Potato Wedges ... 187
- 8.1.3 Balsamic Glazed Carrot and Parsnip Fries ... 188
- 8.1.4 Crispy Brussels Sprouts with Parmesan, ... 190
- 8.1.5 Rosemary and Garlic Roasted Baby Potatoes ... 191
- 8.1.6 Caramelized Rutabaga Fries with Honey Mustard ... 192
- 8.1.7 Smoky Paprika Cauliflower Steaks ... 193

8.2 Fresh and Zesty Salads ... 196
- 8.2.1 Kale and Quinoa Salad ... 196

    8.2.2 Air Fried Caprese Salad 198
    8.2.3 Crispy Asparagus and Strawberry Salad 199
    8.2.4 Air Fryer Falafel Salad 200
    8.2.5 Sweet Potato and Quinoa Salad with Crunchy Cashew 202
    8.2.6 Air-fried halloumi and watermelon salad 204
    8.2.7 Crispy Chickpea and Roasted Vegetable Salad 206
  8.3 Grains and Legume Dishes **209**
    8.3.1 Crunchy Air Fryer Risotto Balls 209
    8.3.2 Fried Garlic Herb Couscous 210
    8.3.3 Lentil and Vegetable Patties 212
    8.3.4 Black Bean and Corn Quinoa Salad 213
    8.3.5 Spiced Lentil Stew with Tomatoes 215
    8.3.6 Sweet Potato and Chickpea Hash 216
    8.3.7 Wild Rice with Cranberries and Pecans 217

9. Breads and Pastries **219**
  9.1 Homemade Breads and Rolls **219**
    9.1.1 Olive and Rosemary Focaccia 219
    9.1.2 Whole Wheat Walnut Bread 220
    9.1.3 Cheddar and Chive Buttermilk Biscuits 221
    9.I.5 Garlic and Herb Tear Apart Bread 223
    9.1.6 Cranberry Orange Pecan Loaf 224
    9.1.7 Sourdough Baguettes 225
  9.2 Sweet Pastries and Desserts **227**
    9. 2.1 Raspberry Almond Frangipane Tart 227
    9.2.2 Chocolate Chip Brioche Rolls 229
    9.2.3 Lemon Curd Danish Pastries 230
    9.2.4 Apricot and Pistachio Pinwheels 231
    9.2.5 Cinnamon Sugar Palmiers 232
    9.2.6 Blueberry Cream Cheese Strudel 233
    9.2.7 Cherry and Almond Galette 235
  9.3 Savory Pies and Quiches **237**
    9.3.1 Tart of Roasted Vegetable and Goat Cheese 237
    9.3.2 Spinach, Feta, and Pine Nut Phyllo Pie 238
    9.3.3 Caramelized Onion and Gruyere Quiche 240
    9.3.4 Broccoli and Cheddar Hand Pies 241
    9.3.5 Prosciutto and Arugula Quiche 242

  9.3.6 Mushroom and Leek Galette 243
  9.3.7 Tomato, Basil and Mozzarella Tart 245
10 The 60-Day Meal Plan **247**
 10.1 Weekly Meal Planners 247
 10.2 Shopping Lists and Prep Guides 249
 10.3 Balanced Meal Ideas 251
11. Troubleshooting and FAQs **296**
 11.1 Common Air Fryer Issues 296
 11.2 Maintenance and Cleaning Tips 297
13. Conclusion **299**

1.1 Introduction

1.2 Embracing the Air Fryer Revolution

So you got an Air Fryer in your kitchen and you are not sure why people are making such a big deal out of it!Let me put it this way: it has changed the way we cook in dramatic fashion and it's not going away – an immediate culinary game changer and revolutionary kitchen gadget we'll walk through below.

Picture some of the filling meals that are made from deep frying, only with much less oil. That is precisely what an Air Fryer does- pure magic! It circulates hot air around your food, making the outside crispy and the inside juicy, meaning you will get the best of both worlds for taste and health! It is indeed a win-win situation for taste buds and bodies!

However, what is your reason for joining this revolution? First of all, it is all about the possibility of eating your favorite fried meals without a sense of guilt. Imagine those delicious fries, golden onion rings, or even crispy chicken wings – with just a fraction of the oil used in regular deep frying. Your waistline will be grateful and you will not have to suffer from the heavy feeling of eating greasy food. And it's not even only about indulging yourself without guilt. When it comes to saving time in the kitchen, the Air Fryer is a superhero. No longer, however, must people wait for oil to warm up or deal with the oily mess of deep frying. With the Air Fryer, you are one button away from having a meal ready in minutes.

Now, you might be thinking, "Does it sacrifice flavor for healthiness?" Absolutely not! In fact, many users swear that their Air Fryer creations taste even better than the traditional versions. The hot air circulation ensures that your food is cooked evenly and retains its natural flavors. You'll be amazed by the culinary wonders you can achieve.
So, consider this chapter your initiation into the Air Fryer club. We're about to explore the ins and outs of this revolutionary kitchen appliance, and by the time you're done, you'll be a bona fide Air Fryer enthusiast. Get ready to embrace the Air Fryer revolution with open arms – your taste buds are in for a treat!

1.2 Health Benefits & Nutritional Perks

Now is the time to explore all of its health and nutritional advantages as an effective means
of cooking for optimal well-being. As you use your Air Fryer as your culinary friend, you are committing yourself to a healthier diet. And since less oil is used as compared to the traditional frying methods, unnecessary fats and calories will be reduced to a great extent; hence, you can indulge in golden and crispy treats without feeling guilty!

What distinguishes an Air Fryer from the traditional deep fryer is that the nutritional value of the ingredients is retained. On one hand, oil will take away all vitamins and nutrients from vegetables and proteins but, on the other hand, hot air circulation will seal all these goodies inside as an insurance against losing them during cooking!

However, the regular frying at high temperatures allows the formation of acrylamide, which is very harmful to health. However, Air Fryers work on much lower temperatures and therefore reduce the risk of acrylamide formation so you can enjoy your favorite treats without having to worry about health concerns!

The Air Fryer simplifies the culinary decision by making home-cooked foods more available and easier to prepare, which are more likely to be made of healthy ingredients and which allows trying tastes and recipes never tried before! This is equally good for health and flavor!

Consider the environment when choosing your cooking method! An Air Fryer is an environment-friendly cooking bid as it consumes less power than the traditional ovens – thus the earth is saved in the name of conservation of energy! By just doing this little thing, you would be getting huge environmental benefits!

1.3 Tips and Tricks for Air Fryer Mastery

Have you just joined the Air Fryer revolution and are eagerly awaiting its health benefits and nutritional advantages? Now let's give you all of the tips and tricks necessary for mastery Air Frying.

1. Preheat for Success

Just like an oven, when using an Air Fryer it is essential to preheat so that you have that initial even cook and the crispiness that you love. If your model has a preheat function, be sure to use it.

2. Avoid Overcrowding

Here are some of the common mistakes that people make when using an air fryer. Crowding the Basket can cause uneven cooking, ensuring enough space between foods that air can flow for crispy perfection. If you are interested in preparing big batches at a time, you may divide your cooking sessions into parts to get the best out of it.

3. Give the Food a Shake

To get even cooking results, make sure to shake your food halfway through the process so that all sides are equally exposed to hot air – this will allow for uniform crispness! Consider it as affording all parties equal opportunities.
Win the hearts of new customers as you air fry with this amazing cooking method!

4. Apply Oil

Since air frying uses far less oil to cook food than traditional deep-frying methods do, a little spritz of oil before they hit the hot basket can make them delightfully crunchy and add that perfect hint of flavor – ideal for air frying! This crucial liquid should be applied using the cooking spray or brush before air frying starts as both methods are effective in delivering it evenly! To obtain the best outcome, start with applying it first and let it set in before air frying starts!

5. Play Around With Seasonings

An Air Fryer offers an amazing chance to try different seasonings and tastes. Be creative, play around with different combinations that enhance the taste of your meals and make them special to you!

6. Monitor Timing

Air fryers cook fast, and it is therefore important to take note of their cooking duration especially for fragile foods. It is best to follow your recipe's suggested timing and make any necessary adjustments at the first sign of trouble; after all, you are in control!

7. Make Smart Additions

Air Fryers are supplemented with such elements as racks, skewers, and baking pans that enable you to go far beyond the mere potato fries or chicken wings by making kebabs, roast vegetables or even allowing you to bake cakes!

8. Stay Curious
Utilize your Air Fryer to the fullest by trying out different recipes and methods with your Air Fryer. With every experiment you perform, its possibilities also manifest themselves and become more obvious' do not hesitate to test it for all that it is capable of in order to find out the potential your creations possess!

2. The Basics of Air Frying

2.1 Essential Air Fryer Tools

Before you embark on your air frying journey, it is vital that you have the right tools. Let your Air Fryer be the center of attraction, with these must-have tools taking their places as supporting actors. Every tool plays a vital role not only for the preparation of palatable dishes but also makes their way from the kitchen up to the table smooth and fun!

Air Fryer Basket
The base of your air frying quest, converts the cooking process into a masterpiece. The holes in the perforated basket are specifically designed for optimal air flow around foods and ensure that they will always cook to perfection – crisp, golden brown each time you use it The non-stick coating on the basket adds a lot of ease to both cooking with this accessory and then cleaning it afterwards – all adding up to great results when used properly!

Cooking Spray or Oil Brush
We also need specific utensils for air frying to get the same crispy effect, not much different from when we are painting a masterpiece – like cooking spray or an oil brush. With the help of these utensils, you can easily apply oil to ingredients uniformly and add the taste as well – it will also assist in achieving that perfect golden-brown exterior with a crispy and golden color. Oil brush ensures better and exact application of oil on different parts for taste improvement and texture.

Meat Thermometer
One of the key weapons in every cook's armada, when grilling meat. This tool eliminates all the guesswork out of cooking, with every bite of your meal being well-cooked, safe and packed with flavor it ensures that you achieve perfect outputs in air frying.

Food Tongs
A must-have accessory for every air fryer user, a perfect cooking buddy that offers an effortless means of handling food during the process with safety and ease, allowing you to flip and turn your favorites to ensure even results with crispiness on all sides or uniform crunch.

Oven Mitts or Silicone Gloves
Keeping safety first in the kitchen, oven mitts or silicone gloves are a must when dealing with hot surfaces like from an air fryer. Often you will have to work with parts that could be hot enough to burn; hence, these gloves are a necessary protection from burns.

Parchment Paper or Liners
Although parchment paper liners or wraps are not essentially required, they can really improve on your air frying. This is because they not only make it easy to clean but also prevent food from sticking to your basket hence making cooking much more simplified and enjoyable as a whole!

Skewers and Racks
Skewers and racks takes another step towards implementing air frying into your life by offering you more options for such culinary creations as kebabs or other roasted vegetables. In addition to this, these appliances permit you to cook multiple items on your air fryer at once and in an efficient manner; as such, they are indispensable add-ons for your air fryer arsenal.

2. 2 Understanding Temperature and Timing

Assuming that we have all the basic tools in place, let us now proceed to air frying. Knowing the temperature and time are just like learning to play musical instruments; they form the basis of your edible music.

Let's first discuss temperature. A good Air Fryer is able to circulate the hot air as efficiently as possible, and the majority of models give the users a choice between 300dF(150C)to 400 F (200°C), depending on which model you choose.

- High Temperatures: For a quick, easy supply of high-intensity heat, choose the upper end of the temperature range. This method works very well for the dishes needing crispy outsides such as French fries or even chicken wings.
- Lower Temperatures: A lower temperature, however, is needed for the fine products or when wanting to dehydrate instead of frying - whether it be fruits and herbs that are being dried.

Considering that preheating your Air Fryer is very necessary for even cooking and also crispiness in every meal, trials are welcome. Trial and error is encouraged, so preheat your oven first to find out what works for each of your recipes.

After that, let's talk about timing – the skill of knowing when and when not to begin cooking. Each dish has its own amount of cooking time, therefore it is quite necessary that you strictly follow the recipes while first using them.

- Cooking Time Frames: For foods such as shrimp or thin cuts of meat that may cook within a few minutes, for instance, one should pay close attention while being away from home to ensure the proper preparation. Do not go too far away from the kitchen!
- Medium Cooking Times: Medium cooking time for most dishes usually varies from 12 to 20 minutes, depending on the temperature and capacity of the Air Fryer. Such examples may be chicken breasts, vegetables or even frozen snacks.
- Air Frying Requires Patience: When you air fry whole chickens or larger cuts of meat, remember that the cooking times might require your patience – it may take up to half an hour.

Remember that variations such as the thickness of ingredients, amount of food in the basket and model will affect the cooking time; hence one should check on his or her food often while learning a new appliance.

Air Frying is like conducting an orchestra, trying to find the balance between heat and time while perfecting the crispy joy. So on our path, we'll find many recipes to test your skills in this gastronomy trip - so get ready to cook magic with your Air Fryer!

2.3 Ingredient Selection and Preparation

Once you've obtained all the essential tools and have mastered temperature and timing, it's time to consider the heart and soul of Air Fryer creations: ingredients This is a proper choice and preparation that makes a vast difference between making the delicious sweets or totally spoiling them.

One of the many wonderful aspects of Air Frying is its versatility: One of the greatest capabilities of an air fryer is that it can cook a diverse range of ingredients, such as vegetables, proteins and even several types of baked goods quite easily. However, air Frying does not bring all the ingredients to success with equal intensity.

- **Vegetables:** When it comes to vegetables, there are many that can be cooked in the Air Fryer including potatoes, sweet potatoes, broccoli, Brussels sprouts and even asparagus – all of these turn crispy. Only remember to make slices equal in size and the heat will be distributed evenly.
- **Proteins:** When seasoned properly and marinated beforehand, the chicken, fish, shrimp, cuts of beef or pork can all be done to perfection when air-fried. And don't forget to blot them dry before air-frying for that crispy outer crunch!
- **Frozen Foods**: Air Fryers make nice tools for making the delicious frozen foods such as chicken nuggets, mozzarella sticks and also frozen veggies that get all crispy in no time.
- **Baked Goods:** Baking can become very fun with your new Air Fryer. Muffins, cookies and even small cakes are very good when using small molds or ramekins that fit in its basket.
- **Prep is Key:** Success depends on its preparation!

Once you've selected your ingredients, it's time for the next critical step of preparation: Seasoning. Don't be afraid to include the flavors because herbs, spices, marinades and rubs are very important in preparing the delicious meals. Try different flavor combos.

- **Coating:** Even more crispiness can be obtained when coating the ingredients in breadcrumbs, panko or a light batter – very convenient for making chicken tenders and onion rings. This works well as chicken-tender substitutes or even onion ring versions.
- **Patting Dry:** It is important to pat anything you air fry down with paper towels before doing so because the excess moisture could prevent a crispy outer skin. This process guarantees a perfect outcome on every single occasion!
- **Spacing**: Do not stuff your Air Fryer basket and leave some space for the air to circulate freely so that your ingredients have enough room to breathe while they cook at their best rate. If necessary, you can cook in batches for the best results.
- **Flipping:** Make sure to flip or turn your ingredients halfway through the cooking time so that they are evenly browned and crispy on all the sides. This guarantees uniformity throughout.
- **Greasing:** For delicate ingredients that stick, such as fish filets, lightly greasing the basket or the parchment paper before placing your ingredients will prevent sticking and make cleaning much easier.

The correct ingredients and cooking techniques make the Air Frying success possible. In this chapter and further on, we will see the interesting recipes that prove its huge potential – brace yourselves for the cooking miracles that are likely to both surprise you personally as well as your dinner companions.

3. Breakfast Delights

3.1 Quick and Nutritious Morning Treats

Welcome to the amazing world of healthy and fast breakfast dishes with your Air Fryer! Breakfast can be challenging in a busy morning; but don't worry; we have compiled an elaborate compilation of mouth-watering recipes specifically for you.

The following Air Fryer recipes are meant to kick-start your morning and keep you energized until lunchtime. Our chefs have specially prepared these quick meals knowing that you are always on the go and strive to save you both, while providing delicious bursts of tasty nutrition – great for starting your busy day!

Do you Hate Boring Breakfasts? May this book lift your day and bring you a new perspective for the early hours of it when you will no longer be bound by breakfast habits. There is a delicious option here for every taste and timetable – from crunchy granola clusters and avocado toast, fluffy pancake bites and stuffed peppers steady to reveal something that fits! Prepare to have a different breakfast today and get out of the cycle!

With the help of these recipes, you can create fast, healthy and delicious breakfast moments –just get your Air Fryer ready, gather all needed ingredients and let us start a cooking adventure to turn every morning into a celebration!

3.1.1 Crispy Granola Clusters

Simply whip them up quickly in an Air Fryer for maximum freshness while providing plenty of healthy nutrients like oats, nuts and seeds - not only as an early morning treat but as an everyday breakfast too.

Ingredients for 4 servings:

- 2 cups of oats
- 1/2 cup of mixed nuts (almonds, walnuts, or your choice)
- 1/4 cup of seeds (chia, flaxseed, etc.)
- 1/4 cup of honey or maple syrup
- 1 teaspoon of cinnamon

Instructions:

In a large mixing bowl, mix oats, mixed nuts, seeds, honey (or maple syrup) and cinnamon. Stir until all the ingredients are evenly coated.

- Heat your Air Fryer to 325°F (1630C for about 2-3 minutes.
- Place the liner in your Air Fryer basket or line it with parchment paper for hassle-free cleanup.
- Arrange the granola mixture in the lined basket evenly. Do not overcrowd; this may require doing it in batches depending on the size of your Air Fryer.
- Air fry the granola clusters at 163°C for about five to seven minutes. It is necessary to keep an eye on them in order not to over-brown them. You can also shake the basket or stir this granola halfway through to ensure even baking.
- When the granola clusters are golden brown and crunchy to your preference, take them out of the Air Fryer.
- Let them sit in the basket for a few minutes to cool; they will continue to harden as they cool.
- Once completely cold, break the granola into clusters.

Cooking Tips:

- Personalize your granola clusters by incorporating raisins, cranberries, or apricots towards the end of air frying.
- Keep the granola clusters crisp by storing them in an airtight container.

3.1.2 Avocado Toast with a Twist

This delectable breakfast staple gives the traditional avocado toast a new direction with an Air Fryer turn. Over warm and slightly crunchy avocado slices on whole-grain toast with a perfectly poached or fried egg, it is a great way to start the day's protein addition. Let's be artistic and turn your breakfast into a real work of art.

Ingredients for 2 servings:

- 2 ripe avocados
- Salt and pepper to taste
- Paprika for seasoning

- four whole-grain bread slices
- 2 poached or fried eggs

Instructions:

- Cut the ripe avocados and take out their pits. Take a spoon and scoop the flesh of an avocado out into a bowl.
- Salt, pepper, and a pinch of paprika must be added to the slices of avocado. Mix gently to coat evenly.
- Heat your Air Fryer to 325°F (163°C) for 2-3 minutes.
- Insert the seasoned avocado slices in an Air Fryer basket arranged uniformly.
- Fry the avocado slices in an air fryer at 325°F (163°C) for around 3-5 minutes until warm and lightly crisp. Monitor them to avoid burning them.
- As the avocados are air frying, toast the whole-grain bread slices in a toaster until they turn golden brown.
- When the avocados are done, take them out of the Air Fryer.
- Spread warm, crisped avocado slices on the toasted slice.
- Finish each avocado toast with a poached or fried egg.
- Add more salt, pepper and paprika to eggs if preferred.

Cooking Tips:

- You can also add other toppings such as slices of tomatoes, red pepper flakes, or a dash of hot sauce to your avocado toast.
- To make it more flavorful you can add grated cheese on top of the avocado prior to frying in the air.

3.1.3 Banana Pancake Bites

These snack bites are perfect when you're craving pancakes but don't have the required time to prepare a full stack. These little Air Fryer pancake bites cook quickly, and inside they are really light and airy with a slight crispness outside. They are great to set up your day with a fresh taste. Let us jump into this recipe because every bite of our breakfast brings a lot of happiness.

Ingredients for 4 servings:

- A cup of your best pancake batter mix.
- 2 ripe bananas, mashed
- Fresh berries for garnish (optional)
- Maple syrup for dipping

Instructions:

- Combine the pancake batter mix with the mashed ripe bananas in a bowl. Mix until the batter is very homogeneous.
- Start the air fryer, and preheat it at 350°F (175°C) for about 2-3 minutes.
- It is recommended to grease the Air Fryer basket or use parchment paper so that the food does not stick.
- Using a spoon, drop small amounts of the banana pancake batter into the basket of the Air Fryer and then shape it to form bite-sized rounds. Ensure each bite has adequate space for even cooking.
- When the temperature is 350°F (175°C), place the pancake bites into an air fryer for cooking; wait until they turn golden brown and crunchy. Nevertheless, cooking time will have to be adjusted depending on the capacity of your Air Fryer and also the sizes of bites.
- Carefully remove the pancake bites from the Air Fryer and allow them to cool for a minute.
- Garnish with some fresh berries if you desire.
- Serve the Banana Pancake Bites with a side of maple syrup for the dipping.

Cooking Tips:

- Get creative with your toppings! In addition to the berries, you may also desire a spoonful of yogurt or some chocolate chips and honey for the taste.
- Be sure to mash the bananas properly so that they mix very well into the pancake batter.

3.1.4 Stuffed Breakfast Peppers

These colorful, fruity peppers are the best start of your day with a taste of healthy goodness. Cutting the bell peppers in half, removing the seeds and filling them with scrambled eggs, diced vegetables sautéed with bacon fat and a pinch of cheese will result in an excellent, colorful breakfast full of nutrients. So let's get down this recipe and add some touch of gourmet to your breakfast.

Ingredients for 4 servings:

- 2 large bell peppers (red, yellow, or green)
- 4 large eggs
- 1/2 cup of diced vegetables (bell peppers, onions, spinach, etc.)
- 1/4 cup of shredded cheese (cheddar, mozzarella, or your choice)
- Salt and pepper to taste
- Cooking spray or a light brushing of oil

Instructions:

- Cut the bell peppers vertically into halves, remove seeds and membranes so you keep four empty pepper halves.
- Beat eggs in a bowl, add salt and pepper.
- Heat your Air Fryer to 350°F (175°C) for 2-3 minutes.
- Use oil or a cooking spray to grease the Air Fryer basket.
- The bell pepper halves should be put into the Air Fryer basket.
- Divide the diced vegetables accordingly between each pepper half.
- After seasoning and whisking the eggs, pour them over each half of all the peppers.
- Top each stuffed pepper with shredded cheese.
- The stuffed peppers are air fried at 350°F (175°C) for about 10-12 minutes until the eggs are set and the peppers have softened.
- Delicately take out the stuffed breakfast peppers from the Air Fryer and allow it to cool for about one minute before serving.

Cooking Tips:

- You have the option to alter your filling by adding cooked bacon bits, sausage or herbs for more aroma.
- If you want a hard yolk, air fry for an extra two to three minutes.

3.1.5 Crispy Breakfast Burritos

For the lovers of savory morning breakfast, these burritos will be an ideal treat. With the help of corn or wheat tortillas wrapped around your favorite breakfast ingredients, you are going to have Air Fryer style crispy, golden, and portable breakfast burritos.

Ingredients for 4 servings:

- 4 large flour tortillas
- 8 large eggs
- 1/2 cup of cooked and crumbled breakfast sausage or your choice of protein.
- 1/2 cup bell pepper dices
- 1/2 cup of diced onions
- Half a cup of shredded cheese (cheddar, Monterey Jack or your favorite)
- Salt and pepper to taste
- Either a few sprays of cooking spray or lightly brush oil

Instructions:

- In a bowl, beat the eggs together with salt and pepper.
- Heat your Air Fryer to 350°F (175°C) for up to 2-3 minutes.
- Apply cooking spray or a very light coat of oil to the Air Fryer basket.
- Lay a tortilla and in the center place scrambled eggs, cooked sausage, diced bell peppers, onions and shredded cheese.
- Fold the sides of the tortilla together and then roll it up to make a burrito. Repeat the same for the remaining tortillas and filling.
- Place the burritos in the basket of the Air Fryer with seam side down and place them uniformly.
- Air fry the burritos at 350°F (175°C) for about 6-8 minutes or until they turn golden brown and crispy.
- Remove the crispy breakfast burritos from the Air Fryer carefully and let them stay for a minute before serving.

Cooking Tips:

- You may add other ingredients to your breakfast burritos such as tomatoes, salsa, avocado or sour cream.
- These burritos can be prepped in advance and reheated in the Air Fryer for a speedy breakfast on hectic mornings.

3.1.6 Fruit-Filled Morning Pastries

Everyone would enjoy beginning their day with these pastries sweetness and an explosion of fruit juice. These pastries are easy to make in your Air Fryer, flaky and delicious treats for the morning. If you have one with your coffee or grab them as a snack on the go, they will surely make an excellent start to the day. Let us take a look at this recipe and enjoy the happiness of homemade breakfast pastry.

Ingredients for 4 servings:

- sheet of puff pastry (thawed)
- 1 cup of sliced fruits (apples, pears, or berries)
- 2 tablespoons of granulated sugar
- 1/2 teaspoon of ground cinnamon
- 1 egg (beaten, for egg wash)
- Powdered sugar for dusting (optional)

Instructions:

- Heat your Air Fryer to 350°F (175°C) for 2-3 minutes prior to using it.
- Flour lightly some working surface and roll out the puff pastry sheet into a square or rectangle.
- Use a knife to cut the pastry into four equal squares or rectangles.
- In a bowl, mix the sliced fruits with granulated sugar and ground cinnamon. Toss to coat fruits evenly.
- Place some of the fruit mixture in the center of each pastry square.
- Wrap the pastry around the fruits to form either a triangular or rectangular shape. Seal the sides by using a fork.
- The beaten egg can be brushed on the surface of the pastries to make them shine like gold.
- As required, gently set the fruit-filled pastries in the Air Fryer basket with space between each.
- Cook the pastries in an air fryer at a temperature of 350°F (175°C) for 8-10 minutes until they turn puffy and golden brown.
- After they are cooked in the Air Fryer, take out the pastries and allow them to cool for a few minutes.
- You can also sprinkle it with powdered sugar before serving.

Cooking Tips:

- You can try different flavors of fruits such as blueberries, strawberries or peaches.
- These pastries are best served hot for the most amazing taste and consistency.

3.1.7 Healthy Veggie Frittata

The frittata is a great way to have an incredible morning meal that is healthy with fresh vegetables and protein. Join me to discuss this recipe and wake up your mornings with some deliciousness!

Ingredients for 4 servings:

- 6 large eggs
- 1/2 cup of diced bell peppers (red, green, or your choice)
- 1/2 cup of diced onions
- 1/2 cup of diced tomatoes
- 1/2 cup of chopped spinach or kale
- 1/2 cup of shredded cheese (your favorite)
- Salt and pepper to taste
- Cooking spray or a light brushing of oil

Instructions:

- Beat the eggs in a bowl and season them with some salt and pepper.
- Turn on your Air Fryer and preheat it to 350°F (175°C) for about 2-3 minutes.
- It is greased with cooking spray or you can lightly oil the Air Fryer basket.
- In a separate bowl, combine the diced bell peppers, onions, tomatoes and also spinach or kale.
- Mix the vegetable mixture with the whisked seasoned eggs.
- Arrange the egg and vegetable mixture in an even layer at the bottom of the Air Fryer basket.
- Arrange the shredded cheese over the frittata.
- Fry the frittata in an air fryer at a temperature of 350°F (175°C) for around ten minutes to twelve minutes or until it is firm and has golden brown edges.
- Cautiously put it out of the Air Fryer and let it stand for a minute before slicing it.
- Cooking Tips:

- You may make the frittata according to your own taste of vegetables, herbs or spices.
- The frittata can be sliced and served alongside some fresh fruit or you can also add a salad to make it a full meal.

3.2 Weekend Brunch Specials

Brunch is that wonder meal where breakfast meets lunch and gives birth to a wonderful culinary treat. It is the golden hour when one can enjoy savory meals, great company, and a slow morning. In this section, we have chosen some recipes that will turn your weekend brunch into a special celebration.

Our Air Fryer recipes will make your weekend brunch extravaganza's with mouthwatering quiches and savory pies, sweet pastries, and indulgent desserts. In any case, whether you are hosting friends and loved ones or just indulging yourself in a delicious meal these dishes will complement your brunch table with some gourmet spirit.

That is why, prepare to discover interesting brunch recipes that are easy to make, so you can enjoy the tastes and the atmosphere. Let's venture into this section and enjoy the weekends as culinary feasts!

3.2.1 Mediterranean Shakshuka with Feta and Fresh Herbs.

Shakshuka is a popular Middle Eastern and Mediterranean dish that refers to the lush, fragrant tomato sauce mixed with poached eggs cooked with spices. In this brunch mix, we have transformed the age-old Shakshuka , by adding creamy feta cheese and fresh herbs, producing a chorus of flavors that will tickle your tongue. However, whether having guests or relaxing on sunday morning, this brunch is a feast of flavors. With this recipe, let us explore the Mediterranean and make it a part of your weekend experience!

Ingredients for 4 servings:

- 2 tablespoons of olive oil
- 1 onion, finely chopped
- 2 cloves of garlic, minced
- 1 red bell pepper, diced
- 1 yellow bell pepper, diced
- 14-ounce can of crushed tomatoes
- 1 teaspoon of ground cumin
- 1 teaspoon of smoked paprika
- 1/2 teaspoon of chili powder (this can be adjusted to taste)
- Salt and pepper to taste

- 4 large eggs
- ½ cup of feta cheese crumbled
- Garnish of fresh herbs (cilantro or parsley)
- For serving, bread – crusty or pita.

Instructions:

- Heat up the olive oil in a big, oven-proof skillet or pan on medium heat.
- Add onion, and sauté until translucent, 3-4 minutes.
- Add the minced garlic, diced red bell pepper and diced yellow bell pepper. Cook 3 to 4 minutes more until the peppers start to become soft.
- Stir in the diced tomatoes, cumin, smoked paprika and chili pepper. Season with salt and pepper. Mix well all the ingredients.
- Simmer the sauce for 10-15 minutes until it thickens and melds its flavors.
- Four indentations should be made in the tomato sauce and gently cradle an egg into each.
- On top of the sauce and eggs sprinkle crumbled feta cheese.
- Set your Air Fryer to 350°F (175°C) and air fry for 6-8 minutes until the egg whites are cooked through but the yolks are still soft.
- With caution, take the skillet out of the Air Fryer and let it sit for a minute.
- Adorn your Mediterranean Shakshuka with chopped herbs like cilantro or parsley and accompany it with crusty bread or pita for dunking.

Cooking Tips:

- Use the amount of chili powder according to your liking for spice.
- Since Shakshuka is usually served straight out of the skillet, ensure that your pan is oven-friendly.

3.2.2 Crispy Chicken and Waffles with Maple Syrup Drizzle

This delicious mix of crunchy fried chicken, soft waffles, and sweet maple syrup is a decadent merger of salty and sugary tastes. If you are celebrating a particular event or indulging in Sunday's brunch of luxury, this dish will tickle your fancy and fill you with craving. So, let's explore this recipe and take your brunch to an altogether new level with this mouthwatering dish!

Ingredients for 4 servings:

For the Chicken:

- 4 boneless, skinless chicken breasts
- 1 cup of buttermilk
- 1 cup of AP flour.
- 1 teaspoon of paprika
- 1 teaspoon of garlic powder
- ½ teaspoon of cayenne pepper (to taste)
- Salt and pepper to taste
- Cooking oil for frying

For the Waffles:

- 2 cups of prepared waffle mix
- A spray of cooking oil or a light brushing using the waffle iron
- For the Maple Syrup Drizzle:
- 1/2 cup of maple syrup
- 1/4 cup of unsalted butter
- 1/2 teaspoon of vanilla extract

Instructions:

For the Chicken:

- Buttermilk should be poured onto the chicken breasts in a bowl. Let them marinate for a minimum of 30 minutes or longer if possible.
- In a different bowl, mix the all-purpose flour, paprika, garlic powder, cayenne pepper, salt and black pepper.
- Set the temperature of your Air Fryer at 375°F (190°C) and heat for about 2-3 minutes.
- Shake off any excess buttermilk from each chicken breast.
- Coat the chicken breasts with the seasoned flour mixture, making sure that they are completely covered.
- Arrange the breaded chicken breasts in the Air Fryer basket so that they are equally spread.

- Cook the chicken breasts in an air fryer for 15-18 minutes at a temperature of 375°F (190°C), or until lightly browned and cooked all the way through. The chicken should be cooked to an internal temperature of 165°F (74°C).
- Gently take the crispy chicken away from the Air Fryer, and let it rest for a bit.

For the Waffles:

- With the chicken cooking, make your waffles following what is stated on the package in a waffle iron. Ensure that they are golden and crispy.

For the Maple Syrup Drizzle:

- Then, in a small saucepan, mix the maple syrup with an unsalted butter and vanilla extract. Simmer over low heat, keeping the mixture warm while stirring until all butter is melted.
- Remove the map syrup from the heat and save it for later.

Assembly:

- Put a piece of crispy chicken breast over the waffle.
- Spread the warm maple syrup mixture liberally over the chicken and waffles.
- Enjoy the delectable infusion of flavors and textures as you serve your Crispy Chicken and Waffles with Maple Syrup Drizzle right away.

Cooking Tips:

- The amount of cayenne pepper added to the flour mixture should be adjusted according to the level of spiciness desired.
- While doing the rest of the chicken, you can keep it warm in a low temperature oven.

3.2.3 Air Fryer Breakfast Burritos

Our Air Fryer Breakfast Burritos should get you up and out with a blast of flavor and energy to start the day. This hearty burrito is stuffed with scrambled eggs, crisp bacon, sautéed bell peppers and onions oozing cheese wrapped in a warm tortilla. It makes them nice and crispy, therefore an ideal treat for a morning breakfast.

Ingredients for 4 Servings:

- 6 large eggs
- 4 large flour tortillas
- 4 bacon strips cooked and crumbled
- 1 red bell pepper, diced
- 1/2 onion, finely chopped
- 1 cup shredded cheddar cheese
- Salt and black pepper, as required
- Cooking spray

Instructions:

- In a bowl, beat the eggs until light and foamy. Salt and pepper it to taste.
- Cook the red bell pepper and onions in a skillet over medium heat. Cook them until they soften and slightly caramelize.
- Beat the eggs and add to the skillet with sautéed vegetables. Cook and scramble the eggs until they are not runny, but still moist. Remove from heat.
- Put the tortilla onto a clean surface. In the middle of a tortilla, spoon out a scoop of scrambled eggs.
- Top the eggs with pieces of crumbled bacon and shredded cheddar cheese.
- The tortilla is then folded over the filling and rolled up tightly into a burrito. Repeat this for the remaining tortillas and filling.
- Turn on your air fryer and preheat it to 350°F (175°C).
- Lightly coat the basket of an air fryer with cooking spray.
- Arrange the breakfast burritos with their seams facing down in the air fryer basket so that they are not touching each other.
- 4 – 6 minutes for air frying the burritos when they are crispy golden brown on the outside.
- Use caution to take out of the air fryer and cool down lightly before serving Air Fryer Breakfast Burritos.
- These great tasting breakfast burritos can be served with the salsa, hot sauce or sour cream of your choice.
- Start your day right and make sure you have a satisfying and crispy Air Fryer Breakfast Burritos.

Cooking Tips:

- By all means, you can choose your favorite filling of sautéed mushrooms, spinach along with diced tomatoes.
- These breakfast burritos can be made ahead and frozen. Heat them in an air fryer for a few minutes when ready to eat until they are hot through.

3.2.4 Lemon Blueberry Scones with Vanilla Glaze

Prepare to try morning perfection, with our "Lemon Blueberry Scones with Vanilla Glaze". You will be taken to breakfast heaven while vivacious lemon and burly blueberries are plush with a sweet vanilla glaze. This rich and delicious combination of flavors and textures makes these scones perfect for hosting a brunch gathering or treating yourself to that special morning treat. Without further ado, let us explore this recipe that adds a little bit of citrusy and sweet sophistication to your mornings.

Ingredients for 8 servings:

For the Scones:

- 2 cups of plain flour
- 1/4 cup of granulated sugar
- 1 tablespoon of baking powder
- 1/2 teaspoon of salt
- 50g of cold unsalted butter, diced
- Zest of 2 lemons
- One cup of fresh or frozen blueberries
- 2/3 cup of heavy cream
- 1 large egg
- 1 teaspoon of vanilla extract

For the Vanilla Glaze:

- 1 cup of powdered sugar
- 2 tablespoons of milk
- 1/2 teaspoon of vanilla extract

Instructions:

For the Scones:

- Set your Air Fryer to 375°F (190°C) preheat for about 2-3 minutes.
- In a big bowl, mix together the all-purpose flour, white sugar, baking power and salt.
- Place the butter in cubes (cold, unsalted) into the dry mixture. With a pastry blender or your bare hands, blend the butter into the flour mixture until it looks like coarse crumbs.
- And then add the lemon zest and blueberries, making sure they are all mixed up.
- In a different bowl, beat together the heavy cream, egg, and vanilla extract.
- Add the wet mixture to the dry ingredients and mix until it comes together as a dough. Be careful not to overmix.
- Put the dough on a lightly floured surface and form it into a roundabout 1 inch thick.
- Divide the dough into 8 equal segments.
- Position the scones in a preheated Air Fryer basket with equal spacing.
- At 375°F(190°C), place the scones in an air fryer and cook for 12-15 minutes or until golden brown and thoroughly cooked.

For the Vanilla Glaze:

- As the scones cool, make the vanilla glaze. In a bowl, combine the powdered sugar, milk and vanilla extract whisking until smooth.
- After the scones have cooled for a moment, pour vanilla glaze over each one.

Cooking Tips:

- It is possible to replace fresh blueberries with frozen ones, but make sure that you do not thaw them prior insertion into the dough.
- Regulate the quantity of lemon zest for stronger or milder tones of lemon flavor.

3.2.5 Spinach and Mushroom Quesadillas for Breakfast

Take your morning to the next level with our "Spinach and Mushroom Breakfast Quesadillas" recipe. Heat up those quesadillas, for they are famous in their melty cheesy goodness. This breakfast twist is a combo of divine spinach sautéed with earthy mushrooms and flavors that will blow your mind! Be it a wholesome breakfast or an invitation to brunch, these quesadillas invite you to celebrate simplicity with a delight. Let's discuss this recipe and let us add texture and flavors to your mornings!

Ingredients for 4 servings:

For the Quesadillas:

- 4 large flour tortillas
- Two cups of fresh spinach leaves.
- One cup of sliced mushrooms such as button or cremini.
- Half a cup of shredded cheddar cheese
- Half a cup of shredded mozzarella cheese.
- 1/4 cup of diced onions
- 1 clove of garlic, minced
- 1/2 teaspoon of dried thyme
- Salt and pepper to taste
- Either cooking spray or a light application of oil

For the Salsa (Optional):

- 1 cup of diced tomatoes
- One fourth of a cup of diced red onions
- 2 tbsp of fresh cilantro, chopped
- 1 tablespoon of lime juice
- Salt and pepper to taste

Instructions:

For the Quesadillas:

- In a skillet, heat a little cooking oil on medium fire.
- Now add the diced onions and minced garlic. Saute for 2-3 minutes to get it fragrant and translucent.
- Stir in the sliced mushrooms and thyme. Cook for further 5 to 7 minutes until the mushrooms are soft and browned. Salt and pepper to taste.
- Add fresh spinach leaves and continue cooking for 2-3 minutes, until the leaves wilt. Remove the skillet from heat.

- Heat your Air Fryer to 350°F (175°C) for about 2-3 minutes.
- Spread a portion of the sautéed mushroom, spinach, and onion combination onto one-half of a flour tortilla.
- Cover the vegetable mixture with a layer of shredded cheddar and mozzarella cheese.
- Fold the tortilla in half so that it covers the filling and forms a half-moon.
- Spray the Air Fryer basket with cooking spray or oil and gently put in the quesadilla.
- You can air fry the quesadilla at 350°F (175°C) for 4-6 minutes on each side or until it is golden brown and the cheese is melted and gooey.
- However, you should cut into the quesadilla after a minute of cooling it down.

For the Salsa (Optional):

- In a bowl, mix the diced tomatoes, red onions, cilantro, lime juice and season with salt and pepper. Toss to combine.
- You can serve the Spinach and Mushroom Breakfast Quesadillas with salsa as an optional side dish to bring in a burst of freshness and flavor.

Cooking Tips:

- Some extra ingredients, such as diced bell peppers or bacon cooked to a crisp could be added on the quesadilla for additional flavor.
- This can be made healthier by using whole wheat tortillas.

3.2.6 Creamy Vanilla French Toast with Caramelized Bananas

. French toast is such a breakfast classic that has withstood the test of time and this version takes it to the opulent new heights. This dish is just a perfect symphony of a vanilla-flavored batter that was creamy and well caramelized bananas. This French toast is bound to become your unforgettable morning if you are celebrating a special occasion, or simply indulging yourself in some little bit of luxury. Let us delve into this recipe and let your taste buds awaken to a world of flavor as well as the comfort.

Ingredients for 4 servings:

For the French Toast:

- 8 pieces of thick-cut bread (such as brioche or challah)
- 2 large eggs
- 1 cup of whole milk
- 1/4 cup of granulated sugar
- 1 teaspoon of vanilla extract
- 1/2 teaspoon of ground cinnamon
- Pinch of salt
- Butter for cooking

For the Caramelized Bananas:

- 2 ripe bananas, sliced
- 2 tablespoons of unsalted butter
- 1/4 cup of brown sugar
- 1/2 teaspoon of ground cinnamon
- Pinch of salt

For Serving (Optional):

- Maple syrup
- Whipped cream
- Sliced strawberries or berries

Instructions:

For the French Toast:

- Whisk the eggs, whole milk, granulated sugar, vanilla extract ground cinnamon and a pinch of salt in a shallow dish to make the creamy batter.
- Set the temperature of your Air Fryer to 375°F (190°C) and allow preheating for 2-3 minutes.
- Dip all slices of bread in the batter thus covering both sides.
- Use medium-high heat to melt a little butter in a skillet.

- After soaking the bread slices in water, cook them until both sides are golden brown and crispy, approximately 3-4 minutes per side, in a skillet. Repeat for all slices.

For the Caramelized Bananas:

- Meanwhile, in a different skillet, melt the unsalted butter over medium heat.
- Next, add the sliced bananas, brown sugar, ground cinnamon and a pinch of salt to this skillet.
- Cook the bananas, stirring them carefully, until they turn caramel and become golden brown – this will take about three to four minutes.

For Serving:

- Put two slices of the creamy vanilla French toast on each plate.
- Serve the bananas on top of the French toast.
- Drizzle with maple syrup, top with a dollop of whipped cream, and finish off by serving with sliced strawberries or your favorite berries.

Cooking Tips:

- Use thick sliced bread for a more decadent sandwich.
- Spice up your French toast with the topping choices like chopped nuts or a sprinkling of the powdered sugar.

3.2.7 BLT Sandwiches with the Garlic Aioli for Breakfast

This is a very decadent version of the classic French toast. It is a sweet, creamy, and utterly delicious mix of vanilla-infused batter and the caramelized bananas. This French toast will make your morning very perfect if it's a special occasion or you want to pamper yourself with something really expensive.

Ingredients for 4 Servings:

For the French Toast:

- 8 bread slices (brioche or challah)

- 2 large eggs
- 1 cup of whole milk
- 1/4 cup of granulated sugar
- 1 teaspoon of vanilla extract
- 1/2 teaspoon of ground cinnamon
- Pinch of salt
- Butter for cooking

For the Caramelized Bananas:

- 2 ripe bananas, sliced
- 2 tablespoons of unsalted butter
- 1/4 cup of brown sugar
- 1/2 teaspoon of ground cinnamon
- Pinch of salt
- For Serving (Optional):
- Maple syrup
- Whipped cream
- Sliced strawberries or berries

Instructions:

For the French Toast:

- To prepare the creamy batter, in a shallow bowl, mix the eggs, whole milk, granulated sugar, vanilla extract with some ground cinnamon and a pinch of salt.
- Start by preheating your Air Fryer at 375°F for approximately 2-3 minutes.
- Dip each slice of bread into the batter such that it is coated well on both sides.
- In the skillet, heat butter on a medium-high level.
- On a griddle, fry the bread slices at 3-4 minutes per side until they become golden and brown on either side.

For the Caramelized Bananas:

- In a separate pan, melt the unsalted butter on medium heat.
- Place in the skillet, bananas that are sliced, brown sugar, ground cinnamon and a bit of salt.
- Slowly cook the bananas until brown and caramelized, about 3 to 4 minutes.

For Serving:

- French toast is a vanilla flavored dish; it should be served on the plate in two slices.
- Then, caramelize the bananas and spread them on the French toast.
- If desired – sprinkle with a little maple syrup, add a portion of whipped cream and sliced strawberries or your choice of berries.

Cooking Tips:

- For a more decadent version of your French toast, try using thick slices of bread. You can also add toppings like chopped nuts or a sprinkling of powdered sugar.

3. Sweet Beginnings and Savory Egg Dishes

This section has got you covered whether it is for a lazy brunch with family or just something sweet to enjoy in your breakfast. Explore a world of flavors where smooth pancakes marry salted quiches and sweet French toast courts hearty omelets. These recipes are designed to excite your palate and elevate your morning routine, inspiring you to make sure breakfast is a meal that you will never forget. Therefore, put on your apron and accompany me as we go through a culinary adventure that celebrates the art of breakfast.

3.3.1 The Cinnamon Roll Pancakes that are Loaded with Cream Cheese Drizzle

Here is a mouth-watering cinnamon rolls and pancakes combo, drizzled with yummy cream cheese glaze that you wouldn't want to miss. Whether it is your special day or just an ordinary morning you want to make extraordinary, these pancakes are the epitome of sweet breakfast bliss. Soon you will be savoring the cinnamon goodness and velvety cream cheese frosting that will make every day feel like paradise. So, here is this recipe that actually fulfills your breakfast dreams!

Ingredients for 4 Servings:

For the Pancakes:

- Two cups of all-purpose flour
- 2 tablespoons of granulated sugar
- 2 teaspoons of baking powder
- 1/2 teaspoon of baking soda
- 1/2 teaspoon of salt
- 2 large eggs
- 1 1/2 cups of buttermilk
- 2 tablespoons of melted unsalted butter
- 1 teaspoon of vanilla extract
- 1 teaspoon of ground cinnamon

For the Cinnamon Swirl:

- 1/4 cup of melted unsalted butter
- 1/4 cup of brown sugar
- 1 tablespoon of ground cinnamon

- For the Cream Cheese Drizzle:
- 4 ounces of cream cheese, room temperature
- 1/2 cup of powdered sugar
- 2-3 tablespoons of milk
- 1/2 teaspoon of vanilla extract

Instructions:

For the Pancakes:

- In a large bowl, mix the all-purpose flour, granulated sugar, baking powder, baking soda, salt and ground cinnamon until well blended.
- In a separate bowl, beat the eggs and then mix in the buttermilk, melted butter, and vanilla extract. Mix until well combined.
- Mix the wet and dry ingredients together, stirring until just combined. Avoid overmixing; a few lumps are acceptable.
- For the Cinnamon Swirl:
- In a small bowl, combine the melted unsalted butter, brown sugar, and ground cinnamon to form the cinnamon swirl.

For the Cream Cheese Drizzle:

- In another bowl, whip the cream cheese until it becomes smooth. Mix the powdered sugar, milk and vanilla extract. Blend until the drizzle becomes silk and creamy.

Assembly:

- Heat your griddle or a non-stick skillet over medium heat and lightly grease it with butter or oil.
- Spread a ladleful of pancake batter into the form of a circle on the hot griddle.
- Drop a spoonful of the cinnamon swirl onto the pancake and use a toothpick or skewer to create a marbled pattern.
- Cook the pancake until bubbles form on the surface and then flip to cook both sides until golden brown.
- Do the same for all other pancakes.
- Spread the cream cheese drizzle liberally over the hot pancakes.

Cooking Tips:

- In order to maintain the warmth of pancakes while cooking the batch, position them on a baking sheet in an oven preheated at 200°F (93°C).
- To control the thickness of the cream cheese drizzle, add more or less milk until you achieve your desired consistency.

3.3.2 Moroccan-Spiced Vegetable Tagine

Moroccan-Spiced Vegetable Tagine is your ticket to a gastronomic tour of North Africa. This vegetarian dish is a delicious blend of aromatic spices, soft vegetables and sweet dried fruits cooked to perfection in a typical tagine. Serve it with couscous or crusty bread to enjoy the flavors of Morocco.

Ingredients for 4 Servings:

For the Tagine:

- 2 tablespoons olive oil
- 1 large onion, finely chopped
- 3 cloves garlic, minced
- 2 teaspoons ground cumin
- 2 teaspoons ground coriander
- 1 teaspoon ground paprika
- 1 teaspoon ground cinnamon
- 1 teaspoon ground ginger
- 1/2 teaspoon ground turmeric
- ¼ teaspoon of cayenne pepper powder (to taste).
- 1 can (400 g) diced tomatoes
- 1 cup vegetable broth
- 1 medium eggplant, diced
- 2 carrots, sliced into rounds
- 1 red bell pepper, diced
- 1 yellow bell pepper, diced
- 1 zucchini, diced
- 1 cup drained and rinsed chickpeas from a can.
- 1/2 cup dried apricots, chopped

- 1/2 cup dried dates, chopped
- Salt and pepper to taste
- Fresh cilantro leaves, for garnish
- Sliced almonds, toasted, for garnish

For Serving:

- Cooked couscous or crusty bread

Instructions:

For the Tagine:

- In a large tagine or skillet with a lid, warm the olive oil over medium heat. Then, add the chopped onion and sauté until it turns translucent; this should take about 3-4 minutes.
- Add the minced garlic and cook for a minute more until it becomes aromatic.
- Add the cumin, coriander, paprika, cinnamon, ginger, turmeric and cayenne pepper. Cook and stir for about 2 minutes until the spices are fragrant.
- Add the diced tomatoes and vegetable broth. Stir well to combine.
- Then add the diced eggplant, sliced carrots, diced red and yellow bell peppers, diced zucchini, canned chickpeas, chopped dried apricots and dates to the tagine. Add salt and black pepper to taste. Mix the ingredients until they are well combined.
- If using a skillet without its lid, cover it with aluminum foil. Lower the heat to low and simmer for 30-40 minutes or until vegetables are tender.

Assembly and Serving:

- Serve the Moroccan-Spiced Vegetable Tagine hot on cooked couscous or with crusty bread.
- Finally, garnish with fresh cilantro leaves and toasted sliced almonds for an added kick of taste and texture.

Cooking Tips:

- Change the amount of cayenne pepper to suit your taste. It can be as light or hot as you want.
- To make it more authentic, use a real Moroccan tagine for cooking and serving.

3.3.3 Stuffed Breakfast Peppers with Sausage and Cheese

This recipe is a wonderful blend of tastes and consistencies that will be perfect for breakfast or brunch. Whether you are hosting or having a luxurious breakfast, these stuffed peppers will not let you down. So here is the recipe, and let's delve into this fantastic world of breakfast in a pepper.

Ingredients for 4 Servings:

For the Stuffed Peppers:

- 4 large red, yellow or green bell peppers
- Breakfast sausage, cooked and crumbled (8 ounces)
- 4 large eggs
- 1/2 cup shredded cheddar cheese
- Salt and pepper to taste
- Chopped fresh chives or parsley to garnish

Instructions:

- Set your Air Fryer to 375°F (190°C) and preheat for 2-3 minutes.
- Remove the tops of the bell peppers and remove seeds and membranes to make hollow pepper cups.
- In a bowl, mix the cooked and crumbled breakfast sausage with the shredded cheddar cheese. Mix well.
- With great caution, crack an egg into each bell pepper cup without breaking the yolk.
- Spoon the sausage and cheese mixture over the eggs in each pepper, distributing it equally.
- Season with salt and pepper as desired.
- Put the stuffed peppers into the preheated Air Fryer basket.
- Air fry at 375°F (190°C) for 15-20 minutes or until the eggs are done to your liking. For runny yolks, the shorter time should be aimed at; for fully set yolks, 20 minutes is much closer.
- Take the stuffed peppers out of the Air Fryer and sprinkle some chopped chives or parsley on top.
- Serve the Stuffed Breakfast Peppers right away, and enjoy!

Cooking Tips:

- You can add other ingredients such as diced tomatoes, spinach, or sautéed mushrooms to the filling.
- Alternatively, you can whisk the eggs before pouring them into the pepper cups if you want your eggs scrambled.

3.3.4 Savory Spinach and Feta Quiche with a Flaky Crust

The combination of the spinach, feta cheese, and homemade crust is the essence of perfection in this dish called quiche that has stood the test of time due to its perfect balance in tastes and texture from a crust which emanates a golden buttery flakiness. Whether you have guests over for brunch or if it's just a lazy weekend breakfast, it is the king of savory delights. So, let's dive right into this recipe and relish the art of creating a perfect quiche that is going to change your mornings for good.

Ingredients for 6 Servings:

For the Flaky Crust:

- 1 ¼ cups of flour.
- 1/2 teaspoon of salt
- ½ cup (1 stick) cold unsalted butter, cut into small pieces
- 2-4 tablespoons of ice water

For the Quiche Filling:

- 6 large eggs
- 1 ½ cups heavy cream
- 1 1/2 cups of chopped fresh spinach.
- 1 cup of feta cheese crumbled
- 1/2 cup grated Parmesan
- 1/2 teaspoon of salt
- 1/4 teaspoon of black pepper
- 1/4 teaspoon of ground nutmeg

Instructions:

For the Flaky Crust:

- In a food processor, mix the all-purpose flour and salt. Pulse a few times to combine.
- Add the cold, cubed unsalted butter to the flour mixture. Process until the mixture looks like coarse crumbs.
- While the food processor is running, gradually add ice water one tablespoon at a time until the dough just holds together.
- Prepare the dough by rolling it out on a floured surface, and then shape the dough into a disk. Wrap it in a plastic wrap and refrigerate for at minimum 30 minutes.

For the Quiche Filling:

- Preheat your Air Fryer at 375 ° F (190 ° C for about two to three minutes.
- In a separate bowl, beat the eggs and heavy cream until thoroughly combined.
- Mix the egg and other ingredients, including fresh spinach that you have chopped into small pieces, crumbled feta cheese, grated Parmesan cheese, salt, black pepper and ground nutmeg. Stir the mixture thoroughly until all ingredients have combined.

Assembling the Quiche:

- Transfer the chilled flaky crust onto a lightly floured surface and roll it into an Air Fryer-sized circle.
- Place the crust gently into a greased Air Fryer basket, with its sides against the walls.
- Fill the crust with the quiche filling.
- Air fry at 190°C for 25-30 minutes or until the quiche is firm and the top has browned.
- Remove the Savory Spinach and Feta Quiche from the Air Fryer and allow to cool slightly before slicing.

Cooking Tips:

- Ensure that the crust is cooled properly before rolling it for best results.

- The filling can also be changed with optional ingredients like onions that have been sautéed, or bacon for added flavor.

---

3. 3.5 Cheddar and bacon breakfast burritos with chipotle mayo

The breakfast burritos are filling and tasty, containing crunchy bacon, cheddar cheese that melts in the mouth and a hint of smoky chipotle mayo. Be it that you are leaving for a hectic day or taking your time on the breakfast table, these burritos are too good to resist and will kick hunger away. Prepare to roll the yumminess and hop on for a breakfast journey that unites the pleasure of taste in every spoon!

Ingredients for 4 Servings:

For the Breakfast Burritos:

- 4 large flour tortillas
- 8 pieces of bacon, fried until crispy
- 4 large eggs, scrambled
- One cup of shredded cheddar cheese.
- Salt and pepper to taste
- Chopped fresh chives for garnish (optional)

For the Chipotle Mayo:

- 1/2 cup of mayonnaise
- 1-2 tablespoons of chipotle sauce (to taste)
- 1 teaspoon of lime juice
- Salt and pepper to taste

Instructions:

For the Chipotle Mayo:

- Take chipotle sauce in a mayonnaise bowl and add lime juice to it along with salt and pepper. Customize the chipotle sauce according to your level of spiciness.
- Preheat your Air Fryer at the temperature of 350°F (175°C) for 2-3 minutes.

- If you want the flour tortillas to remain soft, add them into a preheated Air Fryer for approximately 1-2 minutes.
- Place the scrambled eggs, crispy bacon slices and shredded cheddar cheese on each tortilla in an equal amount till the center.
- Top the filling liberally with chipotle mayo.
- Next, take each tortilla, fold in both sides and roll it very tightly so as to keep the filling inside.
- The burritos are to be placed seam side down in the Air Fryer basket.
- Preheat an air fryer to 350°F (175°C) and cook the burritos for 5-7 minutes or until they are heated through completely, and tortillas become lightly crispy.
- Remove from the Air Fryer Cheddar and Bacon Breakfast Burritos, garnish with chopped fresh chives (optional) and serve.

Cooking Tips:

- Add more ingredients to your breakfast burritos like diced tomatoes, sautéed onions or avocado slices.
- Alter the chipotle sauce in the mayo to your taste of spiciness.

3.3.6 Sweet Potato Hash with Poached Eggs and Avocado

This dish is ideal for those who want a nutritious and filling breakfast or are organizing a brunch party. Sit back and enjoy the delicious combination of ingredients that will invigorate your morning, power you through the day with energy and taste. Let's delve into this recipe and discover the colorful world of energizing breakfast treats!

Ingredients for 4 Servings:

For the Sweet Potato Hash:

- 2 large sweet potatoes peeled and diced.
- 1 red onion, finely chopped
- 2 cloves of garlic, minced
- 2 tablespoons of olive oil
- 1 teaspoon of paprika
- 1/2 teaspoon of ground cumin
- Salt and pepper to taste

- Fresh parsley, chopped, for garnish
- For the Poached Eggs and Avocado:
- 4 large eggs
- 2 ripe avocados, sliced
- Salt and pepper to taste

Instructions:

For the Sweet Potato Hash:

- Set your Air Fryer to 375°F (190°C) and preheat it for about 2-3 minutes.
- In a large mixing bowl, mix together the diced sweet potatoes, finely chopped red onion, minced garlic, olive oil, paprika, ground cumin, salt and pepper. Toss to ensure that the sweet potatoes are evenly coated.
- Put the sweet potato mixture seasoned in an Air Fryer basket that has been preheated.
- Air fry at 375°F (190°C) for about 15-20 minutes or until the sweet potatoes are tender and crispy, turning or shaking the basket occasionally to ensure uniform cooking.
- Once cooked, take the sweet potato hash out of the Air Fryer and place it aside.

For the Poached Eggs and Avocado:

- In a large saucepan, put water and bring it to a low simmer.
- Break one egg into a small bowl.
- Make a gentle vortex in the simmering water by stirring it with a spoon.
- Gently drop the egg into the center of the whirlpool and let it poach for approximately 3-4 minutes for a slightly runny yolk or longer if you want to have a firmer yolk.
- Using a slotted spoon, gently lift the poached egg and place it on a paper towel-lined plate. Repeat the procedure for the rest of eggs.

Assembly:

- Portion the cooked sweet potato hash into four plates.
- Place slices of ripe avocado on each serving.
- Gently top the avocado slices with 1 poached egg.
- Season with salt and pepper, garnish with chopped fresh parsley.

Cooking Tips:

- You can add diced bell peppers or crumbled feta cheese for more flavor to Sweet Potato Hash.

3.3.7 Sausage and Veggie Breakfast Strata with Herbed Breadcrumbs

A breakfast strata is a baked savory casserole composed of layers of bread, eggs, sausage, vegetables and cheese. This is the ultimate in comfort and taste, great for brunch get-togethers or lazy mornings. It's a perfect combination of flavors and aromas coming from herbed breadcrumbs. Let's jump into this recipe and make a breakfast marvel that will leave everyone wanting more!

Ingredients for 6 Servings:

For the Breakfast Strata:

- One pound of breakfast sausage, cooked and crumbled.
- 8 bread slices, cubed (works well with day-old bread)
- 1 cup shredded cheddar cheese
- 1/2 cup diced bell peppers of any color.
- 1/2 cup of diced onions
- 1/2 cup of diced mushrooms
- 8 large eggs
- 2 cups of whole milk
- 1 teaspoon of Dijon mustard
- 1/2 teaspoon of salt
- 1/4 teaspoon of black pepper
- Fresh parsley, chopped, for garnish

For the Herbed Breadcrumbs:

- 1 cup of fresh breadcrumbs from a slice of bread.
- 2 tablespoons of melted butter
- A teaspoon of dried Italian herbs (basil, oregano, thyme)
- Salt and pepper to taste

Instructions:

For the Herbed Breadcrumbs:

- Mix the fresh breadcrumbs, melted butter, dried Italian herbs, salt and pepper in a bowl. Toss so that the breadcrumbs are evenly coated.

For the Breakfast Strata:

- Heat your oven to 350°F (175°C). Grease a 9x13-inch baking dish.
- In a large skillet, brown the breakfast sausage until it is crumbled in medium heat. Take it out of the frying pan and get rid of any remaining fat.
- In the same skillet, place diced bell peppers, onions and mushrooms. Sauté until they soften, about 5 minutes. Remove from heat.
- Add half of the cubed bread to the prepared baking dish. Put half of the cooked sausage, sautéed vegetables, and shredded cheddar cheese on top.
- Repeat the layers with the remaining bread, sausage, vegetables and cheese.
- In a bowl, combine the eggs, whole milk, Dijon mustard, salt and black pepper.
- Pour the egg mixture over the layers in a baking dish to ensure that all of the bread is soaked.
- Spread the ready herbed bread crumbs evenly over the top.
- Put the baking dish in aluminum foil and bake for 30 minutes.
- Remove the foil and bake for 20-25 minutes more, until the strata is golden brown and properly set.
- Leave it to rest for a couple of minutes and garnish with chopped fresh parsley before slicing and serving.

Cooking Tips:

- You can personalize your breakfast strata with whatever vegetables and cheese you like.
- Using day-old or slightly stale bread will provide the best texture.

4. Appetizers and Snacks

Welcome to the delightful realm of appetizers and snacks, where pleasure and health meet in harmony. This chapter is a veritable goldmine of gastronomical delights that will delight your taste buds and take your snacking to the next level. We offer crispy bites, party favorites that are ideal for get-togethers and festivities, healthy snacks, and delicious dips that nourish both the body and soul – all your needs will be met. Moreover, our vegetarian specialities ensure that everyone can enjoy the tasty adventure. Brace yourself to taste a wide variety of flavors, textures and creativity that will make your snack times really memorable.

4.1 Crispy Bites and Party Favorites

In this chapter, we jump into the world of crunch and irresistible snacks. From delightfully seasoned crispy bites that are perfect for parties to finger foods that will turn heads at any event, you'll find a variety of appetizers meant to impress. These recipes offer a happy medium between pleasure and refinement, so your guests will be asking for seconds.

---

4. 1.1 Crispy Baked Zucchini Fritters

Enrich yourselves with the delightful crunch of our Crispy Baked Zucchini Fritters. These healthier versions of the traditional fritter are made with fresh zucchini and a well-seasoned batter. They are a perfect snack or an appetizer that blend crunchiness with freshness from the garden.

Ingredients for 4 Servings:

For the Zucchini Fritters:

- 2 medium zucchinis, grated
- 1 teaspoon salt
- 1/2 cup all-purpose flour
- 1/4 cup grated Parmesan cheese
- 1/4 cup shredded mozzarella cheese
- 1/4 cup chopped fresh parsley

- 1/4 teaspoon black pepper
- 1/4 teaspoon garlic powder
- 2 large eggs, beaten
- Cooking spray

For the Lemon Garlic Dip:

- 1/2 cup Greek yogurt
- 1 tablespoon fresh lemon juice
- 1 clove garlic, minced
- 1/4 teaspoon lemon zest
- Salt and pepper to taste

Instructions:

For the Zucchini Fritters:

- Place the zucchini in a sieve, sprinkle with salt and let stand for 10 minutes. Next, squeeze out the remaining moisture using a clean kitchen towel or even paper towels.
- Preheat your oven to 425 F 220 C. Arrange a baking sheet with parchment papers and apply some cooking oil which should be of light intensity.
- Combine the grated zucchini, all purpose flour, grated Parmesan cheese, shredded mozzarella cheese, chopped fresh parsley leaves and season with black pepper and garlic powder in a mixing bowl.
- The beaten eggs should be added to the mixture and stirred until everything is well blended.
- Divide the mixture into small portions and form fritters from each portion. Spread them on the baking sheet that is ready.
- Lightly coat the tops of the fritters with cooking spray. This will ensure that they brown well in the oven.
- Bake in a preheated oven for about 15-20 minutes or until the fritters are golden and crispy, turning them midway to ensure even cooking.

For the Lemon Garlic Dip:

- Mix Greek yogurt, fresh lemon juice, minced garlic, lemon zest, salt and black pepper in a small bowl. Mix until the dip is homogeneous.

To Serve:

- For a fresh burst of flavor, serve the Crispy Baked Zucchini Fritters while hot with the Lemon Garlic Dip.

Cooking Tips:

- You can flavor your fritters with herbs or spices of your choice.
- It is advisable to use day old or slightly stale bread for the best texture.
- These fritters are best eaten right away to ensure that they remain crispy.

4.1.2 Parmesan and Garlic Roasted Chickpeas

Prepare yourself for a flavorful and moreish snack that is our Parmesan and Garlic Roasted Chickpeas. These little nuggets are perfectly roasted, providing the perfect crunchy texture and a delicious Parmesan-garlic flavor. They are the perfect guilt-free snack that is impossible to resist.

If you want to have a delicious and healthy snack that is crunchy, then Such a great option is these Parmesan and Garlic Roasted Chickpeas. They are simple to prepare and ideal for snacking. This recipe makes about 4 servings.

Ingredients for 4 Servings:

For the Roasted Chickpeas:

- 2 cans (15 ounces each) chickpeas, drained and rinsed
- 2 tablespoons olive oil
- 1/2 cup grated Parmesan cheese
- 1 teaspoon garlic powder
- 1/2 teaspoon onion powder
- 1/2 teaspoon paprika
- Salt and pepper, to taste

Instructions:

- Set your oven to 400°F (200°C) and preheat. Place a baking sheet with parchment paper.
- In a large mixing bowl, stir together the drained and rinsed chickpeas, olive oil, grated Parmesan cheese, garlic powder, onion powder, paprika salt and black pepper. Toss well to coat the chickpeas.
- Arrange the seasoned chickpeas on the prepared baking sheet in an even layer.
- Bake in the preheated oven for about 30-35 minutes, until chickpeas are crispy and golden brown, shaking the pan or stirring them halfway through for even cooking.

Cooking Tips:

- After rinsing, make sure to dry the chickpeas well so that they get crispy.
- The seasoning can be customized by adding your preferred herbs or spices.
- If there are leftovers, store the roasted chickpeas in an airtight container to keep them crunchy.

4.1.3 .Crispy Brussels Sprouts with Balsamic Glaze

Take your appetizer to the next level with our Mini Caprese Skewers with Balsamic Glaze. These little marvels are a feast of flavors with cherry tomatoes, fresh mozzarella cheese, basil leaves and a touch of balsamic glaze. They are a vibrant and sophisticated touch to any event or party.

Ingredients for 4 Servings:

For the Crispy Brussels Sprouts:

- 1-pound Brussels sprouts, trimmed and cut in half
- 2 tablespoons olive oil
- Salt and pepper to taste

For the Balsamic Glaze:

- 1/4 cup balsamic vinegar

- 2 tablespoons honey
- 1/2 teaspoon Dijon mustard

Instructions:

For the Crispy Brussels Sprouts:

- Set your oven to 425°F (220°C) and preheat it. Place a baking sheet with parchment paper.
- In a large bowl, toss the trimmed and halved Brussels sprouts with olive oil, salt and black pepper until well coated.
- Spread the seasoned Brussels sprouts on this prepared baking sheet.
- Bake for 25-30 minutes in a preheated oven or until Brussels sprouts are crispy and caramelized, stirring halfway through the baking process for even cooking.

For the Balsamic Glaze:

- When you have roasted the Brussels sprouts, prepare your balsamic glaze. In a saucepan, combine balsamic vinegar with honey and Dijon mustard.
- Heat the mixture in a pan on medium heat. Allow it to cook for 5-7 minutes or until it is thickened and can coat the back of a spoon.

To Serve:

- After roasting the Brussels sprouts, place them on a serving plate.
- Pour the hot balsamic glaze over the roasted Brussels sprouts.
- Serve this Crispy Brussels Sprouts with Balsamic Glaze as a tasty side dish for about 4 servings.

Cooking Tips:

- To get the best taste and aesthetics, trim off the hard ends of Brussels sprouts and discard any yellowed leaves.
- Patience is necessary when cooling the reduced balsamic glaze, as it will thicken with time.
- It is also possible to garnish with chopped fresh herbs or grated Parmesan cheese for more flavor.

4.1.4 Honey and Spicy Asian Chicken Wings

These wings are a taste explosion, mixing the sweetness of honey with the spiciness of sriracha. They are sticky, juicy and ideal for satisfying your hunger for strong and tangy flavors.

Ingredients for 4 Servings:

For the Chicken Wings:

- 2 lbs chicken wings, divided into drumettes and flats
- 2 tablespoons vegetable oil
- Salt and pepper, to taste

For the Sweet and Spicy Glaze:

- 1/4 cup soy sauce
- 1/4 cup honey
- 2 tablespoons of Sriracha sauce (adjust the amount to your liking).
- 2 cloves garlic, minced
- 1 teaspoon grated fresh ginger
- Optional garnish: sesame seeds and chopped green onions.

Instructions:

For the Chicken Wings:

- Set the oven at 425°F (220°C). Place parchment paper on a baking sheet.
- Toss chicken wings in a large mixing bowl with vegetable oil, salt and black pepper until well coated.
- Arrange the wings on a preheated baking sheet in one layer.
- Roast in a preheated oven for about 25-30 minutes, turning them over halfway through until they are golden and crispy.

For the Sweet and Spicy Glaze:

- As the chicken wings are being cooked, make the sweet and spicy glaze. In a small saucepan, mix soy sauce, honey, Sriracha sauce, minced garlic and grated ginger.

- Simmer the mixture over medium heat. Let it simmer for 5-7 minutes, or until the mixture slightly thickens.
- When the chicken wings are done roasting, place them in a big mixing bowl.
- Warm up the hot sweet and spicy glaze, pour it over the chicken wings and gently toss them until they are evenly coated.
- Sprinkle with sesame seeds and chopped green onions, if desired.
- For about four servings, serve these Sweet and Spicy Asian Chicken Wings as a delicious appetizer or entree.

Cooking Tips:

- Adjust the amount of Sriracha sauce to match your desired level of spiciness.
- If you want an additional crunchy texture, broil the chicken wings for a minute or two after roasting them.
- Serve with rice or vegetables to complete the meal.

4.1.5 Loaded Potato Skins with Bacon and Cheddar

Treat yourself to the ultimate comfort food with our Loaded Potato Skins with Bacon and Cheddar. The bacon is crispy and the cheese used to fill these potato skins is very generous. They are a satisfying and indulgent snack perfect for sharing with friends or family.

Ingredients for 4 Servings:

- 4 large russet potatoes
- 2 tablespoons vegetable oil
- salt and pepper, to taste
- 1 cup shredded cheddar cheese
- 4 slices cooked bacon, crumbled
- 2 green onions, thinly sliced
- Sour cream, for serving (optional)

Instructions:

- Before you start, turn your oven on to 375°F (190°C). Place a baking sheet with parchment paper.

- Prepare potatoes by washing them well and wiping them dry. Using a fork, pierce all potatoes several times.
- Apply vegetable oil on the potatoes, and sprinkle them with salt and black pepper.
- Put the potatoes directly on the rack and bake for 45 to 60 minutes or until they become tender, and their skins turn crispy.
- Remove the potatoes from the oven and allow them to cool for a little while.
- You will cut each potato in half lengthwise and scoop the flesh, making sure there is a quarter-inch of the potatoes on the skin. Set aside the flesh for now.
- Increase the oven temperature to 450°F (230°C).
- Place the skins back onto the baking sheet. Sprinkle the top of each potato skin with shredded cheddar cheese and bacon crumbles.
- Bake your loaded potato skins for 10-15 minutes or until the cheese becomes melted and bubbly.
- Remove the baked potato from the oven and top it with fine slices of green onion.

Cooking Tips:

- It is possible to remove the potato pulp and keep it for mashed potatoes or another recipe.
- Customize your toppings with a variety of ingredients such as diced tomatoes, jalapeños or even a dash of ranch dressing.
- For a little more crunch on the skins, oil them lightly before baking for the second time.

4.1.6 Crispy Coconut Shrimp with Mango Salsa

Let your taste buds travel to a tropical paradise with our Crispy Coconut Shrimp with Mango Salsa. The shrimp are covered in a golden layer of shredded coconut that beautifully compliments the mango salsa which is sweet and tangy. They are a piece of the islands in each bite.

Ingredients for 4 Servings:

For the Crispy Coconut Shrimp:

- 1 lb large shrimp, unshelled with intact tails
- 1 cup shredded coconut
- 1 cup panko breadcrumbs

- 1/2 cup all-purpose flour
- 2 large eggs, beaten
- Salt and pepper to taste
- Cooking spray

For the Mango Salsa:

- 2 ripe mangoes, peeled, pitted and diced.
- ¼ cup finely chopped red onion
- 1/4 cup fresh cilantro, chopped
- 1 jalapeño seeds removed and finely chopped (adjust to taste).
- Juice of 1 lime
- Salt and freshly ground black pepper to taste.

Instructions:

For the Crispy Coconut Shrimp:

- Set your air fryer to 400°F (200°C) and preheat it.
- In a shallow bowl, mix together shredded coconut, panko breadcrumbs, salt and black pepper.
- Dredge each shrimp in all-purpose flour, shaking off the excess.
- Flour the shrimp and dip them into the beaten eggs.
- Coat the shrimp with coconut and breadcrumbs, pressing lightly to secure the coating.
- Put the shrimp in a single layer on the air fryer basket. Based on the size of your air fryer, you may have to cook them in batches.
- Spray the shrimp lightly with cooking spray to make them turn golden brown.
- Cook the shrimp in an air fryer for about 8-10 minutes, turning them over halfway through, until they are crispy and fully cooked.
- Put diced mangos, finely chopped red onion, fresh cilantro, jalapeño, lime juice, salt and black pepper in a mixing bowl. Mix well.
- Crispy Coconut Shrimp is best served hot with Mango Salsa as a side for dipping or drizzling.

Cooking Tips:

- Ensure that the shrimp is designed for both texture and appearance.

- Reduce or increase the amount of jalapeño to change the spiciness of Mango Salsa.

4.1.7 Stuffed Jalapeño Poppers with Cream Cheese

Get ready for an explosion of flavor with our Stuffed Jalapeño Poppers with Cream Cheese! These poppers are spicy with a cream cheese filling and bacon on top. They're the ultimate combination of heat and creaminess, so they are a must-try party staple.

Ingredients:

- 6 large jalapeños, halved and seeded
- 1 cup cream cheese, softened
- ½ cup shredded cheddar cheese
- ¼ tsp garlic powder
- Salt and pepper to taste
- 1 cup breadcrumbs
- Cooking spray

Instructions:

- Begin by halving the jalapeños lengthwise and removing the seeds. Set aside.
- In a bowl, mix together cream cheese, shredded cheddar, garlic powder, and a pinch of salt and pepper.
- Fill each jalapeño half with the cheese mixture, ensuring it's evenly spread.
- Breading: Dip each stuffed jalapeño in breadcrumbs, covering them completely.
- Preheat your Air Fryer to 375°F. Place the breaded jalapeños in the basket in a single layerSpray them with cooking spray.
- Fry in the air for about 8-10 minutes or until jalapenos are warm and breadcrumbs are brown.

To Serve:

- Allow them to cool a little before serving. Relish these as a tasty starter or even tummy fillers!

Cooking Tips:

- However, you can change the time depending on your Air Fryer model and size of jalapeños for the desired level of crispiness.

4. 2 Healthy Nibbles and Dips

Our selection of healthy snacks and dips will be your savior in those times when you feel like nibbling. Jump into healthy choices that are packed with nutrients such as fresh veggies, whole grains, and proteins. Combined with healthy and tasty dips, these snacks are not only enjoyable but also nutritious; hence, they make ideal guilt-free munching.

4.2.1 Air Fryer Crunchy Kale Chips with Herbed Yogurt Dip

Indulge in the perfect guilt-free snack when you pair our Crunchy Air Fryer Kale Chips with a creamy herbed yogurt dip. Kale chips are crunchy, tasty and addictive. They are an ideal balance between crunchiness and creaminess, so they should be tried as a healthy snack.

Ingredients for 4 Servings:

For the Kale Chips:

- 1 bunch kale, stems discarded and leaves torn into bite-sized pieces
- 2 tablespoons olive oil
- 1 teaspoon garlic powder
- 1 teaspoon onion powder
- Salt and pepper, to taste

For the Herbed Yogurt Dip:

- 1 cup Greek yogurt
- 1 tbsp fresh parsley, finely chopped
- 1 tbsp fresh dill, finely chopped
- 1 teaspoon lemon juice
- Salt and pepper to taste

Instructions:

For the Kale Chips:

- Set your air fryer to 350°F (175°C) and preheat.
- Combine the torn kale pieces with olive oil, garlic powder, onion powder, salt and black pepper in a large bowl and toss until well coated.

- Put the kale that has been seasoned into the air fryer basket in one layer, if necessary.
- Cook in an air fryer for about 4-6 minutes, shaking the basket halfway through, until kale chips are crispy and lightly browned. Watch them closely, for they can easily burn.

For the Herbed Yogurt Dip:

- In a small bowl, mix Greek yogurt with finely chopped fresh parsley, finely chopped fresh dill, lemon juice, salt and black pepper. Mix well.
- Taste and adjust seasoning.

To Serve:

- Place the crispy kale chips on a serving platter.
- Offer four servings of Crunchy Air Fryer Kale Chips with Herbed Yogurt Dip as a delicious and healthy snack.

Cooking Tips:

- De-stem the kale leaves to achieve a better texture.
- Trial different spices for the kale chips, either paprika or nutritional yeast.
- You are welcome to make the herbed yogurt dip with your favorite fresh herbs.

4.2.2 Spicy Edamame with Sesame-Ginger Dipping Sauce

Treat your taste buds to our Spicy Edamame that comes with a Sesame-Ginger Dipping Sauce. These soybean pods are cooked to perfection and then tossed in a spicy mix of seasonings, they make great hors-d'oeuvres or snacks.

Ingredients for 4 Servings:

For the Spicy Edamame:

- 2 cups thawed edamame pods
- 1 tablespoon vegetable oil
- 1 tsp. red pepper flakes (to taste)

- 1/2 teaspoon garlic powder
- Salt, to taste
- Lime wedges, for garnish (optional)

For the Sesame-Ginger Dipping Sauce:

- 1/4 cup soy sauce
- 2 tablespoons rice vinegar
- 1 tablespoon honey
- 1 teaspoon sesame oil
- 1 teaspoon grated fresh ginger
- 1 green onion, thinly sliced
- Sesame seeds, for garnish (optional)

Instructions:

For the Spicy Edamame:

- Set your air fryer to 375°F (190°C) and preheat it.
- In a bowl, combine the thawed edamame pods with vegetable oil, red pepper flakes, garlic powder and pinch of salt until they are coated.
- Arrange the seasoned edamame in a single layer in the air fryer basket.
- Air fry for 6-8 minutes, shaking the basket in between, until edamame pods are slightly charred and tender.

For the Sesame-Ginger Dipping Sauce:

In a small bowl, combine soy sauce, rice vinegar, honey, sesame oil, grated fresh ginger and thinly sliced green onions.

To Serve:

- Place the spicy edamame on a serving platter.
- Serve the Spicy Edamame with Sesame-Ginger Dipping Sauce as a spicy and irresistible snack for about 4 servings.

Cooking Tips:

- Adjust the amount of red pepper flakes according to your desired level of spiciness.
- For an extra zesty flavor, squeeze fresh lime juice over the edamame pods before serving.
- For better appearance, sprinkle sesame seeds on the dipping sauce.

4.2.3 Sweet Potato Hummus with Crispy Chickpea Toppers

Treat yourself to the world of flavors with our Sweet Potato Hummus and crispy Chickpeas. This bright hummus is a combination of sweetness and savory, while its crunchy chickpea toppers make it an irresistible texture and taste sensation.

Ingredients for 4 Servings:

For the Sweet Potato Hummus:

- 1 medium sweet potato, peeled and diced.
- 1 can (15 oz) chickpeas, drained and rinsed
- 2 cloves garlic, minced
- 3 tablespoons tahini
- 3 tablespoons olive oil
- Juice of 1 lemon
- 1/2 teaspoon ground cumin
- 1/2 teaspoon paprika
- Salt and black pepper to taste
- Water (as needed for consistency)

For the Crispy Chickpea Toppers:

- 1 can (15 ounces) chickpeas, drained and rinsed
- 1 tablespoon olive oil
- 1/2 teaspoon smoked paprika
- 1/2 teaspoon cayenne pepper (adjust to taste)
- Salt, to taste

Instructions:

For the Sweet Potato Hummus:

- Put the cubed sweet potato in a microwave-safe bowl and microwave until it is soft, 5–7 minutes. Alternatively, you can steam it.
- In a food processor, process the cooked sweet potato, drained and rinsed chickpeas, minced garlic, tahini, olive oil, lemon juice, ground cumin paprika salt black pepper.
- Blend the ingredients to a smooth consistency, adding water as necessary for your preferred hummus texture.

For the Crispy Chickpea Toppers:

- Set the temperature of your air fryer to 375°F (190°C) and preheat it.
- Combine the drained, rinsed chickpeas with olive oil, smoked paprika, cayenne pepper and a pinch of salt in a bowl and toss until well coated.
- Put the spiced chickpeas in a single layer into the air fryer basket.
- Air fry for about 10-12 minutes, shaking the basket in the middle of the process, until chickpeas become crispy and golden brown.

To Serve:

- Put the sweet potato hummus into a serving bowl.
- Top the hummus with crispy chickpea toppers.
- This Sweet Potato Hummus with Crispy Chickpea Toppers is a great appetizer for around 4 servings.

Cooking Tips:

- Spice the crispy chickpea toppers according to your taste.
- You can top the hummus with some drizzle of olive oil and a dash of paprika to add flavor and appearance.
- Serve with pita bread, vegetables sticks or crackers for dipping.

4.2.4 Spicy Lemon-Pepper Zucchini Sticks

Prepare to taste the tart and spicy flavor of our Lemon-Pepper Zucchini Sticks. These sticks offer the perfect blend of citrusy brightness and spicy pepper punch. Either as a starter or as an accompaniment, they will certainly satisfy your taste buds.

Ingredients for 4 Servings:

For the Zucchini Sticks:

- 4 medium zucchini, sliced into sticks
- 2 tablespoons olive oil
- Zest of 1 lemon
- 1 teaspoon lemon juice
- 1 teaspoon black pepper
- 1/2 teaspoon garlic powder
- 1/2 teaspoon onion powder
- Salt, to taste
- Garnish with chopped fresh parsley (optional)

Instructions:

For the Zucchini Sticks:

- Set your air fryer to preheat at 375°F (190°C).
- In a large bowl, whisk the zucchini sticks with olive oil, lemon zest, lemon juice, black pepper, garlic powder and onion powder until they are evenly coated.
- Arrange the seasoned zucchini sticks in a single layer in the basket of an air fryer, cooking them in batches if needed.
- Cook in the air fryer for about 8-10 minutes, turning over the basket halfway through, until the zucchini sticks are tender and lightly browned.

To Serve:

- Place the Zesty Lemon-Pepper Zucchini Sticks on a serving platter.
- If desired, garnish with chopped fresh parsley.
- Serve as a zingy and sour starter or side dish for 4 servings.

Cooking Tips:

- Add the amount of black pepper to suit your desired level of spiciness.
- You can top the zucchini sticks with a dash of grated parmesan cheese just before serving for added taste.
- Serve alongside your preferred dipping sauce – ranch dressing or tzatziki.

4.2.5 Roasted Beetroot and Garlic Dip with Multi-Seed Crackers

Enjoy the earthy richness of our Roasted Beetroot and Garlic Dip along with Multi-Seed Crackers. This bright and colorful beet dip capitalizes on the natural sweetness of roasted beets and the mild taste of garlic, making it a welcome addition to any party.

Ingredients for 4 Servings:

For the Roasted Beetroot and Garlic Dip:

- 2 medium beetroots, roasted and peeled
- 1 head of garlic roasted and cloves removed.
- 2 tablespoons olive oil
- 2 tablespoons Greek yogurt
- 1 tablespoon lemon juice
- 1 teaspoon honey
- Salt and black pepper, to your liking
- Optional garnish: chopped fresh parsley

For the Multi-Seed Crackers:

- 1 cup of multi-seed crackers, either store-bought or homemade.

Instructions:

For the Roasted Beetroot and Garlic Dip:

- Set your oven to 400°F (200°C) and preheat it.

- Individually wrap the beetroots in aluminum foil and place them on a baking sheet. Cook for around 45-60 minutes or until the beetroots are soft when pierced with a fork.
- Cut the top of the whole garlic head to reveal the cloves. Drizzle with a small amount of olive oil, cover it in aluminum foil and bake it on the same baking sheet as the beetroots. Roast for approximately 30-35 minutes or until the cloves of garlic are tender and golden.
- When the beetroots and garlic are roasted, let them cool down a bit.
- Put the roasted beetroots, roasted garlic cloves, olive oil, Greek yogurt, lemon juice, honey, salt and black pepper in a food processor.
- Puree the ingredients to a smooth and creamy consistency.

For the Multi-Seed Crackers:

- Put the multi-seed crackers on a serving plate.

To Serve:

- Move the Roasted Beetroot and Garlic Dip to a serving dish.
- Decorate with chopped fresh parsley if desired.
- Serve the dip along with multi-seed crackers as a colorful and tasty appetizer for about four servings.

Cooking Tips:

- If you want to roast the beetroots, you can wrap them in foil or place them directly on a baking tray. The roasting time may be different depending on the size of the beetroots.
- Alter the quantity of honey, lemon juice, salt and black pepper to your liking.
- You can season the dish with a drizzle of olive oil and a sprinkle of paprika.

4.2.6 Cumin-Spiced Carrot Fries with Avocado Aioli

Ditch that craving for fries and satisfy it in a healthier way with our Cumin-Spiced Carrot Fries paired with creamy Avocado Aioli. These carrot fries are sprinkled with aromatic cumin and baked to a golden brown, while the avocado aioli provides a cool and creamy complement.

Ingredients for 4 Servings:

For the Cumin-Spiced Carrot Fries:

- 4 carrots, large in size, peeled and cut into fries
- 2 tablespoons olive oil
- 1 teaspoon ground cumin
- 1/2 teaspoon paprika
- 1/2 teaspoon garlic powder
- Salt and pepper, to taste

For the Avocado Aioli:

- 2 ripe avocados
- 2 cloves garlic, minced
- 2 tablespoons mayonnaise
- 2 tablespoons Greek yogurt
- Juice of 1 lime
- Salt and pepper to taste

Instructions:

For the Cumin-Spiced Carrot Fries:

- Set your air fryer to 375°F (190°C).
- In a large mixing bowl, combine the carrot fries with olive oil, ground cumin, paprika, garlic powder, salt and black pepper until they are thoroughly coated.
- Arrange the seasoned carrot fries in a single layer in the air fryer basket, if needed, work with batches.
- Air fry for about 10-12 minutes, shaking the basket halfway through, until carrot fries are crispy and golden.

For the Avocado Aioli:

- In a food processor, pulse the ripe avocados, minced garlic, mayonnaise, Greek yogurt, lime juice, salt and black pepper together.
- Blend the ingredients until they are smooth and creamy.

To Serve:

- Place the Cumin-Spiced Carrot Fries on a serving platter.
- Serve the carrot fries with a side of Avocado Aioli as an appetizer or side dish for 4 servings.

Cooking Tips:

- Change the quantity of ground cumin and paprika to match your desired level of spiciness and taste.
- You can spice up the carrot fries with a pinch of red pepper flakes.
- For future use, the Avocado Aioli can be stored in an airtight container in the refrigerator.

4.2.7 Smoked Paprika Cauliflower Bites with Blue Cheese Dip

Get ready to enjoy the smoky flavor of our Smoky Paprika Cauliflower Bites, which are served with a rich Blue Cheese Dip. These bites are full of flavor, and when dipped in the creamy blue cheese sauce they create a perfect blend of smokiness and creaminess.

Ingredients for 4 Servings:

For the Roasted Beetroot and Garlic Dip:

- 2 medium roasted and peeled beetroots.
- 1 whole garlic, roasted and cloves peeled.
- 2 tablespoons olive oil
- 2 tablespoons Greek yogurt
- 1 tablespoon lemon juice
- 1 teaspoon honey
- Salt and black pepper, as desired
- Chopped parsley, fresh, for garnish (optional)

For the Multi-Seed Crackers:

- 1 cup mixed seed crackers (commercial or homemade).

Instructions:

- For the Roasted Beetroot and Garlic Dip:
- Set your air fryer to 375°F (190°C) and preheat it.
- Add roasted and peeled beetroots to the air fryer basket after tossing them with olive oil.
- Air fry for about 15-20 minutes until the beetroots have a slight caramelization and are tender.
- In a food processor, mix the roasted beetroots, roasted garlic cloves, Greek yogurt, lemon juice, honey, salt and pepper.
- Blend the ingredients until they are smooth and creamy.

For the Multi-Seed Crackers:

- Place the multi-seed crackers on a serving dish.

To Serve:

- Place the Roasted Beetroot and Garlic Dip in a bowl to serve.
- Garnish with chopped fresh parsley, if preferred.
- Pair it up with multi-seed crackers to be served as a colorful and flavorful appetizer for around 4 servings.

Cooking Tips:

- Roasting the beetroots and garlic makes it more flavorful and sweet.
- Add the honey and lemon juice according to your taste for sweetness and acidity.
- You can also add your own fresh herbs, such as dill or chives.

4.3 Vegetarian Pleasers

Vegetarian choices have never been so attractive. If you are a vegetarian or would just like to taste some plant-based recipes, this section is all about veggies. From mouth-watering appetizers to stunning inventions that will satisfy the fattest of bellies, these recipes reveal how vegetarian cuisine is not only diverse but also delicious. Get ready to be amazed and inspired by the limitless opportunities that lie in store for you in this chapter.

4.3.1 Stuffed Portobello Mushrooms Air-Fried

Take your appetizers to the next level with this Air-Fried Stuffed Portobello Mushrooms. Every mushroom cap is stuffed with a flavorful blend of herbs, cheese, and breadcrumbs. Air frying makes them crispy on the outside and tender, flavorful inside.

Ingredients for 4 Servings:

- Four large Portobello mushrooms, stems discarded
- 1 cup breadcrumbs
- 1/2 cup grated Parmesan cheese
- 2 cloves garlic, minced
- 2 tablespoons fresh parsley, chopped
- 2 tablespoons olive oil
- Salt and pepper, to taste

Instructions:

- Heat up your air fryer to 375°F (190°C).
- In a bowl, mix breadcrumbs with Parmesan cheese, minced garlic, chopped parsley, olive oil salt and black pepper.
- Place the breadcrumb mixture inside each Portobello mushroom cap.
- The stuffed mushrooms should be placed in the air fryer basket.
- Cook in the air fryer for around 10-12 minutes until the mushrooms are soft and the breadcrumb topping is golden brown.
- These Air-Fried Stuffed Portobello Mushrooms are a delicious appetizer.

Cooking Tips:

- Add some herbs, diced tomatoes or anything else to your liking to the stuffing.

- Based on the size and thickness of your mushrooms, adjust the cooking time.

4.3.2 Crispy Tofu and Veggie Spring Rolls

The roll is filled with tofu that's been marinated and a combination of fresh vegetables and herbs, then rolled up in rice paper and air fried. You can dip them to a sauce of your preference for entrée or as a yummy snack.

Ingredients for 4 Servings:

For the Spring Rolls:

- 8 spring roll rice wrappers
- 8 small tofu slices, marinated
- 1 cup shredded lettuce
- 1 cup shredded carrots
- 1 cup of fresh herbs such as mint, basil or cilantro.
- Rice vermicelli noodles, cooked and chilled
- Your favorite dipping sauce, such as soy sauce or peanut sauce

Instructions:

- Marinate the tofu in your favorite sauce for at least 30 minutes.
- Prepare the spring rolls by softening the rice wrappers in warm water as indicated on the package.
- On a clean plan, put one rice paper and soak it for about three seconds. In the center, add a slice of tofu marinated in soy sauce, shredded lettuce, shredded carrots and fresh herbs with some cooked vermicelli rice noodles.
- Fold the sides of the rice wrapper and roll it into a tight burrito-like shape.
- Heat your air fryer to 375°F (190°C).
- Arrange the spring rolls in a single layer, seam side down, in an air fryer basket.
- The rolls should be crispy and golden brown after about 5-7 minutes of air frying.
- Serve the Crispy Tofu and Veggie Spring Rolls with a dipping sauce of your choice.

Cooking Tips:

- Customize the filling using vegetables and herbs of your choice.
- Make sure not to overstuff the spring rolls in order for them to roll up nicely.

4.3.3 Curried Vegetable Samosas

These golden envelopes encase a medley of spiced vegetables which are enveloped by crunchy pastry. The perfect crisp on the outside gives them that appetizing aspect making them an ideal mirror for a snack in air frying.

Ingredients for 4 Servings:

- 2 cups diced potatoes
- 1 cup diced carrots
- 1 cup frozen peas
- 1 onion, finely chopped
- 2 cloves garlic, minced
- 1 tablespoon vegetable oil
- 2 teaspoons curry powder
- 1/2 teaspoon cumin seeds
- Salt and black pepper, as desired
- Triangles from spring roll pastry sheets (or puff pastry sheets)

Instructions:

- Heat some vegetable oil in a frying pan and cook over medium heat. Put in cumin seeds and let them crackle for a few seconds.
- Sauté after the onions turn translucent.
- Sauté for a couple of minutes until they are slightly tender.
- Add curry powder, salt, and black pepper.
- Add in the frozen peas and cook until all vegetables are soft enough and spices have been well spread out.
- Set your air fryer to 375°F (190°C) and preheat.
- To prepare the samosas, place a spoonful of the vegetable mixture onto each pastry triangle. Seal the edges of this pastry by folding it over and sealing with a little water.

- In the air fryer basket, arrange the samosas in a single layer.
- Air fry for about 10-12 minutes, or until the samosas are golden brown and crispy.
- Enjoy these Curried Vegetable Samosas as a delicious and fragrant appetizer or snack.

Cooking Tips:

- You can also modify the spiciness by adding more or less curry powder.
- For these samosas, you can use spring roll pastry or puff pastry based on your liking.

4.3.4 Balsamic Glazed Brussels Sprouts

Take your side dish to the next level with these Balsamic Glazed Brussels Sprouts. These tiny green jewels are air-fried to a crisp and then dressed with an irresistible balsamic glaze. They are a delicious and elegant complement to any meal.

Ingredients for 4 Servings:

For the Brussels Sprouts:

- 1 lb Brussels sprouts, halved and trimmed
- 2 tablespoons olive oil
- Salt and pepper to taste
- For the Balsamic Glaze:
- 1/4 cup balsamic vinegar
- 2 tablespoons honey
- 1 clove garlic, minced (optional)

Instructions:

- Set your air fryer to preheat at 375°F (190°C).
- In a mixing bowl, combine the halved Brussels sprouts with olive oil, salt, and black pepper to coat them thoroughly.
- The Brussels sprouts should be placed in the air fryer basket so that they lie flat.

- Air fry for about 12-15 minutes, shaking the basket in between, until the Brussels sprouts are crispy and browned.
- As the Brussels sprouts are cooking, make the balsamic glaze. In a small saucepan, mix balsamic vinegar, honey and minced garlic (if using).
- Bring the mixture to a simmer over low heat, stirring occasionally, until it thickens and reduces by half.
- Heat the balsamic glaze.
- Once the Brussels sprouts are cooked, place them in a serving bowl.
- Pour the balsamic glaze on top of the crispy Brussels sprouts.

Cooking Tips:

- Make sure you cut the Brussels sprouts and discard the discolored outer leaves before air frying.
- Alter the sweetness of the glaze as per your preference by adding more or less honey.

4.3.5 Mediterranean Stuffed Peppers

These Stuffed Peppers will transport your taste buds to the Mediterranean. These peppers are stuffed with a flavorful blend of rice, vegetables and herbs which is then air-fried to produce the perfect texture. They provide a hearty and healthy dinner full of Mediterranean flavors.

Ingredients for 4 Servings:

- 4 big bell peppers (any color)
- 1 cup cooked rice (white or brown)
- 1/2 cup diced tomatoes
- 1/2 cup diced cucumber
- 1/4 cup diced red onion
- 1/4 cup sliced black olives
- 2 tablespoons chopped fresh parsley
- 2 tablespoons olive oil
- 1 tablespoon lemon juice
- 1 teaspoon dried oregano
- Salt and freshly ground black pepper, to taste

Instructions:

- Heat your air fryer to 375°F (190°C).
- Trim the tops of the bell peppers and discard seeds and membranes. Set aside.
- In a large mixing bowl, mix cooked rice with diced tomatoes, diced cucumber, diced red onion, sliced black olives, chopped fresh parsley, olive oil, lemon juice, dried oregano salt and black pepper. Combine thoroughly to make the filling.
- Stuff the bell pepper with the rice and vegetable mixture, lightly pressing it.
- Put the stuffed peppers in the air fryer basket.
- Air fry for about 15-20 minutes until the peppers are soft and slightly charred.
- The Mediterranean Stuffed Peppers can be served as a filling and tasty main course.

Cooking Tips:

- The filling can be personalized with your preferred Mediterranean components including feta cheese, artichoke hearts, or roasted red peppers.
- Make sure not to pack the peppers too full so that they will cook evenly.

4.3.6 Garlic herb air fryer falafel

Indulge in the crunchy and delicious taste of our Garlic and Herb Air Fryer Falafel. These small chickpea patties are flavored with fragrant herbs and garlic, then air-fried to crispy goodness. They can be served with tahini sauce or in pita bread for a delicious meal.

Ingredients for 4 Servings:

- 2 cups chickpeas from a can, drained and rinsed
- 1/2 cup fresh parsley, chopped
- 1/4 cup fresh cilantro, chopped
- 1 small onion, chopped
- 2 cloves garlic, minced
- 1 teaspoon ground cumin
- 1 teaspoon ground coriander
- 1/2 teaspoon baking powder

- Salt and pepper to taste
- Olive oil, for brushing

Instructions:

- Heat the air fryer to 375°F (190°C).
- Process chickpeas with parsley, cilantro and onion in a food processor along with garlic, ground cumin, coriander, baking powder, salt and pepper.
- Pulse the ingredients until a coarse mixture is formed. Avoid over-processing; you need a bit of texture.
- Mold the mixture into small patties or balls.
- Brush every falafel with some olive oil.
- The falafel should be placed in the air fryer basket with a single layer.
- Air fry for about 10 to 12 minutes till the falafels are crispy and golden brown.
- These Garlic and Herb Air Fryer Falafel can be served as a delicious appetizer or stuffed in pita bread with your choice of toppings.

Cooking Tips:

- The falafel mix can be tailored by incorporating more herbs and spices according to your preference.
- If the falafel mixture is too runny, you may need to add a little more chickpea flour to help it stick together.

4.3.7 Cheesy Broccoli and Corn Fritters

Our Cheesy Broccoli and Corn Fritters will leave you salivating as you bite into the crunchy delight. These fritters are packed with the healthy goodness of broccoli, sweet corn and melting cheese. If you air fry them, you will get that golden perfection with just the right amount of grease

Ingredients for 4 Servings:

- 2 cups chopped broccoli florets, steamed
- 1 cup sweet corn (fresh or frozen), cooked
- 1 cup shredded cheddar cheese
- 1/4 cup grated Parmesan cheese

- 2 green onions, finely chopped
- 1/4 cup breadcrumbs
- 2 large eggs
- 1/2 teaspoon garlic powder
- Salt and pepper to taste
- Olive oil, for brushing

Instructions:

- Set your air fryer to 375°F (190°C) and preheat.
- In a big bowl, combine broccoli, sweet corn kernels which are previously cooked, shredded cheddar cheese; grated Parmesan cheese; chopped green onions; breadcrumbs eggs garlic powder salt black pepper.
- Combine the ingredients well.
- Shape the mix into patties and fry.
- A little olive oil should be brushed over each fritter.
- Arrange the fritters in one layer inside the air fryer basket.
- Place them into the air-fryer and fry for approximately 8 – 10 minutes or until they are golden-brownish on the outside.
- These Cheesy Broccoli and Corn Fritters can be served as an attractive, healthy snack or side dish.

Cooking Tips:

- You can even experiment with the fritters by adding your preferred herbs and spices to the batter.
- Make sure there is no additional moisture left on the corn and broccoli to prevent fritters from being soggy.

5. Meat and Poultry Magic

5.1 Chicken and Turkey Creations

In this part, we will describe different types of chicken and turkey Cuisines cooked using the power of an air fryer. You will get mouthwatering recipes of crispy wings and tenders, juicy turkey burgers, stuffed chicken breasts to name but a few that are very tasty yet simple to prepare. Here, we will discuss some of the amazing poultry dishes that you can cook using air frying technology; from an easy weeknight supper to a fancy banquet, these are guaranteed to have your taste buds sizzling. Well, let us take a dive into this poultry aerial adventure and see the marvels of air frying in your very own kitchen!

5.1.1 Herbed chicken and mushroom skewers

Savor the joy of tender chicken and earthy mushrooms in our Herbed Chicken and Mushroom Skewers. They are soaked in a high in herb combination and then air fried until perfect. Of these skewers, both outdoor grill and indoor cooking are appetizing and nutritious.

Ingredients for 4 Servings:

- cubed boneless, skinless chicken breast 1 lb.
- 8 ounces fresh mushrooms, stems removed and halved
- 1/4 cup olive oil
- 2 cloves garlic, minced
- 2 tablespoons fresh rosemary, chopped
- 2 tablespoons fresh thyme leaves
- Salt and pepper, to taste
- Wooden skewers, soaked in water for half an hour

Instructions:

- To prepare the marinade, mix olive oil with minced garlic, fresh rosemary, fresh thyme leaves, salt and pepper in a bowl.

- Alternately thread the chicken cubes and halved mushrooms onto soaked wooden skewers.
- Heating your air fryer to 375°F (190°C).
- Arrange the skewers in a single layer in the air fryer basket.
- Cook in an air fryer for about 12-15 minutes, rotating the skewers halfway through, until the chicken is cooked and the edges are golden brown.
- The chicken and mushroom skewers can be accompanied with your most loved dipping sauce or a side salad.

Cooking Tips:

- You can use metal skewers if you wish to avoid soaking the wooden ones.
- Add your favorite herbs and spices to customize the marinade for more flavor.

5.1.2 Crispy Turkey Cutlets with Lemon-Caper Sauce

Enjoy the crunchiness of our Crispy Turkey Cutlets with Lemon-Caper Sauce. These tender turkey cutlets are breaded with a golden breadcrumb crust and crisped to perfection in an air fryer. Doused in a tangy lemon-caper sauce, this dish is an amazing mixture of textures and flavors that will leave your taste buds happy.

Ingredients for 4 Servings:

For the Turkey Cutlets:

- 4 turkey cutlets
- 1 cup breadcrumbs
- 1/2 cup grated Parmesan cheese
- 1 teaspoon of dried Italian herbs (basil, oregano, thyme)
- Salt and pepper, to taste
- 2 eggs, beaten
- Olive oil, for brushing

For the Lemon-Caper Sauce:

- 1/4 cup unsalted butter
- 2 tablespoons capers, drained

- Juice of 1 lemon
- 1 clove garlic, minced
- Salt and pepper, to taste
- Fresh parsley, chopped, for garnish

Instructions:

- In a bowl, mix together the breadcrumbs, grated Parmesan cheese, dried Italian herbs, salt and black pepper.
- Dip each turkey cutlet in the beaten eggs, allowing any excess to drip off, and then cover it with the breadcrumb mixture.
- Set your air fryer to 375°F (190°C) and preheat it.
- Arrange the breaded turkey cutlets in a single layer in an air fryer basket.
- Air fry for 8-10 minutes flipping the cutlets halfway through until crisp and cooked.
- As the turkey cutlets are being prepared, make the lemon-caper sauce. In a small saucepan, melt unsalted butter over low heat. Add in strained capers, lemon juice, minced garlic, salt and black pepper. Simmer for a few minutes until the sauce thickens slightly.
- After the turkey cutlets are cooked, top with lemon-caper sauce and sprinkle with chopped fresh parsley.
- Enjoy these Crispy Turkey Cutlets with Lemon-Caper Sauce as a delicious main course.

Cooking Tips:

- Depending on your preference, season the breadcrumb mixture with more herbs and spices.
- Ensure the turkey cutlets are not overcooked to retain their tenderness and juiciness.

5.1.3 Spicy Orange Glazed Chicken Wings

Our Spicy Orange-Glazed Chicken Wings are ready to give you a burst of flavor. These wings are coated with an orange spicy glaze that will make your taste buds dance. They are air-fried to perfection and ideal for game day, parties or any other time you need a bit of spice and sugary.

Ingredients for 4 Servings:

- 2 lbs of chicken wings, separated into drumettes and flats
- 1 tablespoon olive oil
- Salt and pepper, to taste

For the Spicy Orange Glaze:

- 1/2 cup orange marmalade
- 2 tbsp hot sauce (to taste)
- 2 cloves garlic, minced
- 1 tablespoon soy sauce
- 1 teaspoon grated fresh ginger
- 1/2 teaspoon of red pepper flakes (use more or less depending on the heat level).
- Sesame seeds, for garnish
- Sliced green onions, for garnish

Instructions:

- Heat up your air fryer to 380°F (193°C).
- Toss the chicken wings in a large bowl with olive oil, salt and black pepper until they are well coated.
- Arrange the chicken wings in a single layer inside the air fryer basket, without overcrowding it. You might have to cook them in batches.
- Cook the wings in an air fryer for about 25-30 minutes, flipping them halfway through until they are crispy and fully cooked.
- As the chicken wings are roasting, make the spicy orange glaze. In a saucepan, mix orange marmalade, hot sauce, minced garlic, soy sauce, fresh ginger grated in and red pepper flakes. Cook over low heat, stirring occasionally, until the glaze thickens.
- When the chicken wings are ready, place them in a large bowl.
- Drizzle the spicy orange glaze on crispy wings and toss them to coat evenly.
- Sesame seeds and thinly sliced green onions for garnish.
- The Spicy Orange-Glazed Chicken Wings serve as a spicy and sweet appetizer or main course.

Cooking Tips:

- Modify the spiciness by using more or less hot sauce and red pepper flakes.
- To achieve more crispiness, you can lightly spray the wings with cooking spray before air frying.

5.1.4 Garlic-Lemon Roasted Turkey Breast

This dish unites the traditional pairing of garlic and lemon, adding a flavorful punch to your turkey breast. Air roasting gives a juicy and tender result, which can make it ideal for holiday meals or family dinners.

Ingredients for 4 Servings:

- 1 bone-in turkey breast, approximately 4 pounds.
- 4 cloves garlic, minced
- Zest of 1 lemon
- Juice of 1 lemon
- 2 tablespoons olive oil
- 1 teaspoon dried thyme
- 1 teaspoon dried rosemary
- Salt and pepper, to taste
- Fresh parsley, chopped, for garnish

Instructions:

- Set your air fryer to 325°F (163°C).
- The marinade is formed by mixing minced garlic, lemon zest, lemon juice, olive oil, dried thyme, dried rosemary and salt as well as black pepper in a bowl.
- Wipe the turkey breast dry with paper towels on a clean surface.
- Rub the turkey breast with the garlic-lemon marinade, making sure it is well coated from all directions.
- Place the turkey breast, breast side down, in the air fryer basket.
- Air roast for about 35-40 minutes, then turn the turkey breast.
- Roast in air for an additional 30-35 minutes or until the internal temperature is at least 165°F (74°C) and the skin is golden brown and crispy.
- After that, leave the turkey breast to rest for a little while before cutting it.
- Garnish with chopped fresh parsley.

Cooking Tips:

- Use a meat thermometer to check the internal temperature of turkey breast, which is necessary for safety and juiciness.
- However, if you find that the skin is not as crisp to your liking, then briefly broil it in your oven or air fryer to get the desired crispiness.

5.1.5 Chicken Piccata with Capers

Enjoy the delicious tartness of our Chicken Piccata with Capers. This iconic Italian dish is chicken cutlets bathed in a lemony and salty caper sauce. The air frying of the chicken guarantees a crispy outside but with moist and tasty meat. It's Italian in your own home.

Ingredients for 4 Servings:

For the Chicken Cutlets:

- 4 pounded to even thickness boneless, skinless chicken breasts
- 1 cup all-purpose flour, used for dredging
- Salt and black pepper, as desired
- 2 tablespoons olive oil
- 2 tablespoons unsalted butter

For the Piccata Sauce:

- 1/2 cup chicken broth
- Juice of 2 lemons
- 1/4 cup capers, drained
- 1/4 cup fresh parsley, chopped
- 2 cloves garlic, minced

Instructions:

- Set your air fryer to 375°F (190°C) and preheat.
- Salt and pepper the chicken breasts.
- Dust each chicken breast with all-purpose flour, shaking off any excess.
- Heat the olive oil and butter over medium-high heat in a large skillet until the butter is melted and foamy.
- It takes about 3-4 minutes per side to brown the chicken breasts in the skillet until they are golden and fully cooked. Place them on a plate and cover with foil to keep warm.

- In another skillet, pour in chicken broth, lemon juice, capers minced garlic and chopped fresh parsley. Simmer for a short time until the sauce becomes slightly thick.
- As the sauce simmers, put the cooked chicken breasts in a preheated air fryer for 2-3 minutes to retain their crunch.
- Serve the chicken breasts with the piccata sauce poured over them.
- Have your preferred pasta or a side dish of vegetables with this Chicken Piccata with Capers.

Cooking Tips:

- The amount of lemon juice and capers you use can be adjusted depending on your preference.
- For a more viscous sauce, thicken the piccata sauce with cornstarch slurry and continue cooking until it starts to become oily.

5.1.6 Maple-Dijon Turkey Meatballs

Get ready to have your taste buds tickled by the delightful combination of flavors that our Maple-Dijon Turkey Meatballs offer. These meatballs are made from ground turkey that is free of fats, and it is topped with a delicious combination of maple syrup and Dijon mustard. They are also cooked through air-frying, with crispness on the outside and juiciness on the inside. They would make a wonderful appetizer or the tasty addition to your favorite pasta.

Ingredients for 4 Servings:

- 1 pound lean ground turkey
- 1/2 cup breadcrumbs
- 1/4 cup grated Parmesan cheese
- 1/4 cup milk
- 1/4 cup finely chopped onion
- 1 clove garlic, minced
- 1 egg
- 1 teaspoon dried thyme
- Salt and pepper, to taste
- Olive oil, for brushing

- For the Maple-Dijon Glaze:
- 1/4 cup maple syrup
- 2 tablespoons Dijon mustard
- 1 teaspoon soy sauce
- 1/2 teaspoon garlic powder

Instructions:

- In a large mixing bowl, add lean ground turkey, breadcrumbs, grated Parmesan cheese, milk, finely chopped onion and minced garlics eggs along with dried thyme salt and black pepper.
- Shape the mixture into meatballs with a diameter of 1- inch to 1.5 -inch each.
- Preheat your air fryer to a temperature of 375°F (190°C).
- Brush each meatball with olive oil.
- Place the meatballs in a single layer in the air fryer basket.
- Bake for 12 to 15 minutes, flipping meatballs over halfway through the process, until they are golden brown and clear in the middle.
- While meatballs are getting cooked, the Maple-Dijon Glaze should be first prepared. Combine maple syrup, dijon mustard, soy sauce and garlic powder in a small saucepan. Stir the mixture at low heat to cook until it becomes silky and slightly thick in nature.
- Once the meatballs are cooked, drizzle them with the Maple-Dijon Glaze.
- Garlic-Dijon Turkey Meatballs can be presented as a starter or with any pasta or rice meal.

Cooking Tips:

- You can increase the sweetness or tanginess of the glaze by adding more maple syrup and Dijon mustard respectively.
- However, for those who love a spicy taste, you can include some red pepper flakes to the glaze.

5.1.7 .Szechuan Pepper Chicken with Stir-Fried Vegetables

Get ready to have your taste buds rocked with our Szechuan Pepper Chicken with Stir-Fried Vegetables. This dish has soft pieces of chicken cooked in a spicy Szechuan pepper sauce, along with an assortment of stir-fried vegetables. Air fried chicken has a crispy texture with the right amount of moisture, making it an enjoyable meal with a hint of spice.

Ingredients for 4 Servings:

For the Szechuan Pepper Chicken:

- A pound of boneless, skinless chicken breasts cut into bite-sized pieces.
- 2 tablespoons cornstarch
- 1 tablespoon vegetable oil
- 2 cloves garlic, minced
- 1 teaspoon grated fresh ginger
- 2 tablespoons crushed Szechuan peppercorns (to taste)
- 2 tablespoons soy sauce
- 1 tablespoon rice vinegar
- 1 tablespoon hoisin sauce
- 1 teaspoon sugar
- 1/4 cup chicken broth
- For the Stir-Fried Vegetables:
- 2 cups of mixed vegetables (bell peppers, broccoli, snap peas, carrots etc.) thinly sliced.
- 1 tablespoon vegetable oil
- Salt and pepper, to taste

Instructions:

- In a bowl, dust the chicken pieces with cornstarch so they are well coated.
- Heat your air fryer to 375°F (190°C).
- Spread the coated chicken in a single layer in the air fryer basket. It may be necessary to cook them in batches.
- Air fry the chicken for about 12-15 minutes, shaking the basket or turning over the pieces halfway through until they are crisp and cooked.
- In the meantime, prepare the Szechuan pepper sauce while cooking chicken. Heat vegetable oil in a small saucepan over medium heat. Incorporate minced garlic, grated fresh ginger, and crushed Szechuan peppercorns. Sauté for a minute until aromatic.

- Add soy sauce, rice vinegar, hoisin sauce, sugar and chicken broth to the mixture. Simmer for a couple of minutes to allow the sauce to thicken slightly.
- In another skillet, cook vegetable oil on high heat. Add the sliced mixed vegetables and stir-fry them for 3 to 4 minutes until they are tender crisp. Salt and pepper to taste.
- When the chicken is cooked, coat it with Szechuan pepper sauce and toss.
- Pair the Szechuan Pepper Chicken with stir-fried vegetables for an exciting combination of spices and flavors.

Cooking Tips:

- Regulate the amount of crushed Szechuan peppercorns to manage spiciness.
- The stir-fried vegetables can be tailored to your liking or what you happen to have readily available.

5.2 Beef and Pork Classics Reinvented

In this section, we're transforming traditional beef and pork dishes into a modern air-fried style. You will find new taste notes and revolutionary cooking techniques that take these traditional meats to a whole new level. From juicy steaks to irresistible ribs, prepare yourself for some beef and pork you've never tasted before.

5.2.1 .Smokey BBQ Beef Brisket Sliders

Brace yourself for the delicious and smokey taste of our BBQ Beef Brisket Sliders. We took perfectly cooked tender beef brisket, barbecue sauce and soft slider buns. These sliders are ideal for a casual get-together, game day, or any event where you want to enjoy the true flavor of barbecue.

Ingredients for 4 Servings:

For the BBQ Beef Brisket:

- 1.5 pounds beef brisket
- 1 tablespoon olive oil
- 1 onion, thinly sliced
- 3 cloves garlic, minced
- 1 cup beef broth
- 1 cup barbecue sauce
- 1 teaspoon smoked paprika
- 1/2 teaspoon chili powder
- Salt and black pepper to taste
- For the Slider Buns:
- 12 slider buns
- Butter for toasting

For the Coleslaw:

- 2 cups coleslaw mix
- 1/4 cup mayonnaise
- 1 tablespoon apple cider vinegar
- 1 teaspoon sugar
- Salt and pepper, as desired

Instructions:

- Set your air fryer to 350°F (175°C) and wait for it to preheat.
- The beef brisket should be seasoned with smoked paprika, chili powder, salt and black pepper.
- Heat olive oil in a skillet over medium-high heat. Sear the brisket on all sides, until nicely browned. Set the brisket aside.
- In the same skillet, place thinly sliced onion and minced garlic. Sauté until they become soft and translucent.
- Bring the seared brisket back to the skillet and add beef broth along with barbecue sauce.
- Put the lid on and simmer for 3 to 4 hours or more until the brisket is tender enough.
- While the brisket is cooking you can prepare a coleslaw. In a bowl, mix the coleslaw mix with mayonnaise, apple cider vinegar, sugar, salt and black pepper. Mix well and refrigerate until use.
- After preparing, remove the brisket from the pan and tear it using two forks.
- Return the brisket into the skillet and coat it with this barbecue sauce.
- The buns should be split, and lightly buttered on both sides. Fry it in the air for 2-3 minutes till golden.
- Assemble the BBQ Beef Brisket Sliders by piling a generous portion of brisket on each bun, and top with coleslaw.
- These Smokey BBQ Beef Brisket Sliders can be made into a delicious and filling entrée.

Cooking Tips:

- You also have the option of purchasing barbeque sauce from the shops or preparing your own according to your taste.
- Low-temperature cooking ensures that the brisket is tender and flavorful.

5.2.2 Herb-Crusted Pork Tenderloin with Apple Chutney

Taste the juiciness of our Herb-Crusted Pork Tenderloin with Apple Chutney. This plate brings together the tender texture of piggy's delicate pork fillet and herb covering with a splendid fragrance, which is perfectly balanced by apple chutney sweetly sour. Air frying the pork leaves it with a crispy outside but succulent and tasty meat.

Ingredients for 4 Servings:

For the Herb-Crusted Pork Tenderloin:

- 2 pork tenderloins, about 1 lb.
- 2 tablespoons olive oil
- 2 cloves garlic, minced
- 1 tablespoon fresh rosemary, minced
- 1 tablespoon fresh thyme leaves
- Salt and pepper, to taste

For the Apple Chutney:

- 2 peeled, cored and diced apples
- 1/2 cup apple cider vinegar
- 1/4 cup brown sugar
- 1/4 cup finely chopped red onion
- 1/4 cup dried cranberries
- 1/4 teaspoon ground cinnamon
- 1/4 teaspoon ground allspice
- Salt and black pepper, as desired

Instructions:

- To start, preheat your air fryer to 375°F (190°C).
- Herb crust can be prepared by mixing minced garlic, fresh rosemary, fresh thyme leaves, olive oil, salt and black pepper in a bowl.
- Rub the herb mixture all over the pork tenderloins and make sure that they are well coated.
- Put the pork tenderloins in the air fryer basket.

- Bake in the air fryer for about 20-25 minutes, turning the tenderloins halfway through, until they are done and have a browned crust. The internal temperature should be 145°F (63°C).
- As the pork is air frying, make the apple chutney. Combine diced apples, apple cider vinegar, brown sugar, finely chopped red onion, dried cranberries, ground cinnamon, ground allspice, salt and black pepper in a saucepan.
- Once the mixture is boiling, reduce heat and simmer for 15-20 minutes until apples are soft and chutney thickens.
- When the pork tenderloins are ready, let them sit for a while before cutting.
- Serve the Herb-Crusted Pork Tenderloin slices with a big spoonful of apple chutney on top.

Cooking Tips:

- Ensure that the pork tenderloin is cooked to the desired internal temperature recommended for consumption.
- Adjust the sweetness and spiciness of the apple chutney according to your taste.

5.2.3 Korean-Style Beef Bulgogi Wraps

Go on a gastronomic adventure with our Korean-Style Beef Bulgogi Wraps. The strips of beef are air-fried thinly sliced and marinated in a savory-sweet bulgogi sauce. While wrapped in crisp lettuce leaves and complemented with your preferred toppings, these wraps are a wonderful combination of textures and flavors.

Ingredients for 4 Servings:

For the Beef Bulgogi:

- 1 pound of thinly sliced beef (ribeye or sirloin).
- 1/2 onion, thinly sliced
- 2 cloves garlic, minced
- 1/4 cup soy sauce
- 2 tablespoons sugar
- 1 tablespoon mirin (rice wine)
- 1 tablespoon sesame oil
- 1 teaspoon grated fresh ginger

- 1/4 teaspoon black pepper
- 1 chopped green onion (for garnish)

For the Wraps:

- Large lettuce leaves (e.g., iceberg or butterhead)
- Cooked rice, for serving
- Kimchi, for garnish
- Sesame seeds, for garnish

Instructions:

- In a bowl, mix thinly sliced beef, thinly sliced onion, minced garlic, soy sauce, sugar, mirin sesame oil, grated fresh ginger and black pepper. Stir well to ensure that the beef is completely covered. Marinate for 30 minutes or more.
- Set your air fryer to 375°F (190°C) and preheat it.
- Arrange the marinated beef slices in a single layer in the air fryer basket.
- Cook for about 8-10 minutes in an air fryer, turning the slices of beef halfway through cooking until they are cooked and slightly caramelized.
- As the beef is air frying, prepare the wraps. Place a layer of large lettuce leaves, add some rice to each leaf and then top with the cooked bulgogi beef.
- Decorate the wraps with kimchi, chopped green onions and sesame seeds.

Cooking Tips:

- Modify the length of marinating to make beef taste stronger.
- You are also free to add some extra toppings such as sliced cucumbers, carrots or a dash of sriracha sauce for spiciness.

5.2.4 Italian Stuffed Pork Loin with Balsamic Glaze

Taste the Italian flavor with our Balsamic Glazed Italian Stuffed Pork Loin. This dish has a tender pork loin filled with an aromatic blend of herbs, dried tomatoes, spinach and mozzarella cheese. It is then roasted to perfection and glazed with a scrumptious balsamic sauce, making the combination tasteful.

Ingredients for 4 Servings:

For the Stuffed Pork Loin:

- 1.5 pounds pork loin
- 1/2 cup rehydrated and chopped sun-dried tomatoes.
- 1 cup fresh spinach leaves
- 1 cup shredded mozzarella cheese
- 2 cloves garlic, minced
- 1 teaspoon of dried Italian herbs (basil, oregano, thyme).
- Salt and black pepper to taste
- Butcher's twine for tying

For the Balsamic Glaze:

- 1/2 cup balsamic vinegar
- 2 tablespoons brown sugar
- 1/2 tsp cornstarch (optional as a thickening agent).

Instructions:

- Set the temperature of your air fryer to 375°F (190°C) and preheat.
- Flatten the pork loin by cutting it horizontally without slicing all the way through, and open like a book.
- The inside of the pork loin is seasoned with minced garlic, dried Italian herbs, salt and black pepper.
- Evenly distribute sun-dried tomatoes, fresh spinach leaves and shredded mozzarella cheese over the pork loin.
- With care, roll up the stuffed pork loin and tie it at intervals with butcher's twine.
- Put the pork loin stuffed with stuffing in the air fryer basket.
- Air fry for about 30-35 minutes, turning it occasionally to cook the pork until golden brown and well done. The internal temperature should be 145°F (63°C).
- As the pork is air frying, make the balsamic glaze. In a saucepan, mix balsamic vinegar and brown sugar. Heat over low fire until it reduces and thickens. If you want to make the glaze thicker, you can add cornstarch diluted in water.
- When the pork loin is cooked, take it out of the air fryer and let it rest for a few minutes before slicing.

Cooking Tips:

- Using kitchen twine, tie the stuffed pork loin in order to ensure uniform cooking.

- You can adapt the stuffing to your favorite Italian herbs and ingredients.

5.2.5 Spiced Beef Kofta with Tzatziki

These delicious air-fried beef kofta skewers are spiced with Middle Eastern aromatics. Served with a cool and flavorful tzatziki sauce, they are both delicious and filling.

Ingredients for 4 Servings:

For the Beef Kofta:

- One pound of ground beef (ideally lean)
- 1/2 onion, grated
- 2 cloves garlic, minced
- 1 teaspoon ground cumin
- 1 teaspoon ground coriander
- 1/2 teaspoon ground paprika
- 1/4 teaspoon ground cinnamon
- Salt and pepper to taste
- 2 tablespoons fresh parsley, chopped
- Wooden skewers, soaked in water

For the Tzatziki Sauce:

- 1 cup Greek yogurt
- 1 cucumber, grated and drained
- 2 cloves garlic, minced
- 1 tablespoon fresh dill, chopped
- 1 tablespoon fresh mint, chopped
- 1 tablespoon lemon juice
- Salt and pepper to taste

Instructions:

- Set your air fryer to 375°F (190°C).

- Combine ground beef, grated onion, minced garlic, ground cumin, ground coriander, ground paprika, ground cinnamon salt black pepper and chopped fresh parsley in a bowl. Combine until the spices blend fully with the meat.
- Cut pieces of the seasoned beef mixture and mold them onto wooden skewers to form long slender kofta shapes.
- Arrange the beef kofta skewers in the air fryer basket.
- Air fry for about 10-12 minutes, turning the skewers in half way, until cooked through and evenly browned.
- As the beef kofta is air frying, make the tzatziki sauce. Mix Greek yogurt, grated and drained cucumber, minced garlic, chopped fresh dill, chopped fresh mint, lemon juice, salt and black pepper together in a bowl. Mix well.
- When the beef kofta is cooked, take them out of the air fryer and serve hot with a large spoonful of tzatziki.

Cooking Tips:

- By soaking the wooden skewers in water, they will not burn while air frying.
- Vary the spiciness by introducing more or less ground pepper to the beef mix.

5.2.6 Slow Cooked Pulled Pork with Tangy Coleslaw

Prepare to indulge in the delicious taste of our Slow-Cooked Pulled Pork with Tangy Coleslaw. A classic American dish of tender pulled pork cooked slowly and seasoned to perfection, served with refreshing and tangy coleslaw. It is a delightful blend of smoky, salty, and spicy.

Ingredients for 4 Servings:

For the Slow-Cooked Pulled Pork:

- 2 pounds of pork shoulder or pork butt
- 1 onion, thinly sliced
- 4 cloves garlic, minced
- 1 cup chicken broth
- 1/4 cup apple cider vinegar
- 2 tablespoons brown sugar
- 1 tablespoon smoked paprika

- 1 tsp cayenne pepper (to taste)
- Salt and pepper, to taste
- 1 cup barbecue sauce

For the Tangy Coleslaw:

- 4 cups of shredded green and purple cabbage.
- 1/2 cup mayonnaise
- 2 tablespoons apple cider vinegar
- 1 tablespoon Dijon mustard
- 1 tablespoon honey
- 1/2 teaspoon celery seed
- Salt and pepper, to taste

Instructions:

- Mix the minced garlic, brown sugar, smoked paprika, cayenne pepper, salt, black pepper and barbecue sauce in a bowl to form the pork marinade.
- Now put in the thinly sliced onions at the bottom of your slow cooker.
- Rub the marinade on the pork shoulder or butt, making sure it is well coated.
- Put the pork on top of the sliced onions in the slow cooker.
- Add chicken broth and apple cider vinegar to the pork.
- 8-10 hours in low heat until the pork is tender and falls apart with a fork.
- During the cooking of pork, make a tangy coleslaw. Mix shredded cabbage, mayonnaise, apple cider vinegar, Dijon mustard, honey, celery seed salt and black pepper in a bowl. Toss to coat the cabbage and keep refrigerated until serving.
- After cooking the pork, shred it with two forks and add to the juices in the slow cooker.
- Serve the Slow-Cooked Pulled Pork on buns, with Tangy Coleslaw.

Cooking Tips:

- Increase or decrease the amount of cayenne pepper in the pork marinade to change its spiciness.
- Alternatively, the pork can be cooked in an Instant Pot or oven, but slow-cooking gives incredibly tender results.

5.2.7 Balsamic Glazed Steak Rolls with Vegetables

Our Balsamic Glazed Steak Rolls with Vegetables will help you take your dinner to the next level. These steak rolls are not only aesthetically pleasing but also packed with flavor. Its air-fried thinly sliced beef is filled with a vibrant variety of vegetables and served with balsamic glaze.

Ingredients for 4 Servings:

For the Steak Rolls:

- 4 thinly cut beef steaks (such as flank steak or sirloin).
- 1 red bell pepper, sliced thinly
- 1 thinly sliced yellow bell pepper.
- 1 thinly sliced green bell pepper.
- 1 zucchini, thinly sliced
- 1 carrot, cut into matchsticks
- 4 cloves garlic, minced
- Salt and pepper to taste
- Wooden skewers, soaked in water

For the Balsamic Glaze:

- 1/2 cup balsamic vinegar
- 2 tablespoons brown sugar
- 1/2 tsp cornstarch (optional for thickening)

Instructions:

- Set your air fryer to 375°F (190°C) and preheat.
- Lay the thinned beef steaks on any clean surface.
- Season every steak with garlic, salt and black pepper.
- Place a selection of thinly sliced vegetables over each steak.
- Wrap the steak carefully with the vegetables inside and secure it using wooden skewers.
- Put the steak rolls in the air fryer basket.

- Air fry for about 10-12 minutes, turning the rolls over halfway through cooking, until the beef is done to your specifications and vegetables are soft.
- As the steak rolls are air frying, make the balsamic glaze. In a saucepan, mix balsamic vinegar and brown sugar. Over low heat, simmer until it reduces and thickens. If you want to thicken the glaze even more, you can add cornstarch that has been mixed with a little water.
- Once the steak rolls are cooked, take them out of the air fryer and drizzle with a balsamic glaze.

Cooking Tips:

- Personalize the vegetable fillings according to your liking.
- Pre-soaking the wooden skewers prevents them from burning while air frying.

5.3 Quick and Easy Meaty Morsels

Here is a delicious lineup of recipes that will take you to the taste of honey-mustard glazed ham bites, mini meatball skewers with tomato sauce, quick BBQ pork riblets, chicken satay with peanut sauce, spiced lamb kebabs with yogurt dip, teriyaki beef strips with sesame seeds and buff Such dishes are intended for those times when you need something rich and satisfying but without long preparation. From succulent ham to delectable lamb on a stick, these recipes are all about maximum flavor and minimum effort. Therefore, we should begin a culinary journey that will provide us with tasty and quick-to-prepare meat snacks.

5.3.1 Honey-Mustard Glazed Ham Bites

These scrumptious nibbles are good for any snack, appetizer or buffet. The ham is succulent as it is glazed with honey and mustard, a combination that makes the product irresistible. Now, let us proceed to this quick and easy recipe which will surely tickle your taste buds.

Ingredients for 4 Servings:

- A pound of cooked ham, diced into small cubes
- 1/4 cup honey
- 2 tablespoons Dijon mustard
- 1 tablespoon whole-grain mustard
- 1 tablespoon olive oil

- 1/2 teaspoon garlic powder
- Salt and pepper to taste.
- Toothpicks for serving

Instructions:

- In a bowl, mix honey, Dijon mustard, whole-grain mustard, olive oil, garlic powder, salt and black pepper. Mix until you have a uniform glaze.
- Place the cooked ham cubes on toothpicks.
- Apply the honey-mustard glaze liberally to the ham bites and make sure they are coated well.
- Set your air fryer to preheat at 375°F (190°C).
- Arrange the glazed ham bites in a single layer using the air fryer basket.
- Air fry them for about 5-7 minutes, or till the ham bites are heated through and the glaze is caramelized, making it slightly crispy.
- Take the ham bites out of the air fryer and allow them to cool for a minute or two.

Cooking Tips:

- It is possible to regulate the sweetness and sourness of the glaze by adding more or less honey or mustard.
- Ensure that the air fryer basket is not overloaded to ensure even cooking.

5.3.2 Mini Meatball Skewers with Tomato Sauce

Prepare to enjoy the taste of our Mini Meatball Skewers with Tomato Sauce. These bite-size delicacies are ideal for parties, get-togethers or just as a fun snack. The meatballs are well seasoned and served with a thick tomato sauce. Now, let's get to this quick and easy recipe that will surely satisfy a crowd.

Ingredients for 4 Servings:

- 1 pound ground beef
- 1/4 cup breadcrumbs
- 1/4 cup grated Parmesan cheese

- 1/4 cup milk
- 1/4 cup finely chopped onion
- 1 clove garlic, minced
- 1 egg
- 1 teaspoon dried oregano
- 1/2 teaspoon salt
- 1/4 teaspoon black pepper
- For the Tomato Sauce:
- 1 cup tomato sauce
- 1/2 teaspoon dried basil
- 1/2 teaspoon dried oregano
- Salt and pepper, to taste
- Wooden skewers, soaked in water

Instructions:

- In a bowl, mix ground beef with breadcrumbs, grated Parmesan cheese, milk, finely chopped onion, minced garlic, egg, dried oregano salt and black pepper. Stir until all ingredients are well blended.
- Roll the meat mixture into mini meatballs.
- Place the mini meatballs on wooden skewers.
- Set the air fryer to 375°F (190°C).
- Arrange the meatball skewers in a single layer in the air fryer basket.
- Air fry for around 8-10 minutes, flipping the skewers halfway through, until done and with a crispy exterior.
- As the meatballs are air frying, prepare tomato sauce. In a small saucepan, mix tomato sauce with dried basil, dried oregano, salt and black pepper. Cook over low heat until heated through.
- After cooking the meatballs, take them out of the air fryer and serve with tomato sauce for dipping.

Cooking Tips:

- Personalize the meatballs by spicing up the mixture with your preferred herbs and spices.
- Soaking the wooden skewers prevents them from burning during air frying.

5.3.3 Quick BBQ Pork Riblets

These succulent riblets are covered with a finger-licking barbecue glaze that will make you want another serving. Join us on a flavor-filled journey to master the art of riblets.

Ingredients for 4 Servings:

For the Pork Riblets:

- 2 pounds pork riblets
- 1 tablespoon olive oil
- 1 teaspoon smoked paprika
- 1/2 teaspoon garlic powder
- 1/2 teaspoon onion powder
- Salt and pepper to taste

For the BBQ Sauce:

- 1/2 cup barbecue sauce
- 2 tablespoons honey
- 1 tablespoon apple cider vinegar
- 1/2 teaspoon Worcestershire sauce
- ¼ teaspoon cayenne pepper (to taste)

Instructions:

- In a bowl, mix smoked paprika with garlic powder, onion powder, salt and pepper.
- Coat the pork riblets with olive oil and then season them with spice mixture, making sure they are well covered.
- Heat your air fryer to 375°F (190°C).
- Arrange the seasoned pork riblets in a single layer in the air fryer basket.
- Air fry for 18-20 minutes, turning the riblets halfway through cooking, until they are cooked and charred.
- As the riblets are air frying, prepare the BBQ sauce. In a small saucepan, mix barbecue sauce with honey, apple cider vinegar, Worcestershire sauce and cayenne pepper. Simmer on low heat until it is warm.

- Once the riblets are cooked, take them out of the air fryer and coat them with barbecue sauce.

Cooking Tips:

- Increase or decrease the amount of cayenne pepper to alter the heat level of the BBQ sauce.
- If you prefer a smokier taste, add some liquid smoke to the barbecue sauce.

5.3.4 Chicken Satay with Peanut Sauce

These chicken skewers are not only a treat to the palate but also an excursion down the lanes of Southeast Asia. Let's journey into this recipe together and create a peanut sauce that is impossible to forget.

Ingredients for 4 Servings:

For the Chicken Satay:

- 1 lb of boneless, skinless chicken breasts or thighs cut into strips
- 1/4 cup coconut milk
- 1 tablespoon soy sauce
- 1 tablespoon brown sugar
- 1 tablespoon curry powder
- 1/2 teaspoon turmeric powder
- 1/2 teaspoon ground cumin
- 1/2 teaspoon ground coriander
- 1 clove garlic, minced
- Wooden skewers, soaked in water

For the Peanut Sauce:

- 1/2 cup creamy peanut butter
- 2 tablespoons soy sauce
- 2 tablespoons brown sugar
- 1 tablespoon rice vinegar
- 1 teaspoon sriracha sauce (to taste)

- 1 clove garlic, minced
- Water (to adjust the consistency)

Instructions:

- In a bowl, mix coconut milk, soy sauce, brown sugar, curry powder, turmeric powder, ground cumin and coriander as well as minced garlic. Combine until you have a uniform marinade.
- Thread the chicken strips on wooden skewers and arrange them in a shallow dish.
- Cover the chicken skewers with marinade. Marinate for 30 minutes minimum, or refrigerate and let the flavors mingle for a few hours.
- Heat your air fryer to 375°F (190°C).
- Put the chicken skewers in a single layer in the air fryer basket after marinating them.
- Cook in the air fryer for around 8-10 minutes, turning over the skewers midway through cooking, until the chicken is cooked through and has a slightly charred crust.
- As the chicken is air frying, make the peanut sauce. In a bowl mix creamy peanut butter, soy sauce, brown sugar, rice vinegar, sriracha sauce and minced garlic. Mix well. In the case of too thick sauce, you can add a little water to get your preferred consistency.
- After the chicken skewers are cooked, serve them with peanut sauce for dipping.

Cooking Tips:

- Vary the heat of the peanut sauce by using more or less sriracha sauce.
- Soaking the wooden skewers keeps them from burning while air frying.

5.3.5 Spiced Lamb Kebabs with Yogurt Sauce

The kebabs are a perfect combination of flavorful spices and juicy lamb which goes well with cool, creamy yogurt dip. Come with us on a gastronomic trip to the center of the Mediterranean.

Ingredients for 4 Servings:

For the Lamb Kebabs:

- 1 pound ground lamb
- 1/4 cup finely chopped onion
- 2 cloves garlic, minced
- 1 teaspoon ground cumin
- 1 teaspoon ground coriander
- 1/2 teaspoon ground paprika
- 1/2 teaspoon ground cinnamon
- Salt and pepper, according to taste
- Wooden skewers, soaked in water

For the Yogurt Dip:

- 1 cup Greek yogurt
- 1 tablespoon fresh lemon juice
- 1 clove garlic, minced
- 1 tbsp fresh mint leaves, finely chopped
- Salt and ground black pepper, to taste

Instructions:

- In a bowl, mix ground lamb with finely chopped onion, minced garlic, ground cumin, ground coriander, ground paprika, ground cinnamon salt and black pepper to taste. Stir until the spices are well blended.
- Form kebabs by taking pieces of the lamb mixture and shaping them onto wooden skewers.
- Set your air fryer to 375°F (190°C).
- The lamb kebabs are to be placed in the air fryer basket, in a single layer.
- Air fry for around 8-10 minutes, flipping the kebabs over halfway through, until they are cooked and have a crispy exterior.
- As the lamb kebabs are air frying, prepare the yogurt dip. In a bowl mix Greek yogurt, fresh lemon juice, minced garlic, fresh mint leaves, salt and black pepper. Blend until you get a smooth dip.
- When the lamb kebabs are ready, serve them hot with yogurt dip on the side.

Cooking Tips:

- Change the intensity of spiciness in lamb kebabs by increasing or decreasing ground paprika or ground cinnamon.
- Soaking the wooden skewers prevents them from burning in an air fryer.

5.3.6 Teriyaki Beef Strips with Sesame Seeds

Make the flavors of Japan part of your cooking arsenal with Teriyaki Beef Strips with Sesame Seeds. These tender strips of beef are drenched in a delectable teriyaki sauce and topped with sesame seeds for that delicious crunch. Join us as we explore the art of making this Asian inspired dish.

Ingredients for 4 Servings:

- 1 pound of beef sirloin or flank steak, cut into thin strips
- 1/4 cup soy sauce
- 2 tablespoons of mirin (sweet rice wine)
- 2 tablespoons brown sugar
- 1 clove garlic, minced
- 1 teaspoon grated fresh ginger
- 1/2 teaspoon cornstarch
- Sesame seeds, for garnish
- Sliced green onions, for garnish

Instructions:

- Combine soy sauce, mirin, brown sugar, minced garlic, grated fresh ginger and cornstarch in a bowl. Mix until the sugar has dissolved and the sauce is blended.
- Arrange the thinly sliced beef strips in a resealable plastic bag or shallow dish. Coat the beef with teriyaki sauce. Close the bag or cover the dish and marinate for at least 30 minutes, or refrigerate for a few hours to deepen the taste.
- Set your air fryer to preheat at 375°F (190°C).
- Take the marinated beef strips out of the bag or dish and shake off any excess marinade.
- In a single layer, arrange the beef strips in the air fryer basket.
- Air fry for about 5-7 minutes, turning the strips halfway through, until they reach your desired level of doneness.

- As the beef strips are air frying, you can put the rest of the marinade in a small saucepan and heat it until it thickens to make a glaze for drizzling.
- After the beef strips are cooked, place them on a serving platter, drizzle with teriyaki glaze, and add sesame seeds and sliced green onions.

Cooking Tips:

- If you want a bolder kick, add red pepper flakes to the teriyaki sauce.
- Do not put many foods in the air fryer basket to ensure that they are evenly cooked.

5.3.7 Buffalo Chicken Poppers with Blue Cheese Dip

If you want a little kick and some creamy pleasure, Buffalo Chicken Poppers with Blue Cheese Dip are the perfect choice. These hot, bite-size marvels are a party staple. Come along with us as we delve into the world of buffalo chicken poppers and create a divine blue cheese dip to help you cool your jets.

Ingredients for 4 Servings:

For the Buffalo Chicken Poppers:

- 1 pound boneless, skinless chicken breast cut into little pieces
- 1/2 cup buffalo sauce
- 2 tablespoons melted butter
- 1/2 teaspoon garlic powder
- 1/2 teaspoon onion powder
- 1/2 teaspoon paprika
- To taste, salt and black pepper
- Cooking spray

For the Blue Cheese Dip:

- 1/2 cup mayonnaise
- 1/4 cup sour cream
- 1/4 cup crumbled blue cheese
- 1 clove garlic, minced

- 1 tablespoon fresh lemon juice
- Salt and pepper to taste

Instructions:

- In a bowl, mix buffalo sauce, melted butter, garlic powder, onion powder, paprika, salt and black pepper. Mix until well combined.
- Combine the bite-sized chicken pieces and buffalo sauce mixture, tossing until well coated. At least 30 minutes of marinating, or a few hours in the refrigerator for stronger flavor.
- Heat your air fryer to 375°F (190°C) and coat the basket with cooking spray.
- Arrange the marinated chicken pieces in a single layer without overcrowding in the air fryer basket.
- Air fry for about 10 to 12 minutes, turning the chicken pieces halfway through cooking until they are cooked thoroughly and have a crispy outer layer.
- As the chicken is air frying, make the blue cheese dip. Mix mayonnaise, sour cream, crumbled blue cheese, minced garlic, fresh lemon juice, salt and black pepper in a bowl. Mix until creamy.
- When the chicken poppers are ready, serve them hot with blue cheese dip.
- Get these Buffalo Chicken Poppers as spicy and sour appetizers, with a bold taste.

Cooking Tips:

- Reduce or increase the spiciness by adding more or less buffalo sauce.
- Serve it garnished with celery sticks and carrot slices for a cool reprieve from the spiciness.

6. Fish and Seafood Sensations

6.1 Light and Flavorful Fish Dishes

Welcome to a world of seafood enthusiasts with our assortment of Light and Flavorful Fish Recipes. These recipes are meant to highlight the natural taste of fish with a splash of excitement. Each dish offers a flavourful adventure for your palate ranging from zesty citrus, savory herbs and spicy kicks. Immerse yourself in this sea of culinary delicacies and enjoy the freshness of the ocean.

6.1.1 Lemon-Herb Baked Cod with Zucchini

Enjoy a refreshing seafood treat with our zesty Lemon-Herb Baked Cod with Zucchini. This is a mix of the soft and flaky taste of cod with the brightness of lemon and an assortment of fresh herbs. Combined with the sweet roasted zucchini, it is a hearty and delicious dish that's as simple to prepare as it is to eat.

Ingredients for 4 Servings:

For the Lemon-Herb Cod:

- 4 cod filets
- 2 tablespoons fresh lemon juice
- 2 tablespoons olive oil

- 2 cloves garlic, minced
- 1 tablespoon fresh parsley, chopped
- 1 tablespoon fresh dill, chopped
- Salt and black pepper, as desired

For the Roasted Zucchini:

- 3 zucchini, sliced into rounds
- 2 tablespoons olive oil
- 1 teaspoon dried thyme
- Salt and freshly ground black pepper, to taste

Instructions:

- In a bowl, mix fresh lemon juice, olive oil, minced garlic, chopped fresh parsley and dill, salt and black pepper. Stir until the marinade is homogenous.
- In a resealable plastic bag or in a shallow dish, put the cod filets. The cod filets should be evenly coated with the lemon-herb marinade. Close the bag or cover the dish and refrigerate for at least 30 minutes so that all flavours can be combined.
- Set your air fryer to 375°F (190°C) and preheat it.
- In a separate bowl, coat the zucchini rounds with olive oil, dried thyme, salt and black pepper.
- Arrange the marinated cod filets in a single layer inside the air fryer basket.
- Place the seasoned zucchini rounds around the cod filets in the air fryer basket.
- Cod will be flaky and cooked through within 10-12 minutes of air frying or until the zucchini is tender and slightly browned. Make sure to test for doneness; cooking times can vary according to the thickness of the cod fillet.
- After that, serve the Lemon-Herb Baked Cod together with the roasted zucchini as a side dish.

Cooking Tips:

- One can replace cod with other white fish species such as haddock or halibut.
- Tailor the herbs to your liking, adding basil, tarragon or chives for a more delicious taste.

6.1.2 Chili-Lime Tilapia with Mango Salsa

Our Chili-Lime Tilapia with Mango Salsa will bring a lively and summery taste to your dinner table. Tilapia filets marinated with chili and lime, served on a bed of mango salsa. It is a harmonious fusion of spicy and sweet, good for a light and bright meal that takes you to the sunny heaven with your taste buds.

Ingredients for 4 Servings:

For the Chili-Lime Tilapia:

- 4 tilapia filets
- 2 tablespoons olive oil
- 2 teaspoons chili powder
- 1 teaspoon paprika
- 2 limes zested and juiced
- Salt and pepper to taste

For the Mango Salsa:

- 2 ripe mangoes, diced
- 1/2 red onion, finely chopped
- 1 red bell pepper, diced
- 1/4 cup fresh cilantro, chopped
- Juice of 1 lime
- Salt and pepper to taste.

Instructions:

- In a bowl mix olive oil, chili powder, paprika, lime zest, lime juice, salt and black pepper. Blend until you have a homogenous marinade.
- Arrange the tilapia filets in a resealable plastic bag or a shallow dish. Then, pour the chili-lime marinade over the tilapia to cover each filet evenly. Close the bag or cover the dish and refrigerate for at least 30 minutes to allow flavors to steep.
- Set your air fryer to 375°F (190°C) and preheat it.
- As the tilapia marinades, prepare the mango salsa. Dice the ripe mangoes, finely chop red onion, dice red bell pepper and chop fresh cilantro. Mix them with lime

juice in a bowl along with some salt and black pepper. Mix to produce a colorful salsa.
- Put the marinated tilapia filets in a single layer into the air fryer basket.
- Fry in the air for about 8-10 minutes, turning over halfway through and until cooked through with a crispy skin.
- After this, top the Chili-Lime Tilapia with a large scoop of mango salsa.
- Savor this exciting dish as a vibrant burst of flavors, capturing the heat of chili and the sweetness of mango.

Cooking Tips:

- Alter the heat of the marinade by adding more or less chili powder.
- Tilapia can be substituted with other white fish varieties such as sole and snapper.

6.1.3 Parmesan Crusted Halibut with Lemon Butter.

This is a dish of tender halibut filets in crusty Parmesan, served with a mouthwatering lemon butter sauce. It is the blending of delicious tastes and magnificent texture that every bite is a work of art.

Ingredients for 4 Servings:

For the Parmesan-Crusted Halibut:

- 4 halibut filets
- 1/2 cup grated Parmesan cheese
- 1/4 cup panko breadcrumbs
- 1/4 cup fresh parsley, chopped
- 2 cloves garlic, minced
- 2 tablespoons melted butter
- Salt and freshly ground black pepper, to taste
- Cooking spray

For the Lemon Butter Sauce:

- 1/2 cup unsalted butter
- Juice of 2 lemons
- 2 tablespoons fresh parsley, chopped

- 1 clove garlic, minced
- Salt and black pepper, to your liking

Instructions:

- In a bowl, mix grated Parmesan cheese, panko breadcrumbs, chopped fresh parsley, minced garlic, melted butter, salt and black pepper. Combine thoroughly to form a Parmesan crust mixture.
- Lay the halibut filets on a plate or tray and blot them with paper towels.
- Spread Parmesan crust mixture over each halibut fillet, making sure that an even and generous amount of the mixture is applied.
- Before you begin, preheat your air fryer to 375°F (190°C) and lightly grease the air fryer basket with cooking spray.
- Arrange the Parmesan-crusted halibut filets in the air fryer basket, one layer at a time, without overcrowding.
- Cook in the air fryer for about 10-12 minutes, or until the halibut is cooked through and the crust is golden and crispy.
- As the halibut is air frying, make the lemon butter sauce. In a saucepan, melt the unsalted butter on low heat. Mix in the juice of two lemons, fresh chopped parsley, minced garlic, salt and pepper. Stir until the sauce is well incorporated and heated.
- After the Parmesan-Crusted Halibut is cooked, serve it hot with a little bit of lemon butter sauce.

Cooking Tips:

- Halibut can be substituted with other white fish such as cod or sea bass.
- Taste the lemon butter sauce and add more or less lemon juice to your liking.

6.1.4 - Ginger-Soy Glazed Salmon filets

Our Ginger-Soy Glazed Salmon filets will take your taste buds on a trip. This dish brings together juicy salmon and a perfect balance of ginger and soy for an umami taste. It is a sophisticated and fulfilling seafood treat with its glossy glaze and tender filets.

Ingredients for 4 Servings:

- 4 salmon filets
- 1/4 cup soy sauce
- 2 tablespoons honey
- 1 tablespoon fresh ginger, minced
- 2 cloves garlic, minced
- 1 tablespoon rice vinegar
- 1 teaspoon sesame oil
- Optional garnish: sesame seeds and chopped green onions

Instructions:

- In a bowl, combine soy sauce, honey, minced fresh ginger, minced garlic, rice vinegar and sesame oil. Stir until the glaze is properly mixed.
- Put the salmon filets in a plastic bag with a resealable top or shallow dish. Drizzle the ginger-soy glaze over the salmon filets to coat them evenly. Close the plastic bag or cover the dish and chill for 30 minutes to marry flavors.
- Set your air fryer to preheat at 375°F (190°C).
- Discard the salmon filets from the marinade, shaking off any extra glaze. Reserve the marinade for later.
- The salmon filets should be placed in the air fryer basket such that they are arranged in a single layer.
- Cook for about 10-12 minutes in the air fryer until the salmon is fully cooked and has a shiny coating.
- As the salmon air fries, transfer the reserved ginger-soy glaze to a small saucepan. Heat it over a low heat, stirring from time to time until slightly thickened.
- When completed, serve the Ginger-Soy Glazed Salmon filets hot with a drizzle of the thickened glaze. If desired, garnish with sesame seeds and chopped green onions.
- Relish this delicate combination of the sweetness of honey, ginger spiciness and soy savor.

Cooking Tips:

- Modify the sweetness of the glaze by adding more or less honey to suit your taste.
- To add more flavor, let the salmon marinate for a longer time in the refrigerator, up to 24 hours.

6.1.5 Herbed Tuna Steaks with Olive Tapenade

You will be transported to the Mediterranean with our Herbed Tuna Steaks with Olive Tapenade. The main ingredient of this dish is thick tuna steaks flavored with fragrant herbs and accompanied by a spicy olive tapenade. It's a delicious and healthy seafood dish that captures the spirit of coastal cooking.

Ingredients for 4 Servings:

For the Herbed Tuna Steaks:

- 4 tuna steaks
- 2 tablespoons olive oil
- 2 cloves garlic, minced
- 1 teaspoon dried oregano
- 1 teaspoon dried thyme
- Salt and freshly ground black pepper to taste
- Lemon wedges for serving

For the Olive Tapenade:

- 1 cup pitted Kalamata olives
- 2 cloves garlic, minced
- 2 tablespoons capers
- 2 tablespoons fresh parsley, chopped
- Lemon zest and juice from 1 lemon
- 3 tablespoons olive oil
- Salt and black pepper, as desired

Instructions:

- In a bowl, combine the olive oil with minced garlic, dried oregano, dried thyme and salt and black pepper. Blend until a smooth herb marinade is achieved.

- Place the tuna steaks in a plastic bag or shallow glass dish. Pour herb marinade over tuna steaks, ensuring that they are fully immersed. Cover the dish with a bag and put in the refrigerator for at least 30 minutes to allow flavors to develop.
- Preheat your air fryer to 375°F (190°C).
- While the fish is marinating, make the olive tapenade. In a food processor add the pitted Kalamata olives, minced garlic, capers, chopped fresh parsley together with the lemon zest and juice; then put in olive oil with salt and black pepper. Pulse into a coarse olive tapenade.
- Throw the marinating tuna steaks away, and wipe them dry using paper towels.
- Arrange the tuna steaks in a row on the air fryer basket.
- Air fry for approximately 6 to 8 minutes, depending on the doneness level you desire.
- When done, the Herbed Tuna Steaks should be served hot with a generous scoop of olive tapenade.
- This Mediterranean tuna dish is the ideal fusion of the oily fish and pungent flavors that come from herbs and olives.

Cooking Tips:

- Feel free to alter the herb marinade by adding or reducing your favorite herbs.
- Smoked paprika added should be sprinkled on the tuna steaks before air frying too.

6.1.6 Cajun-Spiced Catfish and Corn Relish

Spice up your seafood dishes with our Cajun-Spiced Catfish with Corn Relish. This is a recipe that brings out the heat and spice of Cajun seasoning in a corn relish. In this tasty catfish recipe, let us divulge the hidden wonders of Cajun cooking.

Ingredients for 4 Servings:

For the Cajun-Spiced Catfish:

- 4 catfish filets
- 2 tablespoons olive oil
- 2 teaspoons Cajun seasoning
- 1 teaspoon paprika

- 1/2 teaspoon garlic powder
- 1/2 teaspoon onion powder
- Salt and black pepper, as desired
- Lemon wedges for serving

For the Corn Relish:

- 2 cups of corn kernels (fresh or frozen)
- 1/2 red onion, finely chopped
- One finely chopped red bell pepper.
- 2 tablespoons fresh cilantro, chopped
- 2 tablespoons olive oil
- Juice of 1 lime
- Salt and pepper, to taste

Instructions:

- Spice up your seafood dishes with our Cajun-Spiced Catfish with Corn Relish. This is a recipe that brings out the heat and spice of Cajun seasoning in a corn relish. In this tasty catfish recipe, let us divulge the hidden wonders of Cajun cooking.
- Combine olive oil, Cajun seasoning, paprika, garlic powder, onion powder, salt and black pepper in a bowl. Stir well until it forms a consistent Cajun spice mixture.
- Place the catfish filets in a plastic bag or on a shallow plate. Now, dust the catfish filets with the Cajun spice mixture and make sure all of them are evenly coated. Seal the bag or you can cover the dish and refrigerate it for at least half an hour so that the flavors become infused.
- Preheat your air fryer to 375°F (190°C).
- While the catfish is being marinated, prepare the corn relish. In the bowl, combine corn kernels, finely chopped red onion, red bell pepper finely chopped, fresh cilantro that has been chopped already and also add olive oil, lime juice salt and ground black pepper. Blend to prepare a vibrant corn relish.
- The catfish filets should be taken out of the marinade and dried with paper towels.
- Arrange the catfish filets in a single layer on the air fryer basket.
- Air-fry for about 8–10 minutes, depending on how thick the filets are, until the catfish is fully cooked and crisp outside.

- When ready, serve the Cajun-Spiced Catfish hot with a large serving of corn relish. Garnish with lemon wedges.
- This Southern-accented dish combines the heat of Cajun spices with the coolness of corn relish.

Cooking Tips:

- Moderate the spiciness by adding more or less Cajun seasoning to the catfish.
- If catfish is unavailable, you can use other white fish varieties such as tilapia or snapper.

6.1.7 Maple-Mustard Glazed Trout with Asparagus

To experience the best of nature, enjoy our Maple-Mustard Glazed Trout with Asparagus. Maple syrup and mustard come together in this recipe to form a glaze that turns trout into an absolute work of art. Let us gather and enjoy the simplicity and beauty of this meal.

Ingredients for 4 Servings:

- For the Maple-Mustard Glazed Trout:
- 4 trout filets
- 1/4 cup pure maple syrup
- 2 tablespoons Dijon mustard
- 1 tablespoon whole-grain mustard
- 1 tablespoon olive oil
- 2 cloves garlic, minced
- Salt and black pepper to taste
- Lemon wedges for serving

For the Roasted Asparagus:

- 1 bunch of asparagus spears, ends removed
- 1 tablespoon olive oil
- Salt and black pepper, as desired.

Instructions:

- Combine pure maple syrup, Dijon mustard, whole grain mustard, olive oil, minced garlic salt and black pepper in a bowl. Stir until a paste with the consistency of maple-mustard glaze is formed.
- Place the trout filets in a zip-lock bag or shallow plate. The maple-mustard glaze should be spread evenly on the trout filets. Cover the plate with a bag or cellophane and place it in the refrigerator for at least half an hour to let flavors seep.
- Preheat your air fryer to 375°F (190°C).
- While the trout is marinating, ready yourself for the roasted asparagus. Coat the asparagus, previously de-stemmed, with olive oil and sprinkle some salt and black pepper over it.
- Remove the trout filets from the marinade and pat them dry with paper towels.
- Place single layers of trout filets in an air fryer basket.
- Air fry for 6 to 8 minutes, depending on the filets' thickness and when the trout is well cooked and has a shiny finish.
- While the trout is air frying, roast the asparagus in an air fryer at 400 degrees for about 5-6 minutes or until tender and crispy.
- The Maple-Mustard Glazed Trout filets are then served with roasted asparagus.
- Enjoy this elegant combination of maple flavor and mustard bite.

Cooking Tips:

- Adjust the amount of sweetness and sourness in the glaze by changing the ratio between quantities of maple syrup and mustard.
- For a hint of freshness, add lemon juice on the trout just before serving.

6.2 Shrimp, Scallops and More

In this article, we take you on a gastronomic trip to enjoy the delicious taste of seafood comprising sweet shrimp and delicate scallops. From the comfort of garlic butter to the zest of Cajun seasoning, these recipes are a reflection of how seafood dishes can be both simple and sophisticated at the same time. Prepare yourself for an unforgettable culinary journey that will take your taste buds on a wild ride.

6.2.1 Garlic Butter Shrimp with Herbed Couscous

This dish brings together plump shrimp sautéed in aromatic garlic butter with fluffy herbed couscous, which makes up a perfect balance of textures and tastes. It's a seafood sensation that is quick and easy to prepare, making it an ideal choice for weeknight dinner or a special occasion.

Ingredients for 4 Servings:

- For the Garlic Butter Shrimp:
- 1 pound of large shrimp, peeled and deveined
- 4 cloves garlic, minced
- 2 tablespoons unsalted butter
- 1 tablespoon olive oil
- 1/4 teaspoon red pepper flakes (to taste)
- Salt and pepper, to taste
- Fresh parsley, chopped, for garnish
- Lemon wedges for serving

For the Herbed Couscous:

- 1 cup couscous
- One and a quarter cups chicken or vegetable stock
- 2 tablespoons unsalted butter
- One fourth cup of fresh herbs {such as parsley, cilantro or dill}, chopped
- Salt and pepper to taste

Instructions:

- First, make the herbed couscous. Boil the chicken or vegetable stock in a saucepan. Add the couscous, cover with a lid and turn off heat. After that, let it sit for 5 minutes and fluff with a fork. Combine the fresh herbs, butter, salt and pepper. Set aside and keep warm.
- In a large skillet, warm olive oil over medium-high heat. Add minced garlic and red pepper flakes, cooking for approximately 30 seconds until the mixture becomes aromatic.
- The shrimp should be added to the skillet after they have been peeled and deveined. Cook for 2-3 minutes per side, until they are pink and translucent.
- Add the unsalted butter and cook for another minute or two, until the butter melts and glazes the shrimp. Salt and black pepper to taste.
- To finish, again fluff the herbed couscous and divide it onto plates. Lay the garlic butter shrimp over the couscous.
- Garnish with parsley and serve lemon wedges to squeeze over the shrimp.
- Savor this delicious meal that brings together the richness of garlic butter shrimp and the freshness of herbed couscous.

Cooking Tips:

- The herbs used in the couscous can also be modified according to your taste.
- To regulate the level of spiciness, increase or decrease the amount of red pepper flakes in the shrimp.

6.2.2 Seared Scallops with Creamy Polenta

Our Seared Scallops with Creamy Polenta will take your dining to a higher level. This dish combines the delicate sweetness of perfectly seared scallops with the creamy comfort of polenta in a symphony that will have your taste buds dancing. It is a fancy yet easy recipe that will surely impress.

Ingredients for 4 Servings:

For the Seared Scallops:

- 16 large sea scallops
- 2 tablespoons olive oil
- Salt and pepper to taste
- Fresh chives, chopped, for garnish
- Lemon wedges for serving

For the Creamy Polenta:

- 1 cup polenta or cornmeal
- 4 cups of chicken or vegetable broth
- 1 cup heavy cream
- 1/2 cup grated Parmesan cheese
- 2 tablespoons unsalted butter
- Salt and pepper, to taste

Instructions:

- First, make the creamy polenta. Boil the broth in a saucepan. Slowly add the polenta while stirring continuously to prevent lumps from forming.
- Lower the heat and simmer, stirring occasionally, for about 15-20 minutes or until the polenta is sufficiently thick and creamy.
- Combine the heavy cream, Parmesan cheese and unsalted butter. Cook for 5 minutes longer or until the polenta is smooth and creamy. Salt and pepper to taste. Keep warm.
- As the polenta is simmering, prepare the seared scallops. Pat dry the scallops with paper towels and season both sides with salt and black pepper.
- Heat olive oil in a large frying pan over high heat until it shimmers.
- Carefully place the scallops into the skillet so that they do not overlap. Sear for 2-3 minutes per side until golden brown and opaque in the middle.
- For serving, place a large dollop of creamy polenta on each plate. Top with seared scallops.
- Serve with freshly chopped chives and lemon wedges for squeezing over the scallops.
- This refined dish features the blissful union of sweet scallops and rich polenta.

Cooking Tips:

- Make sure your scallops are dry before searing them to get a good crust.
- Change the consistency of the polenta by increasing or decreasing heavy cream to your liking.

6.2.3 Spicy Cajun Shrimp Skewers

These delicious shrimp skewers are marinated in a zesty Cajun spice blend, grilled to crispy perfection and accompanied by a refreshing yogurt dip. It's a spicy and tasty dish for those who appreciate some heat in their seafood.

Ingredients for 4 Servings:

For the Spicy Cajun Shrimp:

- 1 pound deveined and peeled large shrimp
- 2 tablespoons olive oil
- 2 Tbsp Cajun seasoning (adjust to taste).
- 1 tablespoon lemon juice
- Salt and pepper to taste.
- Soaked wooden skewers

For the Yogurt Dip:

- 1 cup Greek yogurt
- 1 tablespoon lemon juice
- 1 teaspoon honey
- 1/2 teaspoon paprika
- Salt and ground black pepper to taste

Instructions:

- First, make the spicy Cajun shrimp. In a bowl, mix together olive oil, Cajun seasoning, lemon juice, salt and black pepper. Mix well.
- Place the peeled and deveined shrimp in the marinade, making sure that they are well-coated. Let them sit for at least fifteen minutes.

- Heat your grill or air fryer to medium-high.
- Put the shrimp through the soaked wooden skewers to thread them and space evenly.
- Cook the shrimp skewers for about 2-3 minutes per side, or until they are pink and have grill marks. If an air fryer is used, cook for 5–6 minutes at 375°F (190°C).
- As the shrimp are cooking, make up the yogurt dip. In a bowl, mix Greek yogurt with lemon juice, honey, paprika, salt and black pepper. Mix until well combined.
- When the shrimp skewers are ready, serve them hot with a creamy yogurt dip on the side.
- Savor the rich and hot tastes of these Cajun shrimp skewers complemented with the refreshing and sour yogurt sauce.

Cooking Tips:

- For the level of spiciness, add more or less Cajun seasoning to the shrimp marinade.
- Water soaked wooden skewers do not burn in the grill or air fryer.
- Alternatively, these spicy shrimp skewers can be served with a plate of rice or a fresh salad for a full meal.

6.2.4 Cajun-Spiced Catfish with Corn Relish

Add a little extra flavor to your dinner with our Cajun-Spiced Catfish with Corn Relish. This Southern-style dish consists of filets of catfish covered with a Cajun spice mix and cooked in an air fryer. It comes with a spicy corn relish that provides freshness to every mouthful.

Ingredients for 4 Servings:

- For the Cajun-Spiced Catfish:
- 4 filets of catfish (6-8 ounces each).
- 2 tablespoons olive oil
- 2 tablespoons Cajun seasoning
- 1/2 teaspoon garlic powder
- 1/2 teaspoon paprika
- 1/2 teaspoon dried thyme

- Salt and pepper, to taste
- Lemon wedges for serving

For the Corn Relish:

- 2 cups of fresh corn kernels (from 2-3 ears of corn)
- 1 red bell pepper, diced
- 1/2 red onion, finely chopped
- 1/4 cup fresh cilantro, chopped
- Juice of 1 lime
- 2 tablespoons olive oil
- 1/2 teaspoon chili powder (according to taste)
- Salt and black pepper to taste

Instructions:

- Begin with the Cajun-spiced catfish. In a small bowl, mix Cajun seasoning, garlic powder, paprika, dried thyme, salt and black pepper.
- Dry the catfish filets with paper towels and then brush them lightly with olive oil.
- Coat both sides of each catfish filet with the Cajun spice mixture.
- Set your air fryer to 375°F (190°C) and preheat it.
- Arrange the catfish filets in the air fryer basket such that they are not touching each other.
- Cook the catfish in an air fryer for 10-12 minutes, turning them over halfway through or until they are golden brown and cooked. Internal temperature must be 145°F (63°C).
- As the catfish is being cooked, make corn relish. In a bowl, mix fresh corn kernels, diced red bell pepper, finely chopped red onion, cilantro chopped chili powder salt and black pepper. Mix well.
- When the catfish is cooked, serve it hot with a big dollop of corn relish on top.
- Garnish with more cilantro and serve lemon wedges to squeeze over the catfish.
- Savor the robust and spicy notes of Cajun-Spiced Catfish accompanied by the lively and rejuvenating Corn Relish.

Cooking Tips:

- Tweak the amount of Cajun seasoning and chili powder to match your spice levels.

- Should you not have catfish, other kinds of white fish can be used, such as tilapia or snapper.
- Make sure that the catfish filets are thoroughly coated with the Cajun spice mixture for optimal flavor.

6.2.5 Honey-Lime Tilapia with Zesty Quinoa

Get a taste of our refreshing and tangy Honey-Lime Tilapia served with zesty quinoa. As you indulge your taste buds, this dish also offers a wholesome and healthy meal.

Ingredients for 4 Servings:

Four filets of tilapia- 6-8 ounces per each

- 1/4 cup honey
- Juice of 2 limes
- 1 teaspoon lime zest
- 1 tablespoon soy sauce
- 2 cloves garlic, minced
- Lime wedges for serving

For the Zesty Quinoa:

- 1 cup quinoa, rinsed
- 2 cups vegetable broth
- 1/4 cup corn kernels
- 1-¼ cup black beans, rinsed and drained
- 1 teaspoon chili powder
-

Instructions:

- First, prepare the honey-lime marinade. In a medium-sized mixing bowl, combine honey, lime juice and zest, soy sauce, minced garlic cloves as well as salt and black pepper.

- First set your air fryer at 380°F (193°C) and preheat it.
- Apply the honey-lime marinade on the tilapia filets, leaving some in a dish for serving. Marinating time of the filets is 10 minutes.
- Boil the vegetable broth in a saucepan. Add in your quinoa, stir it a little bit to mix with the other ingredients then put on the cover while you reduce heat for simmering and let it sit there for 15 minutes or wait until all liquid is absorbed.
- After the quinoa is ready, fluff it with a fork and stir in bell pepper, corns, black beans, as well as chili powder. Add salt and pepper, to taste.
- Arrange the marinated tilapia in a single layer inside the air fryer basket. Cook in an air fryer for 6-10 minutes per side or until the fish breaks apart easily with a fork and is lightly browned.
- Garnish the honey-lime tilapia on top of the zest bed; quinoa. Dribble with the remainder of honey-lime marinade.
- For that extra zing, garnish with cilantro leaves and lime wedges on the side.

Cooking Tips:

- You may also need to increase or decrease the chili powder, according to your desired heat level for a milder or spicier quinoa.
- Serve the quinoa with a sprinkle of roasted almonds or pumpkin seeds for extra crunch.
- The remaining quinoa might be stored in a fridge and utilized as the foundation of salads or served alongside other dishes.

6.2.6 Coconut-Coated Shrimp with Pineapple Salsa

Get away to a tropical paradise with our Coconut-Crusted Shrimp with Pineapple Salsa. These succulent shrimp are battered in a crispy coconut breading and served with a fantastic pineapple salsa that is full of freshness. It's a wonderful dish that brings the taste of the tropics to your table.

Ingredients for 4 Servings:

For the Coconut-Crusted Shrimp:

- 1 pound large deveined and peeled shrimp
- 1 cup shredded coconut

- 1/2 cup breadcrumbs
- 1/2 teaspoon paprika
- 1/2 teaspoon garlic powder
- 2 eggs
- Salt and black pepper to taste
- Cooking spray

For the Pineapple Salsa:

- 1 cup fresh pineapple, diced
- 1/2 red onion, finely chopped
- 1/2 red bell pepper, diced
- 1/2 small jalapeño pepper, minced (to taste)
- Juice of 1 lime
- 2 tablespoons fresh cilantro, chopped
- Salt and black pepper, as desired

Instructions:

- First, make the pineapple salsa. In a bowl, mix diced fresh pineapple, finely chopped red onion, diced red bell pepper, minced jalapeño pepper, lime juice and chopped cilantro. Mix and season with salt and black pepper to taste. Store the salsa in a refrigerator before serving.
- Set your air fryer to 400°F (200°C) and preheat.
- In a bowl, mix shredded coconut, breadcrumbs, paprika, garlic powder, salt and black pepper.
- In another dish, whip the eggs.
- Dip each shrimp in the beaten eggs and let any excess drip away.
- Roll the shrimp in the coconut and breadcrumb mixture, pressing slightly to coat.
- Arrange the coated shrimp in a single layer inside the air fryer basket so that they do not touch. It may be necessary to cook them in batches.
- Spritz the shrimp lightly with cooking spray to ensure uniform browning.
- Air fry the shrimp at 400°F (200°C) for 5-7 minutes, flipping them halfway through, or until they turn golden brown and crispy.
- Serve the coconut-crusted shrimp hot with chilled pineapple salsa on the side.

Cooking Tips:

- Change the cooking time as necessary for shrimp that is cooked until opaque and crispy coating.
- The salsa can be made using either fresh or frozen pineapple, depending on what is available and what is preferred.
- If you want more heat, leave the seeds in the jalapeño pepper or add a pinch of cayenne to the salsa.

6.2.7 Garlic Lemon Scallops with Spinach

Up your seafood ante with our Air Fryer Garlic Lemon Scallops with Spinach. This air fryer scallops recipe is the best in its class because it uses perfectly cooked scallops filled with garlic and lemon flavors while keeping them tender inside and crispy outside. This dish, which is served on a bed of sautéed spinach, is an orchestra of textures and flavors.

Ingredients for 4 Servings:

For the Scallops:

- 1 pound large scallops
- 2 tablespoons olive oil
- 4 cloves garlic, minced
- Zest of 1 lemon
- Juice of 1 lemon
- Salt and pepper to taste
- 2 tablespoons fresh parsley, chopped
- Lemon wedges for serving

For the Sautéed Spinach:

- 10 ounces of fresh spinach leaves, washed and trimmed
- 2 cloves garlic, minced
- 1 tablespoon olive oil
- Salt and black pepper to taste
- Optional crushed red pepper flakes for heat

Instructions:

- First, sauté the spinach. In a large skillet, heat one tablespoon of olive oil on medium heat. Add chopped garlic and fry for about 30 seconds until aromatic.
- Then add the fresh spinach leaves to the skillet. Salt and pepper to taste. Sauté for 2-3 minutes, stirring occasionally, until spinach wilts and softens. Optionally, add some red pepper flakes for a slight kick. Place the spinach in a serving dish and keep it warm.
- Dry the surface of the scallops gently with a paper towel and season them lightly with salt and freshly ground black pepper.
- Plug in the air fryer and set it to 375°F (190°C) and let it preheat.
- Place the scallops in a bowl and season them with two tablespoons of olive oil, minced garlic, lemon zest and juice. Throw in scallops and mix thoroughly.
- Fill the basket of your air fryer with the marinated scallops such that they lay in one flat layer. Air fry for a period of 6-8 minutes or until the surfaces of the scallops turn golden and they are fully cooked. Ensure that you shake the basket or turn the scallops upside down when halfway through cooking so that they brown evenly.
- Serve with sautéed spinach, a small amount of which should be placed on each plate and topped with the crispy air-fried scallops.
- Sprinkle some fresh chopped parsley and accompany with lemon wedges for a tangy taste.
- Treat yourself to the one of a kind taste and texture that Air Fryer Garlic Lemon

Cooking Tips:

- Diversifying the scallops cooking time depends on their size, so they are well prepared.
- The quantities of garlic, lemon juice and red pepper flakes can be adjusted as per individual tastes.
- Complete the meal by offering this dish with rice, pasta or bread that is crusty.

6.3 Seafood Snacks and Appetizers

Whether you plan any celebration or feel like eating something from the ocean, these recipes will make you salivate and crave for more. Each dish is a splendid example of how lightness of seafood flavors and textures in combination with crispy calamari and zesty shrimp ceviche can be achieved using an air fryer. So, dive into this sea food fiesta and enjoy the lip smacking delicacies that are waiting for you in this tasty part of the page.

6.3.1 Crispy Calamari with Spicy Marinara

These golden rings of calamari are battered with a seasoned breadcrumb mixture and fried in air creating crispy outer crust while tender interior. With a tangy homemade marinara sauce, this is a great seafood snack or appetizer that will keep your taste buds happy.

Ingredients for 4 Servings:

For the Crispy Calamari:

- 1 lb calamari rings, thawed if frozen
- 1 cup breadcrumbs
- 1/2 cup grated Parmesan cheese
- 1 teaspoon garlic powder
- 1 teaspoon paprika
- 1/2 teaspoon salt
- 1/4 teaspoon black pepper
- Cooking spray

For the Spicy Marinara:

- 1 cup marinara sauce
- 1/2 teaspoon of red pepper flakes (adjust to taste).

- 1 teaspoon sugar
- 1 teaspoon dried basil
- 1/2 teaspoon dried oregano
- Salt and pepper, to your liking

Instructions:

For the Crispy Calamari:

- In a bowl, mix the breadcrumbs with grated Parmesan cheese, garlic powder, paprika, salt and black pepper. Mix well.
- Dip each calamari ring in the breadcrumb mixture, making sure it is completely covered. Adhere the calamari with pressed breadcrumbs.
- Heat up your air fryer to 400°F (200°C).
- Spray the air fryer basket lightly with cooking spray.
- Place the breaded calamari rings in a single layer in the air fryer basket so that they do not touch.
- Fry with air for 8-10 minutes, turning the rings over halfway through the cooking time until golden brown and crispy.

For the Spicy Marinara:

- As the calamari cooks, make the spicy marinara sauce. In a cast iron skillet, mix the marinara sauce with red pepper flakes, sugar, dried basil, dried oregano, salt and black pepper. Warm over medium-low heat, stirring occasionally.
- Depending on your preference, add more or fewer red pepper flakes to adjust the spice level.
- Serve the Air Fryer Crispy Calamari with Spicy Marinara for dipping.

Cooking Tips:

- Be sure not to fill the air fryer basket too full because you want the calamari to cook evenly.
- To adjust the spice level of the marinara sauce, simply modify the number of red pepper flakes used.

6.3.2 Smoked Salmon and Cream Cheese Pinwheels

Enjoy our Air Fryer Smoked Salmon and Cream Cheese Pinwheels, a superb seafood appetizer that will definitely suit any occasion. These pinwheels blend the plush tastes of smoked salmon and luscious cream cheese, all enveloped in an ultralight phyllo pastry that's fried to a golden hue. These pinwheels with a hint of fresh dill and a sprinkle of lemon are guaranteed to wow your guests.

Ingredients for 4 Servings:

For the Pinwheels:

- 8 thawed phyllo pastry sheets
- 4 ounces smoked salmon slices
- 4 ounces cream cheese, softened
- 2 tablespoons fresh dill, chopped
- Zest of 1 lemon
- 2 tablespoons unsalted butter, melted
- Cooking spray

For the Dipping Sauce:

- 1/4 cup sour cream
- 1 tablespoon fresh lemon juice
- 1 teaspoon capers, chopped
- Salt and black pepper, to taste.

Instructions:

For the Pinwheels:

- Place one sheet of phyllo pastry on a clean surface and lightly brush it with melted butter. Place another sheet over it and repeat this action until you have four sheets.
- Spread one-quarter of the softened cream cheese over the phyllo pastry, leaving a border around the edges.
- Place a quarter of the smoked salmon slices on top of the cream cheese.

- Season the salmon with dill and lemon zest.
- Roll the phyllo pastry into a log, tucking in the edges as you go. Repeat the process for the remaining sheets to produce four pinwheels.
- Set your air fryer to 375°F (190°C).
- Spray the air fryer basket lightly with cooking spray.
- Seam side down, place the pinwheels in the air fryer basket and ensure they are not touching.
- Cook in the air fryer for 8-10 minutes or until pinwheels are golden brown and crispy.

For the Dipping Sauce:

- Mix the sour cream, fresh lemon juice, chopped capers, salt and black pepper in a small bowl. Mix until well combined.
- It is recommended to serve the Air Fryer Smoked Salmon and Cream Cheese Pinwheels with a tart dipping sauce on the side.
- Savor this divine appetizer that combines the rich taste of smoked salmon and cream cheese with the crunchiness of air-fried goodness.

Cooking Tips:

- Work fast with phyllo pastry because it dries up quickly. Cover the unused sheets in a damp kitchen towel to keep them from drying out.
- You can customize your pinwheels with a thin slice of cucumber or avocado before rolling to add freshness.

6.3.3 Coconut Shrimp with Mango Salsa

With our Air Fryer Coconut Shrimp with Mango Salsa, you can travel to a tropical paradise with your taste buds. These coconut-breaded succulent shrimp are air-fried to a delectable golden brown. Served with a mango salsa that is fresh and zesty, this dish has a balance of sweet and salty flavors that make it perfect for an appetizer or even a light meal.

Ingredients for 4 Servings:

For the Coconut Shrimp:

- 1 lb. large shrimp, shelled and deveined with tails on
- 1 cup shredded coconut
- 1 cup panko breadcrumbs
- 1 teaspoon garlic powder
- 1 teaspoon paprika
- 1/2 teaspoon salt
- 1/4 teaspoon black pepper
- 2 large eggs, beaten
- Cooking spray

For the Mango Salsa:

- 1 ripe mango, diced
- ¼ cup chopped red onion
- ¼ cup finely chopped red bell pepper
- 2 tablespoons fresh cilantro, chopped
- Juice of 1 lime
- Salt and pepper, to taste

Instructions:

For the Coconut Shrimp:

- In a bowl, mix together the shredded coconut, panko breadcrumbs, garlic powder, paprika salt and black pepper. Mix well.
- Dip each shrimp in the beaten eggs, shaking off any excess.
- Roll the shrimp in the coconut and breadcrumb mixture, gently pressing to stick. Put them on a cookie sheet.
- Set your air fryer to 375°F (190°C) and preheat it.
- Spray the air fryer basket lightly with cooking spray.
- Place the coated shrimp in one layer in the basket of the air fryer so that they do not touch each other.
- Air fry 6-8 minutes flipping halfway through or until golden brown and cooked through.

For the Mango Salsa:

- In a bowl, mix the diced mango with the finely chopped red onion, red bell pepper, fresh cilantro leaves, lime juice, salt and black pepper. Mix until well combined.
- Modify the seasoning and lime juice according to your preference.
- For a delicious appetizer or light meal, serve the Air Fryer Coconut Shrimp with Mango Salsa.

Cooking Tips:

- Be sure to peel and devein the shrimp, but leave the tails on so they are easy to handle.
- Adjust the spiciness of the mango salsa by adding a pinch of hot sauce or finely chopped jalapeno if you prefer it hot.

6.3.4 Crab-Stuffed Mushrooms

Take your appetizer to the next level with these decadent Air Fryer Crab-Stuffed Mushrooms. These delicious bite-sized morsels have mushroom caps that are soft and a crab filling that is creamy and savory, crisping up in the air fryer. These garlic-infused stuffed mushrooms with a dash of Parmesan cheese delight any crowd and are great for parties or get-togethers.

Ingredients for 4 Servings:

- 16 large cleaned and stemmed mushroom caps
- 8 oz lump crabmeat, drained and flaked
- 1/2 cup cream cheese, softened
- 2 cloves garlic, minced
- 1/4 cup grated Parmesan cheese
- 2 tablespoons fresh parsley, chopped
- Salt and pepper to taste
- Cooking spray

Instructions:

- Mix the lump crabmeat, softened cream cheese, minced garlic, grated Parmesan cheese and fresh parsley in a bowl. Stir until everything is combined. Salt and pepper to taste.
- Fill the mushroom cap with crab mixture using a spoon.
- Set your air fryer to preheat at 375°F (190°C).
- Spray the air fryer basket lightly with cooking spray.
- Place the stuffed mushrooms in a single layer inside the air fryer basket so that none of them are touching.
- Air fry for 8 to 10 minutes until the mushroom caps are soft and the filling is golden and bubbly.

Cooking Tips:

- A piping bag or a zip-top bag with the corner snipped off can be used to neatly fill the mushroom caps.
- You could also add a pinch of Old Bay seasoning or cayenne pepper for an additional taste boost to the crab filling.

6.3.5 Oysters Kilpatrick

Enjoy the lavish and smoky taste of our Air Fryer Oysters Kilpatrick. This is a classic Australian appetizer that has plump oysters with a delicious combination of bacon, Worcestershire sauce and barbecue sauce all cooked in the air fryer. These oysters, smothered in a crispy bacon and slightly tangy topping are a delight for any seafood enthusiast.

Ingredients for 4 Servings:

- Fourteen oysters, fresh and shucked on the half shell
- 4 pieces of bacon, cooked and crumbled
- 2 tablespoons Worcestershire sauce
- 2 tablespoons barbecue sauce
- Fresh parsley, chopped, for garnish
- Lemon wedges, for serving

Instructions:

- In a small bowl, mix the Worcestershire sauce and barbecue sauce. Mix well.
- Put the shucked oysters on the half shell in the air fryer basket.
- Place a teaspoon of the sauce mixture on each oyster.
- The crumbled bacon should be sprinkled over the oysters.
- Set your air fryer to preheat at 375°F (190°C).
- Cook the oysters in an air fryer for 6-8 minutes, or until they are ready and the bacon turns crispy.
- Top the Air Fryer Oysters Kilpatrick with chopped fresh parsley and serve them with lemon wedges.

Cooking Tips:

- Make sure the oysters are properly seated on the half shell to avoid any spills in the air fryer.
- These Air Fryer Oysters Kilpatrick deliver a blast of smoky, savory and slightly tart flavors that go well with the salty oysters. Serve them as an appetizer sensation or a part of a seafood fest. Enjoy your culinary adventure!

6.3.6 Zucchini and Corn Fritters with Spicy Aioli

Are you in search of a crispy as well as delicious appetizer? If you like, give our Air Fryer Zucchini and Corn Fritters with Spicy Aioli a go. The golden-brown fritters are loaded with fresh zucchini, sweet corn and seasonings. These are served with an invigoratingly spicy dipping sauce known as aioli which is a great accompaniment to the dish, and could also be had as snacks or appetizers that will enthrall your taste buds.

Ingredients for 4 Servings:

For the Zucchini and Corn Fritters:

- 2 medium zucchinis, grated and drained
- 1 cup corn kernels, fresh or frozen
- 1/2 cup all-purpose flour
- 1/4 cup grated Parmesan cheese
- 2 cloves garlic, minced
- 1/2 teaspoon smoked paprika
- 1/2 teaspoon chili powder

- 1/2 teaspoon salt
- 1/4 teaspoon black pepper
- 2 large eggs, beaten
- Cooking spray

For the Spicy Aioli:

- 1/2 cup mayonnaise
- 1 tbsp sriracha sauce (to taste)
- 1 clove garlic, minced
- 1 teaspoon lemon juice
- Salt and pepper, to taste

Instructions:

For the Zucchini and Corn Fritters:

- Combine the grated and squeezed zucchini with corn kernels, all-purpose flour, Parmesan cheese, minced garlic, smoked paprika, chili powder, salt and black pepper in a large bowl.
- Whisk the eggs and pour them into the mixture; whisk until a smooth uniform texture is achieved.
- Preheat your air fryer to 375°F (190°C).
- Lightly coat the air fryer basket with cooking spray.
- Using a spoon or your palm, form the mixture into small fritters and place them in an even layer inside the air fryer basket but without crowding.
- Place the cakes in the air fryer and cook them for 8 to 10 minutes with a flip in between or until they turn golden brown and crispy.

For the Spicy Aioli:

- So, in a little bowl combine the mayonnaise, sriracha sauce, minced garlic, lemon juice and pinch of salt and pepper. Adjust the spice level of sriracha to taste.
- Mix thoroughly until the aioli is smooth.
- For an appetizer, snack, or something to serve at a party, here is the recipe of Air Fryer Zucchini and Corn Fritters with Spicy Aioli.

Cooking Tips:

- In case the fritter batter seems overly moist, you may add a little flour in order to make it denser.
- Alternatively, you can increase the amount of the herbs or spices in your aioli to make it more flavorsome.

6.3.7 Garlic and Herb Mussels

Indulge in the savory flavors of the ocean with our Air Fryer Garlic and Herb Mussels. This dish features juicy and delicious mussels infused with the aroma of garlic, herbs, and a hint of white wine. It is a delicious treat that will impress your guests, and it is also easy to cook using an air fryer.

Ingredients for 4 Servings:

- 2 lbs of fresh mussels, cleaned and washed their beards
- 4 cloves garlic, minced
- 2 tablespoons white wine
- 2 tablespoons olive oil
- Lemon wedges, for serving

Instructions:

- Preheat your air fryer to 375°F (190°C).
- Combine the cleaned mussels, garlic cloves minced, parsley chopped, cilantro and basil with white wine and olive oil in a large bowl.
- Stir the ingredients until the mussels are thoroughly covered with herbs.
- Place the seasoned mussels in the air fryer basket in a single layer.
- Place the mussels in an air fryer and cook them at a temperature of 180 degrees Celsius for 8-10 minutes, shaking the basket halfway through or until they are well opened and cooked.
- Air Fryer Garlic and Herb Mussels should be served with side lemon wedges immediately.

Cooking Tips:

- Discard any mussels which do not open during the cooking process as they could be poisonous.

- Alter the quantity of garlic and herbs according to how strong you want your dish to taste.

7. Vegetarian and Vegan Varieties

7. 1 Plant-Based Main Courses

In this chapter we will discuss an enchanting variety of dishes that highlight the exciting tastes and mouth feels of vegetables, legumes, and other plant-based proteins. If you are a vegan veteran, a curious flexitarian or just someone who wants to add more plant based dishes to your diet, these recipes will not only satisfy your taste buds but also allow you to use the full potential of your air fryer. Whether savory tacos or hearty shepherd's pie, each recipe provides a healthier and nutritious take on traditional comfort foods proving that plant-based eating is not only satisfying but extremely delicious. Thus, let us delve into these scrumptious vegetarian mains and explore the vast potential of air fryers in making healthy plant based meals.

7.1.1 Falafel Platter with Tahini Sauce

Explore the exciting new world of plant-based superfoods with our Falafel Platter. This recipe combines the bold tastes of air-fried falafels, crunchy pita bread and a rich tahini sauce. The air fryer performs its miracles to produce falafel that is crispy on the outside and soft inside, making this a vegetarian's dream. We will take you on a culinary adventure that is influenced by the Mediterranean, and we will accompany you as you prepare this delicious vegan dish.

Ingredients for 4 servings:

For the Falafel:

- 1 can (15 oz) of chickpeas, drained and rinsed
- 1/2 cup fresh parsley, chopped
- 1/2 cup fresh cilantro, chopped
- 1 small onion, chopped
- 3 cloves garlic, minced
- 1 teaspoon ground cumin
- 1 teaspoon ground coriander
- ¼ teaspoon cayenne pepper (to taste)

- Salt and pepper to taste
- 1 tablespoon lemon juice
- 1 teaspoon baking powder
- 2-3 tablespoons of all-purpose flour (for binding).
- Cooking spray or olive oil (Air fry)

For the Tahini Dressing:

- 1/4 cup tahini
- 2 tablespoons lemon juice
- 2 tablespoons water
- 1 clove garlic, minced
- Salt to taste

For the Platter:

- Pita bread or flatbreads
- Sliced cucumbers, tomatoes and red onions.
- Fresh lettuce leaves
- Pickles (optional)

Instructions:

Prepare the Falafel Mixture:

- In a food processor, blend chickpeas, parsley, cilantro, onion, garlic, cumin, coriander, cayenne pepper salt and black pepper with lemon juice.
- Pulse until the mixture is homogeneous but not completely smooth.
- Add 2 tablespoons of flour and baking powder. Re-pulse to form the mixture. However, if the dough is too sticky, add more flour as required.
- Shape the mixture into small patties or balls, about 1.5 inches in size.
- Set your air fryer to 375°F (190°C).
- Spray the air fryer basket or tray with a little cooking spray or olive oil.
- First, arrange the falafel patties in the air fryer making sure there is enough space between them.
- Cook in an air fryer for 10-12 minutes flipping halfway through until golden brown and crispy outside.
- To prepare the Tahini Dressing combine tahini, lemon juice, water, minced garlic and a pinch of salt in a small bowl; whisk until smooth.

- Heat up the pita bread or flatbreads.
- Put some lettuce leaves on each piece of bread.
- Place falafel patties on top and garnish with sliced cucumbers, tomatoes, and red onions.
- Drizzle with the tahini dressing.
- Serve with pickles as a side dish if you want to.

Cooking Tips:

- If you have spare time, you can refrigerate the falafel mixture for about 30 minutes before shaping to make it less sticky.
- Adjust the cayenne pepper intensity to your liking.
- Pair with your favorite hot sauce or hummus for added taste.

7.1.2 Spicy Sweet Potato and Black Bean Tacos

These marvels of vegetarian nature are full to bursting with a perfect harmony between the taste and mouthfeel. To create a taco that will leave an impression, make you want more and titillate your taste buds all at the same time, combine roasted sweet potatoes, seasoned black beans and flavor chipotle sauce in hot tortillas.

Ingredients for 4 Servings:

- 2 big sweet potatoes, cubed
- 1 can 15 ounces black beans, rinsed and drained
- 2 tablespoons olive oil
- 1 teaspoon ground cumin
- 1 teaspoon chili powder
- 1/2 teaspoon smoked paprika
- Salt and pepper to taste

For the Chipotle Sauce:

- 1/2 cup vegan mayonnaise
- Adobo sauce – 1-2 tablespoons, to taste; you can use one taken from canned chipotle peppers.
- 1 clove garlic, minced

- 1 tablespoon lime juice

For Serving:

- Sliced avocado
- Chopped fresh cilantro
- Lime wedges

Instructions:

- Preheat the air fryer by adjusting it to a temperature of 375°F (190°C).
- Toss the diced sweet potatoes with olive oil ground cumin, chili powder, smoked paprika salt and black pepper mixture in a bowl.
- Put the sweet potatoes coated in seasoning onto the air fryer basket making sure they are all spread out, in a single layer.
- Air fry sweet potatoes for 15-20 minutes, shaking the basket halfway until tender but still crispy.
- Meanwhile, the black beans are mixed with a little pinch of salt in another bowl.
- Combine vegan mayonnaise with adobo sauce, minced garlic lime juice salt and black pepper in a small bowl. You can adjust the spice of adobo sauce to suit your preferences.
- On every tortilla, spread a layer of roasted sweet potatoes and black beans.
- Drizzle with chipotle sauce.
- Put avocado into slices and cut cilantro.
- Serve with a side of lime wedges.

Cooking Tips:

- Control the heat of the chipotle sauce by adding more or less adobo sauce.
- To add more variety to your tacos, you may also include other toppings such as chopped tomato, red onion or vegan cheese.

7.1.3 Grilled Portobello Mushroom Steaks

The texture of these meaty mushrooms has a steak-like nature when marinated well and air-fried. These mushroom steaks are also a great alternative if you are vegetarian or just want to have something that replicates meat but is tasty and healthy.

Ingredients for 4 Servings:

- 4 portabella mushroom caps, large
- 1/4 cup balsamic vinegar
- 2 tablespoons olive oil
- 2 cloves garlic, minced
- 1 teaspoon dried thyme
- Salt and black pepper to taste
- Fresh parsley, chopped

Instructions:

- To make the marinade, one needs to put balsamic vinegar, olive oil, minced garlic, thyme dried in a special way , salt and black pepper all into a bowl.
- Place the cleaned Portobello mushroom caps in a shallow pan and pour over the marinade.
- Leave the mushrooms for at least half an hour to marinate, turning them from time to time so that they can be coated evenly.
- Preheat your air fryer to 375°F (190°C).
- Arrange the marinated Portobello mushrooms in the air fryer basket.
- Air fry them for between 12 and 15 minutes, turning them over midway until they become tender and have a grilled look.
- For the grilled Portobello mushroom steaks, chopped fresh parsley should be applied.
- If you want it to taste more, top it with a balsamic glaze.

Cooking Tips:

- You can alter the marinade ingredients to suit your taste buds. If you want more taste, increase the quantity of garlic or herbs.

7.1.4 Vegan Shepherd's Pie with Lentils

Enjoy the soothing taste of our Vegan Shepherd's Pie with Lentils. This vegetarian variation of a familiar dish offers the combination of rich lentils, assorted vegetables and light air fryer-baked mashed potatoes. It is a wholesome and filling dish that can be enjoyed on cold nights or family get-togethers.

Ingredients for 4 Servings:

For the Lentil Filling:

- 1 cup dry green or brown lentils, rinsed and drained
- 2 1/2 cups vegetable broth
- 1 onion, finely chopped
- 2 cloves garlic, minced
- 2 carrots, diced
- 1 cup frozen peas
- 1 cup frozen corn kernels
- 1 teaspoon dried thyme
- Salt and pepper, as desired

For the Mashed Potato Topping:

- 4 large russet potatoes, peeled and diced
- Four tablespoons of unsweetened almond milk (or any plant-based milk)
- 2 tablespoons vegan butter
- Salt and pepper to taste

Instructions:

For the Lentil Filling:

- Mix the rinsed lentils and vegetable broth in a large saucepan. Heat to boiling, then lower heat, cover and simmer for about 25-30 minutes or until lentils become tender. Drain all the extra liquid and keep it aside.
- In a different pan, heat some olive oil over medium heat. Add diced onions and fry until they turn pale, approximately 3-4 minutes.
- Add minced garlic, diced carrots, frozen peas, frozen corn, dried thyme salt and black pepper. Alternatively, cook for 5-7 more minutes to allow the vegetables to soften.
- Stir the cooked lentils into the vegetable mixture. Cook for some more minutes until the flavors blend.

- Put the peeled and diced potatoes in a pot of boiling water. Cook until fork-tender, about 15-20 minutes. Drain.
- Mash the cooked potatoes in a mixing bowl along with unsweetened almond milk, vegan butter, salt and black pepper until it is smooth and creamy.
- Set your air fryer to 375°F (190°C) and preheat it.
- In an appropriate air fryer-safe dish, spread the lentil filling evenly.
- Spread the mashed potato topping carefully over the lentil filling, using a spatula to flatten it.
- Put the dish in the air fryer basket and air fry for 10-12 minutes, until the top is lightly golden and the filling is heated through.

Cooking Tips:

- Personalize the mash topping by adding a bit of vegan cheese or nutritional yeast for more taste.

7.1.5 Stuffed Bell Peppers with Quinoa and Black Beans

These colorful bell peppers are stuffed with a rich blend of quinoa, black beans, tomatoes, and flavorful seasonings that have been perfectly cooked in the air fryer. This meal is not only aesthetically pleasing but also healthy and fulfilling at any time of the day.

Ingredients for 4 Servings:

- 4 large bell peppers (any color), cored
- 1 cup of rinsed and drained quinoa
- 2 cups vegetable broth
- 1 can (15 ounces) of black beans, drained and rinsed
- One can (14.5 ounces) of diced tomatoes, drained
- One cup of corn kernels (fresh, frozen or canned).
- 1 small onion, finely chopped
- 2 cloves garlic, minced
- 1 teaspoon chili powder
- 1/2 teaspoon ground cumin
- Salt and pepper, to taste
- (Optional topping) 1 cup of vegan shredded cheese.

- Cilantro or parsley, for garnish (fresh)

Instructions:

For the Quinoa and Black Bean Filling:

- Combine quinoa and vegetable broth in a saucepan. Bring it to a boil, reduce the heat, cover and simmer for about 15-20 minutes or until the quinoa is completely cooked and all liquid absorbs. Remove from heat and fluff with a fork.
- On the other hand, in a separate frying pan fry the sliced onions and crushed garlic with a little olive oil on medium heat until they turn translucent, which should take about 3-4 minutes.
- Add black beans that have been drained and rinsed, diced tomatoes, corn kernels, chili powder, ground cumin salt and pepper into the skillet. Simmer for an additional 5 minutes to allow the flavors to amalgamate.
- Combine the quinoa that has been cooked with the black bean mixture and stir until fully combined.
- Preheat the air fryer to 375°F (190°C).
- Fill each bell pepper tightly with the quinoa and black bean mixture, packing it down gently.
- Then place the eggplant bell peppers into your air fryer basket. This will be cooked in a batch depending on the size of your air fryer.
- Air fry the stuffed bell peppers for 18-20 minutes or until they are soft and lightly browned on the outside.
- Instead, for the last 5 minutes of air frying, you can finish off by topping your stuffed bell peppers with vegan shredded cheese to give them a cheesy taste.
- Garnish the Stuffed Bell Peppers with Quinoa and Black Beans with fresh cilantro or parsley.

Cooking Tips:

- And of course, you can tailor the filing to your liking by adding other veggies or even spices.
- The stuffed bell peppers can be consumed as full course meals or tasty side orders.

7.1.6 Ratatouille with Herbed Couscous

Immerse yourself in the beautiful Provencal countryside with our Ratatouille and Herbed Couscous. This classic French dish includes a blend of vibrant and fragrant vegetables cooked slowly, served with a cushion of herbed couscous. Get ready to embark on a cozy and rich culinary adventure with this delicious plant-based treat.

Ingredients for 4 Servings:

For the Ratatouille:

- 2 medium-sized eggplants, diced
- 2 medium zucchinis, diced
- 2 red bell peppers, diced
- 1 yellow bell pepper, diced
- 1 large onion, finely chopped
- 4 cloves garlic, minced
- 14.5 ounces canned diced tomatoes
- 2 tablespoons tomato paste
- 2 teaspoons dried thyme
- 2 teaspoons dried oregano
- Salt and pepper to taste
- Olive oil for sautéing
- Fresh basil leaves, for garnish

For the Herbed Couscous:

- 1 cup couscous
- 1 cup vegetable broth
- 2 tablespoons olive oil
- 1 teaspoon dried basil
- 1 teaspoon dried parsley
- Salt and black pepper, to your taste

Instructions:

For the Ratatouille:

- In a large skillet, heat some olive oil on medium fire. Heat the onion and garlic in a sauté pan until they begin to brown, about 3-4 minutes.
- Sauté the diced eggplants, zucchinis and bell peppers in the skillet. Cook and stir for 5-7 minutes, or until the vegetables start to soften.
- Incorporate the diced tomatoes, tomato paste, dried thyme, dried oregano, salt and black pepper. Mix well to incorporate all the ingredients.
- Lower the heat to simmer, cover the skillet and cook for about 20-25 minutes stirring occasionally until the vegetables are tender and all flavors blend.
- Boil vegetable broth and olive oil in a saucepan. Remove from heat.
- Incorporate the couscous, dried basil, dried parsley, salt and black pepper. Seal the saucepan and leave it for 5 minutes.
- Using a fork, fluff the couscous to separate the grains and mix with the herbs.
- Ladle a healthy serving of the Ratatouille onto a bed of herbed couscous.
- Add fresh basil leaves for a splash of color and flavor.

Cooking Tips:

- Ratatouille is even better the day after because the flavors have more time to combine, so do not hesitate to make some extra for leftovers.

7.1.7 Moroccan-Spiced Vegetable Tagine:

Moroccan-Spiced Vegetable Tagine will take you on a culinary adventure to North Africa. This vegetarian dish is an explosion of aromatic spices,tender vegetables and the subtle sweetness of dried fruits simmered to perfection in a traditional tagine. Serve it with couscous or crusty bread to enjoy the flavors of Morocco.

Ingredients for 4 Servings:

For the Tagine:

- 2 tablespoons olive oil
- 1 large onion, finely chopped
- 3 cloves garlic, minced
- 2 teaspoons ground cumin
- 2 teaspoons ground coriander
- 1 teaspoon ground paprika

- 1 teaspoon ground cinnamon
- 1 teaspoon ground ginger
- 1/2 teaspoon ground turmeric
- 1/2 teaspoon cayenne powder (to taste)
- 1 can (14.5 ounces) tomatoes, diced
- 1 cup vegetable broth
- 1 medium eggplant, diced
- 2 carrots, sliced into rounds
- 1 red bell pepper, diced
- 1 yellow bell pepper, diced
- 1 zucchini, diced
- 1 cup drained and rinsed canned chickpeas
- 1/2 cup dried apricots, chopped
- 1/2 cup dried dates, chopped
- Salt and pepper to taste
- Fresh cilantro leaves, for garnish
- Sliced almonds, toasted, for garnish
- Cooked couscous or crusty bread

Instructions:

For the Tagine:

- In a big tagine or in a deep skillet with a cover, warm up olive oil over medium heat. Sauté the chopped onion in a pan until it turns translucent, about 3-4 minutes.
- Add the minced garlic and cook for another minute until fragrant.
- Include the ground cumin, ground coriander, ground paprika, ground cinnamon, ground ginger, ground turmeric and the ground cayenne pepper. Cook and stir for 2 minutes to brown the spices so that their flavors are released.
- Add the diced tomatoes and vegetable broth. Stir well to combine.
- The tagine should be added with diced eggplant, sliced carrots, diced red and yellow bell peppers, diced zucchini chickpeas canned from a can, chopped dried apricots and dried dates. Season with salt and pepper as desired. Stir well to mix the ingredients.
- If you do not have a lid, cover the tagine with aluminum foil. Lower the heat to a simmer and continue cooking for 30–40 minutes, or until the vegetables are cooked through and the flavors have melded together.

- Serve this Moroccan-Spiced Vegetable Tagine hot with cooked couscous or crusty bread.
- Serve garnished with fresh cilantro leaves and toasted sliced almonds for an additional flavorful bite.

Cooking Tips:

- Increase or decrease the amount of cayenne pepper to suit your spice level. It can be as mild or spicy as you desire.

7.2 Vegan Snacks and Sides

With vegetarian food, you can be as creative as possible to make snacks and sides that are not only tasty but also made from plants. So, if you are looking for something new and crispy snacks or a selection of side dishes that can complete your main courses – this section is your detailed plan on how to make the perfect plant-based snacking and sides. Prepare to relish the flavors, feel and aroma of these vegan delights that are bound to leave you craving for more. From all the light and savory to rich hearty ones, our recipes cover it all; we provide delicious vegan snacks and sides for your table. Therefore, we shall delve into this wonderful realm of gourmet vegan goodies and trimmings as each recipe takes you on a tantalizing journey through flavors.

7.2.1 Air Fryer Avocado Fries

Crispy Air Fryer Avocado Fries is a healthy version of an old favorite. These fries have a crispy outside but maintain the avocado's creamy richness inside. With a tangy dipping sauce they become the perfect guilt-free snack or appetizer that you won't be able to resist.

Ingredients for 4 Servings:

For the Avocado Fries:

- 2 ripe avocados, cut into fries.
- 1 cup panko breadcrumbs
- 1/2 cup grated Parmesan cheese
- 1 teaspoon garlic powder
- 1/2 teaspoon paprika
- Salt and freshly ground black pepper, to taste
- Cooking spray

For the Zesty Dipping Sauce:

- 1/2 cup Greek yogurt
- 1 tablespoon fresh lemon juice
- 1 teaspoon fresh dill, chopped
- 1 teaspoon fresh parsley, chopped
- Salt and pepper to taste

Instructions:

For the Avocado Fries:

- Mix the panko breadcrumbs, grated Parmesan cheese, garlic powder, paprika, salt and black pepper in a bowl. Mix well.
- For each slice of avocado, cover it with the breadcrumb mixture and press lightly to ensure that the breadcrumbs stick onto the avocado.
- Set your air fryer to preheat at 375°F (190°C).
- Arrange the coated avocado fries in a single layer in the basket of an air fryer, not touching each other. It may be necessary to cook them in batches if your air fryer is small.
- Spray the avocado fries lightly with cooking spray to give them a crispy coat.
- Cook the avocado fries in an air fryer for 6-8 minutes, turning them halfway through the cooking process, until they are golden brown and crispy.

For the Zesty Dipping Sauce:

- Whisk together the Greek yogurt, fresh lemon juice, chopped dill, chopped parsley, salt and black pepper in a small bowl. Mix until well blended.
- Serve the Crispy Air Fryer Avocado Fries warm with the spicy dipping sauce.

Cooking Tips:

- Be sure to use ripe but firm avocados in order to maintain their shape while frying.
- Adjust the seasonings in the breadcrumb mixture to your liking.
- You can adjust the dipping sauce by adding more herbs or spices to make it tastier.

7.2.2 Air Fryer Vegan Cauliflower Buffalo Wings

If you enjoy the strong flavors of Buffalo wings but want a vegan alternative? Look no further! We have a vegan version of our air fryer cauliflower buffalo wings, which is a plant-based take on an old favorite. These Buffalo cauliflower bites are dipped in spicy sauce, giving each bite a fiery touch. Get ready to treat your tongue.

Ingredients for 4 Servings:

For the Cauliflower Wings:

- 1 cauliflower head, cut into florets.
- 1 cup of all-purpose flour (or chickpea flour for a gluten-free alternative).
- A 1-cup unsweetened almond milk (or any other plant-based milk)
- 1 teaspoon garlic powder
- 1 teaspoon onion powder
- 1/2 teaspoon smoked paprika
- 1/2 teaspoon salt
- 1/4 teaspoon black pepper
- Cooking spray

For the Buffalo Sauce:

- Hot sauce 1/2 cup (to your taste)
- 1/4 cup vegan butter, melted
- 1 tablespoon apple cider vinegar
- 1/2 teaspoon garlic powder
- 1/2 teaspoon smoked paprika
- Salt and pepper, to taste

For the Vegan Ranch Dip:

- 1/2 cup vegan mayonnaise
- Two tablespoons of unsweetened almond milk (or any plant-based milk)
- 1 teaspoon apple cider vinegar
- 1/2 teaspoon dried dill
- 1/2 teaspoon dried parsley
- 1/4 teaspoon garlic powder
- Salt and black pepper, as desired

Instructions:

For the Cauliflower Wings:

- Combine the all-purpose flour (or chickpea flour), unsweetened almond milk, garlic powder, onion powder, smoked paprika, salt and black pepper in a bowl to make a smooth batter.
- Dip each cauliflower floret into the batter, making sure it is fully coated and letting any excess drip off.
- Set your air fryer to 375°F (190°C) and preheat.
- Arrange battered cauliflower florets in the air fryer basket to form a single layer, making sure they do not touch. You might have to cook them in batches.
- Spray the cauliflower lightly with cooking spray to make them crispy.
- Cook the cauliflower in an air fryer for 15-20 minutes, flipping them halfway through the cooking time until they are golden and crispy.

For the Buffalo Sauce:

- In a separate bowl, mix together the hot sauce, melted vegan butter, apple cider vinegar, garlic powder, smoked paprika salt and black pepper. Mix until well blended.
- When the cauliflower wings are cooked, move them to a large bowl.
- Coat the Buffalo sauce over the cauliflower wings and stir until evenly distributed.

For the Vegan Ranch Dip:

- In a small bowl, mix the vegan mayonnaise, unsweetened almond milk, apple cider vinegar, dried dill, dried parsley, garlic powder, salt and black pepper together. Blend until the dip is homogeneous.
- The Vegan Air Fryer Cauliflower Buffalo Wings are best served hot with the vegan ranch dip and celery sticks as side dishes.

Cooking Tips:

- Change the amount of hot sauce in the Buffalo sauce according to your desired level of spiciness.
- Add extra herbs or spices to the vegan ranch dip for more flavor.

7.2.3 Black Bean and Sweet Potato Taquitos:

Enjoy the deliciousness of our Air Fryer Sweet Potato and Black Bean Taquitos. This is a mouth-watering snack, appetizer or light meal that combines sweet potatoes with black beans and spices to give you crispy savory rolls. With the help of air fryer magic, you can have a lower calorie version of this popular Tex-Mex dish.

Ingredients for 4 Servings:

For the Sweet Potato and Black Bean Filling:

- 2 medium sweet potatoes, peeled and chopped
- 1 can (15 ounces) of black beans, drained and rinsed
- 1 small onion, finely chopped
- 2 cloves garlic, minced
- 1 teaspoon ground cumin
- 1/2 teaspoon chili powder
- Salt and pepper, to taste
- Cooking spray

For the Assembly:

- 12 small corn tortillas
- 1 cup of vegan shredded cheese (optional).
- Salsa, guacamole or sour cream for dipping (optional).

Instructions:

- For the Sweet Potato and Black Bean Filling:
- Put the sweet potato cubes in a microwave-safe bowl, cover with a wet paper towel and cook for 4-5 minutes or until softened. Or, you can steam or boil them until tender with a fork.
- In a large skillet, spray with a small amount of cooking spray over medium heat. Sauté the chopped onion and minced garlic. The onion should sauté for 2-3 minutes until it turns translucent.
- Combine cooked sweet potatoes, black beans, cumin along with the chili powder in a large skillet and mix them together. Using a potato masher or a fork, slightly mash the mixture while stirring until they are all combined well. Cook for another 2-3 minutes until the taste is absorbed.

- Set the skillet aside and let the filling cool for a little bit.

For the Assembly:

- Preheat the air fryer to 375°F (190°C).
- If corn tortillas are too stiff, you can microwave them for a few seconds or heat in a hot skillet.
- Spread a spoonful of the sweet potato and black bean mixture on each tortilla and add some vegan shredded cheese, if desired.
- Roll each tortilla tightly and pin with a toothpick.
- Lightly spray the taquitos with cooking oil ensuring that all of them are coated.
- Put taquitos in the basket of an air fryer making sure they are not touching one another. They might need to be cooked in portions.
- Place the taquitos in an air fryer and cook for 8 to10 minutes until cooked through and golden brown.
- You can also serve your Air Fryer Sweet Potato and Black Bean Taquitos warm with salsa, guacamole or sour cream for dipping.

Cooking Tips:

- You can also spice up the filling to your liking or even throw in some jalapeños for a hotter flavor.
- If you want to air fry, make sure the taquitos are secured by toothpicks so that they do not crumble.

7.2.4 Crispy chickpeas and roasted peppers bites:

Get the best of both worlds with our Air Fryer Crispy Chickpea and Roasted Pepper Bites, which combine amazing flavors and textures. These crispy bites marry the creaminess of chickpeas, the depth of roasted peppers, and the crispness of air-frying to a dish that is as tasty as it is healthy.

Ingredients for 4 Servings:

- 15 oz can chickpeas, drained and rinsed.
- A half a cup of roasted red bell peppers, diced.
- 2 tablespoons olive oil

- 1 teaspoon smoked paprika
- 1/2 teaspoon garlic powder
- Salt and freshly ground black pepper to taste
- 12 mini filo pastry cups (readily available in stores)

Instructions:

- In a bowl of medium size, combine chickpeas with finely diced roasted red bell peppers along with olive oil, smoked paprika, garlic powder salt and black pepper. Combine chick peas and bell peppers with the mixture of spices along with oil until there is even coating.
- Adjust your air fryer to a preheat temperature of 375°F (190°C).
- Lay the chickpea and pepper mixture in one layer over the air fryer basket ensuring that they are not overly packed.
- Put the mixture in an air fryer and bake for 8-10 minutes, giving it a good shake halfway through or until chickpeas have gone crispy and peppers slightly caramelized.

For the Assembly:

- Meanwhile, following the preparation instructions on the package of mini filo pastry cups, cook them as you air fry the chickpea and pepper mix.
- Once the chickpea mixture is good to go, be sure to fill every mini filo pastry cup with this crispy peas and roasted pepper filling as soon as possible.
- Add a little chopped fresh parsley to the top as well if you want.
- Lemon wedges may also be provided as a side for an extra zing.

Cooking Tips:

- If you wish, you may vary the seasoning to your own liking by putting more smoked paprika or garlic powder or whatever spices pleases your palate.
- These crispy bites must be served straight away to retain their crispiness.

7.2.5 Roasted Brussels Sprouts with Balsamic Glaze and Garlic:

Make Brussels sprout a gourmet meal using our Air Fryer Garlic-Roasted Brussels Sprouts with Balsamic Glaze. These young sprouts are soaked in garlic, cooked to golden perfection with the help of an air fryer and drizzled with sweet n sour balsamic glaze. This is a condiment that will make you crave for these miniature green treasures.

Ingredients for 4 Servings:

For the Brussels Sprouts:

- 1 lb. Brussels sprouts, trimmed and halved
- 2 tablespoons olive oil
- 3 cloves garlic, minced
- Salt and black pepper to taste

For the Balsamic Glaze:

- 1/2 cup balsamic vinegar
- 2 tbsp honey or maple syrup (for a vegan alternative)
- Salt, to taste

Instructions:

For the Brussels Sprouts:

- Add to a large bowl the halved Brussels sprouts, olive oil, minced garlic, salt and black pepper. Toss with the oil and seasonings to evenly coat the sprouts.
- Heat your air fryer to 375°F (190°C).
- Arrange the Brussels sprouts in a single layer, avoiding overcrowding, in an air fryer basket.
- Air fry the Brussels sprouts for about 12-15 minutes, shaking the basket or tossing them halfway through, until they are tender and golden brown with crispy edges.

For the Balsamic Glaze:

- As the Brussels sprouts are air frying, make the balsamic glaze. In a small saucepan, mix the balsamic vinegar and honey (or maple syrup).

- Heat the saucepan on medium heat and simmer the mixture.
- Let it simmer for 5-7 minutes or until it thickens and reduces by half. Stir occasionally.
- Heat the glaze and season with a pinch of salt. It will become thicker as it cools.

Assembly and Serving:

- After air frying the Brussels sprouts, transfer them to a serving plate.
- As soon as the Brussels sprouts are roasted, drizzle balsamic glaze over them.
- Gently toss the sprouts with the glaze.
- Serve the Air Fryer Garlic-Roasted Brussels Sprouts with Balsamic Glaze as a delicious side dish that is full of taste.

Cooking Tips:

- Vary the sweetness of balsamic glaze, add more or less honey or maple syrup depending on your preference.
- You can add more flavor by sprinkling the Brussels sprouts with some grated Parmesan cheese or toasted pine nuts before drizzling them with the glaze.

7.2.6 Stuffed Mushrooms with Pesto and Pine Nuts

These delicious mushrooms are stuffed with a pesto and pine nut paste that is then air fried to perfection. They are a perfect finger food appetizer or party snacks.

Ingredients for 4 Servings:

For the Stuffed Mushrooms:

- Sixteen large white mushrooms, cleaned and stemmed.
- 1/2 cup pesto sauce
- 1/4 cup grated Parmesan cheese
- 2 tablespoons pine nuts, toasted
- Salt and pepper, to taste

For Garnish:

- Fresh basil leaves, for garnish

Instructions:

- In a bowl, mix the pesto sauce with grated Parmesan cheese and toasted pine nuts. Mix until well combined.
- Heat up your air fryer to 350°F (175°C).
- Fill each cleaned mushroom cap with the pesto mixture and press gently to ensure it's well-packed.
- Arrange the stuffed mushrooms in a single layer in the air fryer basket without overcrowding.
- Air fry the stuffed mushrooms for 10-12 minutes until cooked through and the tops are lightly browned.
- When the stuffed mushrooms are ready, place them on a serving plate.
- Garnish with fresh basil leaves to add color and flavor.
- Serve the Air Fryer Stuffed Mushrooms with Pesto and Pine Nuts as an appetizer that will not last long at any party.

Cooking Tips:

- For convenience, you can use ready-made pesto sauce or make homemade pesto for a personal touch.
- Pine nuts can be toasted by placing them in a dry pan over medium-low heat. Stir occasionally, until they become golden brown and aromatic which takes about 2-3 minutes. Do not over-toast them because they burn quickly.

7.2.7 Vegan Mozzarella Sticks and Marinara Dip

Enjoy a vegan take on the classic delicacy with our Air Fryer Vegan Mozzarella Sticks with Marinara Dip. These mozzarella sticks are 100% vegan, and they are sure to satisfy anyone who wants a delicious snack without harming animals. They need to be dipped in zesty marinara sauce for a delicious mixture of flavors.

Ingredients for 4 Servings:

For the Vegan Mozzarella Sticks:

- 8 store-bought or homemade vegan mozzarella sticks.
- 1 cup all-purpose flour
- 1 cup breadcrumbs (preferably panko)
- 1/2 cup of unsweetened plant-based milk (e.g., almond or soy).
- 1 teaspoon garlic powder
- 1 teaspoon dried oregano
- 1/2 teaspoon paprika
- Cooking spray

For the Marinara Dip:

- One cup of marinara sauce (store bought or homemade).
- 1/2 teaspoon dried basil
- 1/2 teaspoon dried oregano
- 1/4 tsp red pepper flakes (optional).
- Salt and pepper, to taste

Instructions:

For the Vegan Mozzarella Sticks:

- Freeze the vegan mozzarella sticks for about 30 minutes to make them firm.
- Prepare three bowls with the breading station. The first bowl should be filled with all-purpose flour. In the second bowl, mix the plant-based milk with garlic powder, dried oregano, and paprika. In the third bowl, place the breadcrumbs.
- So, take the mozzarella sticks out of the freezer and dust them all with flour so that they are covered completely. Shake off any excess flour.
- Dip the floured mozzarella sticks into the plant-based milk mixture, making sure to shake off any excess liquid.
- Squeeze the mozzarella sticks in breadcrumbs, so that the crumbs adhere evenly.
- Put the breaded mozzarella sticks on a plate or tray and freeze them for another thirty minutes to solidify the coating.
- Set your air fryer to 375°F (190°C) and preheat it.
- Spray the air fryer basket lightly with cooking spray.
- Place the frozen mozzarella sticks in a single layer in the air fryer basket, making sure they do not touch.
- Cook the mozzarella sticks in an air fryer for 6-8 minutes or until golden brown and crispy, flipping them halfway through cooking.

For the Marinara Dip:

- As the mozzarella sticks are being air fried, prepare the marinara dip. Mix the marinara sauce, dried basil, dried oregano, and red pepper flakes (if applicable) in a small saucepan.
- Heat the sauce on low-medium heat, occasionally stirring it until it is warm. Salt and pepper to taste.
- After the Vegan Mozzarella Sticks are cooked, take them out of the air fryer and allow them to cool for a minute.
- Serve the hot mozzarella sticks with a warm marinara dip on the side.
- Indulge in these vegan treats as a guilt-free snack or appetizer that will undoubtedly leave your cravings satisfied.

Cooking Tips:

- Some grocery stores sell vegan mozzarella sticks, or you can shape and freeze vegan mozzarella cheese into stick shapes to make your own.
- In order to ensure that they keep their shape and do not melt too fast while air frying, make sure to freeze the mozzarella sticks twice.

7.3 Tofu and Tempeh Innovations

In this section, we'll discuss the adaptability of tofu and tempeh, two plant-based protein superheroes that can turn themselves into a wide range of mouthwatering meals. From stir-fries to sandwich recipes, you will discover various ways to add these ingredients in your daily meals and explore new flavors and textures that make your vegan diet interesting. Prepare for a gastronomic adventure that shatters the boundaries of tofu and tempeh in the kitchen.

7. 3.1 Smoky BBQ Tempeh Ribs:

Prepare for a plant-based barbecue marvel with our Air Fryer Smoky BBQ Tempeh Ribs. These ribs are a vegan take on the classic BBQ, with tempeh marinated in smoky barbecue flavors and air-fried for that perfect crisp. They are aromatic, smokey and will definitely cure your appetite.

Ingredients for 4 Servings:

For the Smoky BBQ Tempeh Ribs:

- 8 ounce tempeh, cut into rib-sized strips
- 1/2 cup barbecue sauce (vegan-friendly)
- 1 tablespoon liquid smoke
- One tablespoon of soy sauce or tamari
- 1 teaspoon smoked paprika
- 1/2 teaspoon garlic powder
- 1/2 teaspoon onion powder
- 1/2 teaspoon black pepper
- Cooking spray
- For Serving:
- Extra barbecue sauce for dipping
- Pickles and coleslaw (optional)

Instructions:

- For the Smoky BBQ Tempeh Ribs:
- Begin by preparing the marinade. In a bowl, mix the barbecue sauce, liquid smoke, soy sauce (or tamari), smoked paprika, garlic powder, onion powder and black pepper. Combine the ingredients to form a smoky BBQ marinade.

- Cover the tempeh strips with marinade and place them in a shallow dish or resealable bag. Coat the tempeh evenly. Close the bag or cover the dish and marinate in the refrigerator for at least 30 minutes, so that flavor penetrates.
- Heat your air fryer to 375 degrees Fahrenheit (190 degrees Celsius).
- Spray the air fryer basket with a little cooking spray.
- The marinated tempeh strips are taken out of the fridge and put in the air fryer basket in a single layer, making sure they do not occupy too much space.
- Cook the tempeh ribs in an air fryer for about ten to twelve minutes, flipping them half way through cooking. Ribs should be crisp with a delicious barbecue glaze.
- The Air Fryer Smoky BBQ Tempeh Ribs can be served hot with additional barbecue sauce for dipping once they are cooked.
- Serve them with pickles and coleslaw, if desired, for the ultimate plant-based BBQ.
- Delicious as a main course or perfect for sharing, these vegan tempeh ribs are ideal for any BBQ party.

Cooking Tips:

- Tempeh is a vegetarian protein that takes flavors well. The secret to getting that true BBQ flavor is marinating it in the smoky BBQ sauce.
- You can play with the cooking time a little to get your desired crispiness for the tempeh ribs.

7.3.2 Crispy Tofu Nuggets with Sweet Chili Sauce

Get ready to be amazed by the crunchy and delicious taste of our Air Fryer Crispy Tofu Nuggets with Sweet Chili Sauce. These delicious tofu nuggets are breaded and air-fried, resulting in a crunchy shell seasoned with spices. Dip them in a sweet and sour chili sauce for a wonderful vegan appetizer or snack.

Ingredients for 4 Servings:

For the Crispy Tofu Nuggets:

- 1 block (14 ounces) extra-firm tofu, drained and cut into cubes
- 1/2 cup all-purpose flour
- 1 teaspoon garlic powder

- 1 teaspoon onion powder
- 1/2 teaspoon paprika
- 1/2 teaspoon salt
- 1/4 teaspoon black pepper
- Half a cup of unsweetened plant-based milk (almond or soy)
- 1 cup breadcrumbs (preferably panko)
- Cooking spray

For the Sweet Chili Sauce:

1/2 cup sweet chili sauce

- 1 tablespoon rice vinegar
- ½ tsp soy sauce or tamari
- 1/2 teaspoon minced garlic
- ¼ tsp red pepper flakes (to taste)

Instructions:

For the Crispy Tofu Nuggets:

- First, squeeze the tofu to get rid of any excess liquid. Place the tofu block between two clean kitchen towels and put something heavy on top, such as a cast iron skillet or a couple of cans. Let it sit for at least 30 minutes.
- When the tofu is pressed, slice it into nuggets.
- Mix all-purpose flour, garlic powder, onion powder, paprika, salt and black pepper in a shallow bowl.
- In a different bowl, add the unsweetened plant-based milk.
- In a third bowl, add the breadcrumbs.
- Dip each tofu nugget into the flour mixture, then in the plant-based milk, and finally coat with breadcrumbs. Press the tofu with breadcrumbs.
- Set your air fryer to preheat at 375°F (190°C).
- Lightly spray the air fryer basket with cooking oil.
- Place the coated tofu nuggets evenly on the air fryer basket without touching each other.
- Fry the tofu nuggets for about 10-12 minutes, turning them halfway through or until golden brown and crispy.

For the Sweet Chili Sauce:

- While the tofu nuggets are air frying, make the sweet chili sauce. In a little saucepan, mix sweet chili sauce, rice vinegar, soy sauce (or tamari), minced garlic, and red pepper flakes. Simmer the sauce on low-medium heat, stirring occasionally until it is warm and has slightly thickened.
- Add or subtract red pepper flakes in the sauce according to your preferred spice level.
- When the Air Fryer Crispy Tofu Nuggets are ready, serve them hot and offer a side of sweet chili sauce for dipping.
- These Tofu nuggets are a great snack, appetizer or even as part of the main dish.

Cooking Tips:

- Tofu pressing is an important step to help create a firmer texture that removes excess water.
- Make the sweet chili sauce spicy according to your preference by using a different amount of red pepper flakes.

7.3.3 Tempeh and Vegetable Stir-Fry with Peanut Sauce

Take your plant-based meal to the next level with our Air Fryer Tempeh and Vegetable Stir-Fry with Peanut Sauce. This dish brings together the earthiness of tempeh with a rainbow of vegetables, all crisped in an air-fryer. It is drizzled with a delicious peanut sauce, vegetarian stir fry that will make your taste buds happy.

Ingredients for 4 Servings:

For the Tempeh and Vegetable Stir-Fry:

- 1 block (8 ounces) tempeh cut into cubes
- 2 cups broccoli florets
- 1 red bell pepper, sliced
- 1 yellow bell pepper, sliced
- 1 carrot, thinly sliced
- 1/2 cup snap peas, trimmed
- 1/2 cup sliced mushrooms
- 1 tablespoon sesame oil

- Salt and pepper, to taste

For the Peanut Sauce:

- 1/4 cup smooth peanut butter
- 2 tablespoons of soy sauce or tamari
- 2 tablespoons rice vinegar
- 1 tbsp maple syrup or agave nectar
- 1 teaspoon minced garlic
- 1/2 teaspoon grated ginger
- ¼ teaspoon of red pepper flakes (to taste)
- 2-4 tablespoons hot water (for desired thickness)

Instructions:

For the Tempeh and Vegetable Stir-Fry:

- Start by marinating the tempeh. Mix the cubed tempeh with a little sesame oil, salt and black pepper in a shallow bowl. Toss to coat well and marinate for 10-15 minutes.
- Set your air fryer to preheat at 375°F (190°C).
- Put the marinated tempeh cubes in the air fryer basket and air-fry for 8 to 10 minutes, shaking the basket half way through until golden brown and slightly crispy. Take the tempeh out of the air fryer and let it cool.
- In a large bowl, mix the broccoli florets, red and yellow bell peppers, carrot slices, snap peas, and sliced mushrooms. Drizzle with sesame oil and season with salt and pepper. Coat the vegetables with a toss.
- Place the prepared vegetables in a single layer in the air fryer basket, making sure they are not too tightly packed together. It might be necessary to fry the vegetables in batches.
- Air fry vegetables for 8-10 minutes, shaking the basket occasionally until they are tender and slightly charred.

For the Peanut Sauce:

- As the tempeh and vegetables are air frying, prepare the peanut sauce. In a small bowl, combine the peanut butter with soy sauce (or tamari), rice vinegar, maple syrup (or agave nectar), minced garlic, grated ginger and red pepper flakes.

- Add warm water to the sauce, one tablespoon at a time; continue adding until you have achieved your desired consistency. Whisk until the sauce is smooth and homogenous.

Assembly and Serving:

- When the tempeh, vegetables, and peanut sauce are prepared, toss them together in a large bowl. Gently stir to coat the tempeh and vegetables in peanut sauce.
- Serve the Air Fryer Tempeh and Vegetable Stir-Fry hot with sesame seeds and chopped fresh cilantro as a garnish if desired.
- Enjoy this delicious vegan stir fry as a healthy and filling meal.

Cooking Tips:

- Choose the vegetables that will appeal to you, adding or removing any as preferred.
- Adjust the amount of red pepper flakes used in the peanut sauce to your desired spiciness.

7.3.4 Tofu Tikka Masala

This vegan delight has crisp air fried tofu cubes soaked in a flavorful and fragrant tomato based tikka masala sauce. Served with steamed rice or warm naan bread, it's a vegetarian dish that is filled with savory and spicy notes.

Ingredients for 4 Servings:

For the Air-Fried Tofu:

- 1 block (14 ounces) extra-firm tofu, drained and cubed
- 2 tablespoons olive oil
- 1 teaspoon ground cumin
- 1 teaspoon ground coriander
- 1 teaspoon ground paprika
- 1/2 teaspoon ground turmeric
- 1/2 teaspoon garam masala

- Salt and black pepper, as needed

For the Tikka Masala Sauce:

- 1 tablespoon vegetable oil
- 1 onion, finely chopped
- 3 cloves garlic, minced
- grated ginger, 1-inch piece.
- One can (14.5 ounces) diced tomatoes
- One can (14 ounces) of full-fat coconut milk
- 2 tablespoons tomato paste
- 1 teaspoon ground cumin
- 1 teaspoon ground coriander
- 1 teaspoon ground paprika
- 1/2 teaspoon ground turmeric
- 1/2 teaspoon garam masala
- ¼ teaspoon cayenne pepper (to taste).
- Salt and freshly ground black pepper, to taste
- Fresh cilantro leaves, for garnish
- Serve with steamed rice or naan bread.

Instructions:

For the Air-Fried Tofu:

- First, squeeze out the water from the tofu. Set the tofu between two clean kitchen towels and put a heavy object (like a cast-iron skillet) on top. Let it press for at least half an hour.
- When the tofu has been pressed, cut it into chunks.
- In a mixing bowl, mix the olive oil with ground cumin, ground coriander, ground paprika, ground turmeric, garam masala salt and black pepper. Mix thoroughly to form a marinade.
- The tofu cubes should be tossed in the marinade and coated evenly. Allow them to marinate at least for 15-20 minutes so that they can absorb the flavors.
- Set your air fryer to 375°F (190°C) and preheat it.
- Air fry the marinated tofu cubes in a single layer without overcrowding them. It may be necessary to cook the tofu in batches using an air fryer.
- Fry the tofu in air for 15-18 minutes, shaking the basket halfway through or until it turns light brown and crispy. Take the tofu out of the air fryer and let it rest.

For the Tikka Masala Sauce:

- In a large skillet, sauté the vegetable oil over medium heat. Add the diced onion and sauté for 3-4 minutes, or until it turns transparent.
- Add the chopped garlic and ginger, and cook for another minute or two until aromatic.
- Saute the diced tomatoes, tomato paste, cumin powder, coriander powder, paprika powder, turmeric powder and garam masala with salt and black pepper. Combine all the spices with the tomatoes by stirring thoroughly.
- Add the coconut milk and mix until all of the ingredients are blended.
- Lower the heat to simmer and cook for 10-15 minutes, letting the flavors develop and the sauce thicken.

Assembly and Serving:

- Lightly incorporate the air-fried tofu cubes into the tikka masala sauce, making sure they are fully covered in the delicious and spicy sauce.
- Serve the Air Fryer Tofu Tikka Masala hot with fresh cilantro leaves as a garnish.
- Serve it with steamed rice or warmed naan bread to make a balanced and satisfying meal.

Cooking Tips:

- Modify the cayenne pepper in the sauce according to your preferred level of spiciness.
- To make the sauce creamier, you can add a tablespoon of vegan yogurt or cashew cream when simmering.

7.3.5 Balsamic-Glazed Tempeh Steaks

Taste the explosion of flavors with our Air Fryer Balsamic-Glazed Tempeh Steaks. These plant-based steaks are marinated and air fried to allow a tender interior with caramelized, balsamic glaze exterior. If you are an expert vegan or simply want to enjoy a meatless meal, these tempeh steaks will satisfy your taste buds.

Ingredients for 4 Servings:

For the Tempeh Steaks:

- 2 (8-ounce) blocks of tempeh
- 1/2 cup balsamic vinegar
- 2 tbsp soy sauce or tamari
- 2 tablespoons olive oil
- 2 cloves garlic, minced
- 1 teaspoon dried thyme
- 1 teaspoon dried rosemary
- 1/2 teaspoon smoked paprika
- Salt and black pepper to taste

For the Balsamic Glaze:

- 1/4 cup balsamic vinegar
- 2 tablespoons maple syrup

Instructions:

For the Tempeh Steaks:

- Start by dividing each tempeh block into four steaks of equal size. You may cut them horizontally or diagonally, according to your choice.
- Whisk together balsamic vinegar, soy sauce or tamari, olive oil, minced garlic, dried thyme, dried rosemary, smoked paprika , salt and black pepper in a mixing bowl.
- Put the tempeh steaks in a shallow bowl, pouring the marinade over it and making sure that they are evenly coated. Let them sit for at least half an hour or up to 4 hours in the refrigerator to marinate more intensely.

For the Balsamic Glaze:

- In a small saucepan, mix the balsamic vinegar and maple syrup. Heat the mixture on medium heat until it simmers.
- Lower the heat and let it simmer for about 10-15 minutes or until the glaze becomes thick enough to coat the back of a spoon. Remove it from heat.

For Air Frying:

- Set your air fryer to 190°C and preheat it.
- Grease the air fryer basket slightly to prevent sticking on it.
- After pouring the marinade off, take out the tempeh steaks from the dish.
- Put the tempeh steaks in the air fryer basket without overcrowding them and air fry for about 10-12 minutes, flipping them halfway through the cooking process.
- When completed, the tempeh steaks should be golden brown and have a caramelized glaze.

Assembly and Serving:

- Just before serving, drizzle the balsamic glaze over the Air Fryer Balsamic-Glazed Tempeh Steaks.
- Have these delicious tempeh steaks with your favorite side dishes like roasted vegetables, quinoa or a fresh salad.
- From these Air Fryer Balsamic-Glazed Tempeh Steaks, you can get a delicious and appetizing vegan meal. Their sauce and balsamic glaze are the ideal combination of sweet and savory that appeals to both vegans those who do not practice veganism.

Cooking Tips:

- You can also add other herbs or spices that you prefer to the marinade.
- Ensure that the tempeh steaks are properly arranged in the basket of an air fryer for uniform cooking.
- Depending on the unit model of your air fryer and thickness of tempeh steaks, change the cooking time. Once done, they should have a nice golden-brown crust on them.

7.3.6 Szechuan Tofu and Peppers with Peanuts

Add some flavor to your daily dinners with our Air Fryer Szechuan Tofu with Peppers and Peanuts. This vegan recipe contains tofu that is air-fried until crispy and served with a spicy Szechuan sauce, bell peppers, and peanuts. It is a delightful and fulfilling meal that you can quickly prepare in your air fryer.

Ingredients for 4 Servings:

For the Szechuan Tofu:

- 1 (450-gram) block extra-firm tofu, drained and cut into cubes
- 2 tablespoons cornstarch
- 1 tablespoon vegetable oil
- For the Szechuan Sauce:
- 3 tablespoons soy sauce
- 2 tablespoons rice vinegar
- 2 tablespoons hoisin sauce
- 1 tablespoon toasted sesame oil
- 1 tbsp. maple syrup or agave nectar
- 2 teaspoons crushed Szechuan peppercorns (to taste).
- Red pepper flakes (adjust to taste) 1 teaspoon.
- 1 teaspoon minced ginger
- 2 cloves garlic, minced

For the Stir-Fry:

- 1 thinly sliced red bell pepper.
- 1 sliced green bell pepper
- 1/2 cup unsalted peanuts
- Sliced green onions, for garnish
- Cooked rice, for serving

Instructions:

For the Szechuan Tofu:

- First, squeeze the tofu to drain off excess moisture. Put the tofu block between two clean kitchen towels or paper towels and put a heavy object such as a cast-iron skillet on it. Allow it to squeeze for at least 30 minutes.
- After pressing, cut the tofu into cubes.
- In a mixing bowl, toss the tofu cubes with cornstarch until they are completely coated.
- Set your air fryer to 375°F (190°C) and preheat.
- Use vegetable oil or a cooking spray to lightly grease the air fryer basket.
- Place the tofu cubes with a coating in one layer inside the air fryer basket, making sure they do not touch.

- Fry the tofu in an air fryer for about 15-20 minutes, flipping them after 10 minutes or until crispy and golden brown.

For the Szechuan Sauce:

- As the tofu air fries, make the Szechuan sauce. In a small bowl, mix soy sauce, rice vinegar, hoisin sauce toasted sesame oil, maple syrup or agave nectar crushed Szechuan peppercorns red pepper flakes minced ginger and minced garlic

For the Stir-Fry:

- In a large skillet or wok, heat some vegetable oil at medium-high.
- Add the thinly sliced red and green bell peppers and stir-fry for 2-3 minutes until they begin to soften.
- Toss the peppers with the prepared Szechuan sauce.
- In the skillet, add the air-fried tofu cubes and unsalted peanuts. Toss everything together gently to coat the peppers and tofu with the sauce.
- Proceed to cook for a further 2-3 minutes until the tofu is well coated and heated.

Assembly and Serving:

- Serve the Air Fryer Szechuan Tofu with Peppers and Peanuts on top of cooked rice.
- For a burst of color and freshness, garnish with sliced green onions.
- Include this Air Fryer Szechuan Tofu with Peppers and Peanuts in your repertoire of tasty plant-based meals that offer strong flavors and textures.

Cooking Tips:

- Modify the spiciness by changing the amount of crushed Szechuan peppercorns and red pepper flakes to your liking.
- To add some extra crunch you can lightly toast the peanuts before putting them in the stir-fry.
- Make sure the tofu cubes are coated with cornstarch for a crispy texture when air frying.

7.3.7 Teriyaki Tempeh and Pineapple Skewers

Prepare to indulge in a delectable treat that comes in the form of Teriyaki Tempeh and Pineapple Skewers, specifically designed for air fryer use. These skewers feature marinated tempeh, sweet pineapple chunks and bright bell peppers, all grilled to perfection and drizzled with a luscious teriyaki sauce. It is a vegetative type of cooking that will suit your next barbecue or weekday dinner.

Ingredients for 4 Servings:

For the Teriyaki Marinade:

- Half a cup of low-sodium soy sauce or tamari
- 1/4 cup water
- 2 tablespoons rice vinegar
- 2 tablespoons brown sugar
- 2 cloves garlic, minced
- 1 teaspoon ginger, minced
- 1 teaspoon sesame oil
- 1 tsp of cornstarch (optional, for thickening)

For the Skewers:

- 8 ounces tempeh, cut into cubes.
- 1 cup fresh pineapple chunks
- A red bell pepper, cut into small pieces.
- 1 green bell pepper, diced
- 1 yellow bell pepper, diced
- Wooden skewers soaked in water for 30 minutes

Instructions:

For the Teriyaki Marinade:

- In a small saucepan, mix the low-sodium soy sauce or tamari, water, rice vinegar, brown sugar, minced garlic, minced ginger and sesame oil.
- Whisk the mixture together and bring it to a low simmer over medium heat.

- For a thicker sauce, combine the cornstarch with one tablespoon of water to create a slurry and stir it into the sauce. Cook further for a minute until slightly thickened.
- Place the saucepan off heat and let teriyaki marinade cool.

For the Skewers:

- Cut the tempeh into cubes and put it in a bowl. Half of the teriyaki marinade must be poured over tempeh and let to stay for at least 30 minutes or longer if needed.
- Thread the tempeh cubes, fresh pineapple slices and bell pepper pieces onto the soaked wooden skewers, interspersing them as you thread.
- Set your air fryer to 400°F (200°C) and preheat.
- To prevent sticking, lightly grease the air fryer basket.
- Arrange the Teriyaki Tempeh and Pineapple Skewers assembled in the air fryer basket in a single layer without touching.
- Cook the skewers in an air fryer for 10-12 minutes, turning halfway through cooking time or until charred and cooked to your desired doneness.
- Spread the rest of the teriyaki marinade on the skewers in the last few minutes of cooking to form a delicious glaze.
- Take out the Teriyaki Tempeh and Pineapple Skewers from the air fryer steaming hot.
- These skewers go perfectly with steamed rice or a fresh green salad.
- Dig into the sweet-savory flavor of these Teriyaki Tempeh and Pineapple Skewers for a delicious meal that is also healthy.

Cooking Tips:

- If you are using wooden skewers, be sure to soak them in water for at least 30 minutes before placing your meat on it. This shields them from getting burnt during the cooking process.
- In addition, you may add cherry tomatoes, red onion or mushrooms to the skewers for an alternative flavor and a bit more diversity.

8. Sides and Salads

8. 1. Vegetables and Potatoes Air Fryer

Get ready for a culinary adventure that will transform your kitchen into an oasis of flavors. Here, we need to consider vegetables and potatoes that are being air fried. Instead of having to bid farewell to regular sides and snacks, prepare yourself for a symphony of tastes and sensations that will treat your palate. If you are a fan of crisp tender vegetables or fall victim to the lure of potatoes cooked just right, this is the place for you. Join us as we step on the journey and discover all that we can do with your air fryer, preparing stunning dishes. Prepare to level up your cooking and savor the taste of each bite of these delightful air-fried treats.

8.1.1 Herbed Root Vegetable Medley

This mixture consists of root plants from the earth's crust, such as carrots, parsnips and sweet potatoes with a blend of fragrant herbs and a drizzle of olive oil. This produces a crispy tasty and healthy meal that can be taken at any time.

Ingredients for 4 Servings:

- 2 carrots, peeled and sliced into sticks.
- 2 medium-sized parsnips, peeled and sliced into sticks
- 2 medium sweet potatoes, peeled and cut into wedges
- 2 tablespoons olive oil
- 2 teaspoons dried thyme
- 2 teaspoons dried rosemary
- 2 teaspoons dried oregano
- Salt and pepper to taste

Instructions:

- Place the carrot sticks, parsnip sticks and sweet potato sticks in a large bowl.
- Put the vegetables in a bowl and pour olive oil over them, tossing so that they are coated evenly.
- Sprinkle the veggies with the dried thyme, rosemary and oregano. Season with salt and pepper to taste.

- Give the vegetable another toss for all the herbs and seasonings to be well-distributed.
- Preheat your air fryer to a temperature of 375°F (190°C).
- The basket of the air fryer should be sprayed with cooking oil so as to prevent it from sticking.
- Arrange herbed root vegetables sticks in a layer on the fryer basket ensuring that they are placed side by side and not one over the other.
- Vegetable medley should be air fried for 20-25 minutes, with the basket shaken or vegetables turned over halfway through. Deep fry until crisp and slightly soft inside.
- Then remove it from the air fryer and transfer Herbed Root Vegetable Medley to a serving plate.
- You may also sprinkle some fresh herbs or a few drops of olive oil if you wish.
- Use the herbed root vegetables as a tasty side dish for a variety of chicken, beef or pork dishes.
- Enjoy the sweetness from nature and the herbaceous taste of these crunchy tubers alongside any dish.

Cooking Tips:

- It is possible to adjust herbs and seasonings according to one's taste. In case you have some fresh herbs at hand, do use them to achieve a much more vivid flavor.
- To ensure that the vegetables are evenly cooked and crispy, do not overcrowd the air fryer basket.

8.1.2 Spicy Cajun Sweet Potato Wedges

These wedges bring out the natural sweetness of sweet potatoes and spice them up with Cajun flavor, creating a crispy, savory, slightly spicy snack or side dish.

Ingredients for 4 Servings:

- 4 medium sweet potatoes, washed and cut into wedges.
- 2 tablespoons olive oil
- 2 teaspoons Cajun seasoning
- 1/2 teaspoon garlic powder

- 1/2 teaspoon paprika
- 1/2 teaspoon onion powder
- Salt and pepper to taste

Instructions:

- In a large mixing bowl, place the sweet potato wedges.
- Drizzle olive oil over the sweet potato wedges and toss to coat evenly.
- In another bowl, mix the Cajun seasoning, garlic powder, paprika, onion powder salt and black pepper.
- Cover the sweet potato wedges with the spice mixture and toss them again so that all of them have an even coating.
- Set your air fryer to preheat at 375°F (190°C).
- Using cooking spray, grease the air fryer basket lightly to prevent sticking.
- Place the sweet potato wedges, which have been seasoned, in a single layer in the air fryer basket so that they are not too crowded.
- Air-fry the wedges for 15 to 20 minutes, shaking the basket or tossing the wedges at midway point during cooking. They should be cooked until they are soft inside and crispy outside.
- After that, take the Spicy Cajun Sweet Potato Wedges out of the air fryer and put them on a serving plate.
- These sweet potato wedges are best served hot as a snack or side dish, where the sharpness of Cajun spices blends with the natural sweetness of the potatoes.
- Prepare yourself for a taste sensation as you bite into these tasty wedges.

Cooking Tips:

- Adjust the amount of Cajun seasoning and spices, depending on how much heat you want.
- You are free to make a dip sauce from ingredients such as mayonnaise, Greek yogurt, or sour cream with a little lime or lemon juice for some cooling counterbalance against the spiciness of the Cajun seasoning.

8.1.3 Balsamic Glazed Carrot and Parsnip Fries

Up your side dish game with these Balsamic Glazed Carrot and Parsnip Fries cooked in an air fryer. These savory-sweet fries are a delicious change from the standard potato ones. They are roasted to crispy perfection and glazed with a rich balsamic sauce, making them an irresistible complement to any meal.

Ingredients for 4 Servings:

- For the Balsamic Glazed Carrot and Parsnip Fries:
- 4 large carrots, peeled and cut into thin strips
- Four parsnips, peeled and cut into thin fries
- 2 tablespoons olive oil
- 2 tablespoons balsamic vinegar
- 2 cloves garlic, minced
- 1 teaspoon dried thyme
- Salt and pepper, as desired
- Fresh parsley, chopped (for garnish)

Instructions:

- Combine the carrot and parsnip fries in a large mixing bowl.
- Drizzle the olive oil over the fries and toss to make sure that they are evenly covered.
- To the fries add balsamic vinegar, minced garlic, dried thyme, salt and black pepper. Re-toss to season them.
- Set your air fryer to 375°F (190°C) and preheat.
- Spray the air fryer basket with cooking spray lightly to prevent sticking.
- The seasoned carrot and parsnip fries should be arranged in a single layer in the air fryer basket, with care to avoid overcrowding.
- Fry the fries for 15-20 minutes, shaking the basket or tossing the fries in between. They should be cooked until they are tender and have a crispy skin.
- As the fries are cooking, prepare a small saucepan.
- Heat the rest of the balsamic vinegar in a saucepan over low heat. Simmer for a short time until it reduces and becomes slightly thicker forming glaze. Remove from heat.
- When complete, take out the Balsamic Glazed Carrot and Parsnip Fries from the air fryer.
- Pour the balsamic glaze over hot fries and sprinkle with fresh parsley.
- Serve these delicious fries as a side dish, and enjoy the combination of sweetness and savory with a slight balsamic kick.
- Such a healthy alternative to potato fries, these Balsamic Glazed Carrot and Parsnip Fries are perfect for your cooking arsenal.

Cooking Tips:

- Alter the quantity of balsamic vinegar and spices depending on your personal taste.
- During the final few minutes of cooking, observe the fries to prevent them from getting too crunchy or burnt.

8.1.4 Crispy Brussels Sprouts with Parmesan,

Brussels sprouts are given a delicious makeover with our Crispy Brussels Sprouts with Parmesan, which can be made easily in an air fryer. These green jewels are turned into crunchy, golden-brown nuggets with a cheesy aftertaste. This recipe is a perfect example of how an air fryer can transform an often despised vegetable into a delectable and habit-forming side dish.

Ingredients for 4 Servings:

For the Crispy Brussels Sprouts:

- One pound of Brussels sprouts, trimmed and cut in half.
- 2 tablespoons olive oil
- 1/2 cup grated Parmesan cheese
- 1/2 teaspoon garlic powder
- 1/2 teaspoon onion powder
- 1/2 teaspoon paprika
- Salt and ground black pepper, to taste
- Cooking spray

Instructions:

- In a large bowl, mix the halved Brussels sprouts with olive oil until they are well-coated.
- Stir in the grated Parmesan cheese, garlic powder, onion powder, paprika, salt and black pepper with the Brussels sprouts. Toss again so that the seasoning and cheese are evenly distributed.
- Set your air fryer to 375°F (190°C).
- Spray the air fryer basket with cooking spray to ensure it does not stick.

- Put the seasoned Brussels sprouts in a single layer in the air fryer basket and ensure that they are not overcrowded.
- Air fry the Brussels sprouts for around 15-20 minutes, shaking the basket or tossing the sprouts halfway through cooking. Cook until they are soft inside and have browned on the outside.
- Upon completion, take out the Crispy Brussels Sprouts with Parmesan from the air fryer.
- Place them on a serving plate, and finish with leftover Parmesan for an extra cheesy touch.

Cooking Tips:

- Modify the amount of seasoning and cheese to your liking. You can also try other spices for variety.
- Watch the Brussels sprouts in the last few minutes of cooking to prevent them from becoming too crispy or burned.

8.1.5 Rosemary and Garlic Roasted Baby Potatoes

Take your side dish to the next level with our Rosemary and Garlic Roasted Baby Potatoes, expertly prepared in an air fryer. The baby potatoes are seasoned with the subtle scent of rosemary and the salty richness of roasted garlic, which combine to form a delicious blend of taste and texture that will go well with any main meal.

Ingredients for 4 Servings:

- 1 pound baby potatoes, washed and cut into halves.
- 2 tablespoons olive oil
- 2 cloves garlic, minced
- 1 tablespoon fresh rosemary leaves, minced
- Salt and black pepper, as desired

Instructions:

- In a large bowl, combine the halved baby potatoes with olive oil, minced garlic and rosemary leaves that have already been chopped. Throw 12 times to coat the potatoes with the aromatic mix. Seasons with salt and pepper.

- Preheat your air fryer to the temperature of 375°F (190°C).
- The tray of the air fryer should be sprayed lightly with cooking oil spray to prevent sticking.
- Transfer the seasoned baby potatoes into the basket of an air fryer and spread them as a single layer, without overcrowding.
- Shake or toss the potatoes after about 10 minutes and put back for another 10-15 minutes. Cook until the insides have softened up and the outside has turned crispy.
- From here, remove the Rosemary and Garlic Roasted Baby Potatoes from the air fryer.
- Transfer onto a serving dish and garnish with fresh rosemary leaves for an added touch of color and flavor.

Cooking Tips:

- The cooking time varies with the size of baby potatoes and how crispy you want them to be.
- The spice can be changed according to your taste buds as per the herbs and spices you desire, thus providing various options for this tasty side dish.
- You can serve the Rosemary and Garlic Roasted Baby Potatoes with your preferred protein or use them in a complete breakfast buffet.

8.1.6 Caramelized Rutabaga Fries with Honey Mustard

Prepare to treat your palate with our Honey-Mustard Glazed Rutabaga Chips done in an air fryer. The chips are sweetened like honey, flavored with mustard and savoring the tastiness of a rutabaga; this makes it a completely different snack or side dish.

Ingredients for 4 Servings:

- 2 peeled rutabagas in thin chips
- 2 tablespoons olive oil
- 2 tablespoons honey
- 1 tablespoon Dijon mustard

Instructions:

- In a bowl, combine the olive oil, honey, Dijon mustard and black pepper. Continue stirring until the paste is smooth and similar to honey-mustard sauce.
- In a bowl, mix the rutabaga chips with the thinly sliced glaze. Toss the chips for an even coating.
- Preheat your air fryer to 375°F (190°C).
- Spray the air fryer basket with a little cooking spray to prevent sticking.
- Lay the glazed rutabaga chips in a single layer over the air fryer basket, making sure they are not crowded.
- Air fry the chips for about 10-12 minutes, turning them over halfway through the cooking time, or until they become crispy and golden brown.
- After that take out the Honey-Mustard Glazed Rutabaga Chips from the air fryer.
- Put them into a serving bowl, decorate with fresh parsley (optional), and serve as a nice snack or one-of-a-kind side dish that everyone will ask for the recipe.

Cooking Tips:

- Change the amount of honey and mustard to match your desired level of sweetness and sharpness.
- However, it is important to watch the chips as they are air-fried because cooking times may differ based on the thickness of the slices and your particular air fryer model.
- These chips taste best when they are fresh and crispy, so serve them immediately for the ultimate enjoyment of the flavor.

8.1.7 Smoky Paprika Cauliflower Steaks

Take your vegan dining to the next level with our Smoky Paprika Cauliflower Steaks made in an air fryer. These cauliflower steaks have a smoky paprika flavor that enhances the natural sweetness of the cauliflower. Brace yourself for every delectable bite.

Ingredients for 4 Servings:

For the Smoky Paprika Cauliflower Steaks:

- 1 large cauliflower head
- 2 tablespoons olive oil

- 2 teaspoons smoked paprika
- 1 teaspoon garlic powder
- 1/2 teaspoon onion powder
- 1/2 teaspoon cumin
- Salt and pepper, to taste.
- Fresh parsley, for garnish (optional)

Instructions:

- Begin by preparing the cauliflower. Trim the stem and discard the outer leaves, leaving only the core. Cut the cauliflower into steaks that are approximately 1 inch (2.5 cm) thick, taking care in doing so. The number of steaks you can get from one cauliflower head depends on its size; usually, two to three steaks are enough.
- In a small bowl, mix together the olive oil, smoked paprika, garlic powder, onion powder, cumin, salt and pepper. Blend until you get a tasteful paprika spice mix.
- Spread the paprika mixture on both sides of each cauliflower steak. Ensure that the steaks are properly coated.
- Set your air fryer to 375°F (190°C).
- Spray the air fryer basket with cooking spray to prevent sticking.
- Arrange the cauliflower steaks in a single layer in the air fryer basket. If your air fryer is big enough, you may have to cook them in batches.
- Cook the cauliflower steaks in an air fryer for about 12-15 minutes, turning them over midway through. They should soften and acquire a delicious golden crust.
- After this, gently take out the Smoky Paprika Cauliflower Steaks from the air fryer and place them on a serving platter.
- If desired, garnish with parsley.
- Serve these scrumptious cauliflower steaks as a mouthwatering main or an amazing side dish.

Cooking Tips:

- Change the amount of smoked paprika to suit your desired level of smokiness and heat.
- When air frying the cauliflower steaks, be careful not to allow them to become too dark. However, cooking times may differ from one air fryer model to another.
- If you want to add more flavor complexity, customize the seasoning with other herbs or spices.

8.2 Fresh and Zesty Salads

Goodbye to the tasteless green and welcome a combination of freshly flavored ingredients with piquant dressings, and innovative new additions that will bring your senses to life. But for those who are into salads and would want something light, healthy and delicious, prepare to be amazed. So, let us dive into the art and science of making salads that are not only eye-catching but tasty as well. So gear up to elevate the choices of your salads and relish these rejuvenating cuisines with each mouthful.

8.2.1 Kale and Quinoa Salad

Elevate your salad game with our Crispy Kale and Quinoa Salad featuring crunchy kale leaves baked in an air fryer. This dish is a great combination of flavors and textures because it features the natural taste of quinoa, crispiness from kale chips, and tang in its dressing. So, get ready for a wholesome and satiating journey of salads!

Ingredients for 4 Servings:

- 1 bunch kale, stems removed and torn into pieces.
- 1 tablespoon olive oil
- Salt and pepper to taste
- For the Quinoa Salad:
- 1 cup of quinoa, properly rinses and drained.
- 2 cups vegetable broth
- 1 cucumber, diced
- Because the fresh mint is optional, you may choose not to include it.
- If using, ¼ cup feta cheese crumbled

For the Lemon Vinaigrette:

- 2 tablespoons lemon juice
- 1 teaspoon Dijon mustard
- 1 clove garlic, minced

Instructions:

- Preheat your air fryer up to 375°F (190°C).
- In a large bowl, drizzle the olive oil over the torn kale leaves.
- Salt and black pepper to taste.
- Make sure the kale leaves are evenly coated with oil and seasoning by tossing.
- The kale leaves should be arranged in a single layer in the air fryer basket. You may have to operate in batches if your air fryer is large.

- Air fry the kale for 3-5 minutes, shaking the basket or tossing them halfway through to get crispy and lightly browned. Observe them carefully to avoid burning.
- Cool the crispy kale chips after removing them from the air fryer.

For the Quinoa Salad:

- In a medium saucepan, mix the rinsed quinoa with vegetable broth. Heat to a boil and then simmer, covered. Cook for 15-20 minutes or until the quinoa is cooked and the liquid has been absorbed. Heat off and fluff with a fork. Let it cool.
- Add the cooked quinoa, halved cherry tomatoes, diced cucumber, finely chopped red onion, parsley leaves and mint leaves (if using) to a large salad bowl. Toss gently to mix.
- If desired, top the salad with crumbled feta cheese.

For the Lemon Vinaigrette:

- In a small bowl, whisk together 1/4 cup extra-virgin olive oil, lemon juice, Dijon mustard, minced garlic, salt and black pepper until well blended.
- Pour the lemon vinaigrette over top of the Crispy Kale and Quinoa Salad, mix everything together to evenly coat the salad with its zesty dressing.
- After plating, top the salad with crispy kale chips to add a little crunch.

Cooking Tips:

- To save time during salad preparation, the kale chips and quinoa can be prepared in advance.
- Personalize the salad by incorporating your favorite vegetables or protein options including grilled chicken, chickpeas, and roasted sweet potatoes.

8.2.2 Air Fried Caprese Salad

Prepare to take your salad to the next level with our Air Fried Caprese Salad. This variation of the traditional Caprese salad gives you a crunch and warmth in texture, courtesy of the air fryer. It is a cool, crunchy dish that you don't want to miss. Let's dive into the details:

Ingredients for 4 Servings:

- Two large tomatoes, cut into 1/2-inch rounds
- 8 ounces (225 g) fresh mozzarella cheese, cut into 1/4-inch slices
- Fresh basil leaves
- Balsamic glaze, for drizzling
- Olive oil, for brushing
- Salt and pepper to taste

Instructions:

- First, prepare your tomatoes and mozzarella. Cut the tomatoes into 1/2-inch thick rounds. In the same way, cut fresh mozzarella cheese into 1/4-inch rounds.
- Begin constructing your Caprese stacks by alternating the tomato slice, mozzarella slice and then a fresh basil leaf. Repeat this process until you come up with a flavor tower.
- Preheat your air fryer to 375°F or about 190°C.
- To add a golden touch, brush both sides of the Caprese stacks lightly with olive oil.
- Gently put the Caprese stacks in the air fryer basket. This may need to be done in batches though, depending on the size of your air fryer.
- Cook the Caprese stacks in the air fryer for 4-5 minutes or until they turn beautifully crispy and the cheese melts.
- Then, remove the Air Fried Caprese Salad from the air fryer and transfer them to a plate.
- Afterward, pour the succulent balsamic glaze over it and add salt and black pepper to taste.
- This delicious version of the classic Caprese salad can serve as an original appetizer or a side dish and has its own unique taste.

Cooking Tips:

- Do not allow the Caprese stacks to overcook because crisps should be achieved while maintaining freshness.
- To make it taste better, you can include a high quality balsamic glaze in your salad.

8.2.3 Crispy Asparagus and Strawberry Salad

Prepare yourself for an explosion of taste with our Crispy Asparagus and Strawberry Salad that combines the best flavors and gives you a food experience that will satisfy different aspects of your senses. Earth crunchiness meets strawberry sweet juice in asparagus salad for a refreshing vibrant dish.

Ingredients for 4 Servings:

- 1 bunch of fresh asparagus, trimmed
- One cup of fresh strawberries, de-stemmed and sliced.
- 1/4 cup sliced almonds, toasted
- Fresh mint leaves, for garnish
- Olive oil, for drizzling
- Balsamic glaze, for drizzling
- Salt and pepper, to your liking

Instructions:

- Begin by preparing your asparagus. Discard the tough ends. They will be tender spears that you would like to keep.
- Preheat your air fryer to 375°F (190°C).
- Arrange the trimmed asparagus on the air fryer basket with one layer to ensure uniform cooking.
- Drizzle some olive oil over the asparagus, add a dash of salt and freshly ground black pepper. Toss them lightly to coat evenly.
- Fry the asparagus in an air fryer for 5-6 minutes, until they are nicely crunchy and soft.
- As the asparagus is being air fried, let's prepare strawberries. Peel and cut them into thin rings.

- When ready, take the asparagus out of the air fryer and let them rest for a minute or two.
- It is now time to prepare your salad. Place the crispy asparagus on a serving platter and distribute the sliced strawberries over them.
- Finish the salad with toasted sliced almonds for a touch of crunch.
- To enrich the taste, pour both olive oil and balsamic glaze on the salad; it will add a nice balance of richness and sourness.
- Add fresh mint leaves to your Crispy Asparagus and Strawberry Salad as a garnish for the additional freshness and fragrance.
- This salad is a perfect appetizer or side dish that you can use to surprise your guests with something different.

Cooking Tips:

- Take care not to overcook the asparagus, because you want them crisp and tender, but not mushy.
- You can also add a pinch of goat cheese or feta to the salad for some creamy twist.

8.2.4 Air Fryer Falafel Salad

Prepare to enjoy the taste of the Mediterranean with our Air Fryer Falafel Salad. This salad is a delicious combination of the crunchiness of falafel with fresh vegetables and a tangy tahini dressing for an appetizing meal. Let's dive into creating this culinary masterpiece:

Ingredients for 4 Servings:

For the Air Fryer Falafel:

- One can (15 ounces) of drained and rinsed chickpeas
- 1/4 cup chopped fresh parsley
- 1/4 cup chopped fresh cilantro
- 1/2 small onion, chopped
- 3 cloves garlic, minced
- 1 teaspoon ground cumin
- 1 teaspoon ground coriander

- ¼ teaspoon cayenne pepper (adjust to taste).
- Salt and pepper to taste
- 2-3 tablespoons all-purpose flour
- Olive oil, for brushing

For the Salad:

- Mixed fresh greens (lettuce, spinach, arugula etc.)
- Cherry tomatoes, halved
- Cucumber, sliced
- Red onion, thinly sliced
- Kalamata olives
- Feta cheese, crumbled (optional)

For the Tahini Dressing:

- 1/4 cup tahini
- 2 tablespoons lemon juice
- 1 clove garlic, minced
- 2 tablespoons water
- Salt and pepper, to taste

Instructions:

For the Air Fryer Falafel:

- Process chickpeas, chopped parsley, chopped cilantro, chopped onion, minced garlic, ground cumin, ground coriander and cayenne pepper until fine. Season with salt and black pepper.
- Pulse the mixture until it is well blended, but still has some body. You don't want it to be too smooth.
- Add 2-3 tablespoons of all-purpose flour to the falafel mixture in a bowl and stir it in order to help bind the mixture. Begin with 2 tablespoons and add more if necessary.
- Form the mixture into small falafel patties or balls, each 1-2 inches in diameter.
- Set your air fryer to 375°F (190°C) and preheat.
- Lightly brush the falafel patties with olive oil to make them crisp up in the air fryer.
- Arrange the falafel in one layer on the air fryer basket, making sure that there is a space between them and they are not overcrowded.

- Air fry the falafel for 10-12 minutes, turning them halfway through, or until golden brown and crispy.

For the Tahini Dressing:

- In the meantime, make tahini dressing. In a bowl, mix the tahini with lemon juice, minced garlic, water salt and black pepper until you get a smooth dressing. If necessary, adjust the thickness using more or less water.

Assembling the Salad:

- In serving bowls, place a bed of fresh mixed greens.
- If you wish, add cherry tomatoes, cucumber slices, red onion slices, Kalamata olives and crumbled feta cheese.
- When the falafel is ready, put them on top of the salad.
- Pour the tahini dressing over the salad.
- If desired, garnish with more fresh parsley or cilantro.

Cooking Tips:

- Make the falafel mixture according to your taste. If you want it more spicy, add some more cayenne pepper.
- You can also bake the falafel in an oven at 375°F (190°C) for approximately 20-25 minutes, flipping them over halfway through if you do not have an air fryer.

8.2.5 Sweet Potato and Quinoa Salad with Crunchy Cashew

Let's take your taste buds on a trip with our Air Fryer Sweet Potato and Quinoa Salad featuring Crunchy Cashews. The air fryer brings that perfect crunch to this vibrant and nutritious salad, which beautifully blends the natural sweetness of sweet potatoes with the protein-packed goodness of quinoa. Here's how to create this delicious dish:

Ingredients for 4 Servings:

For the Air Fryer Sweet Potatoes:

- 2 medium sweet potatoes, peeled and cut into small cubes

- For a light coating, olive oil
- Salt and pepper to taste
- For the Quinoa Salad:
- 1 cup of rinsed and drained quinoa
- 2 cups of water or vegetable broth for cooking quinoa.
- 1/2 cup chopped fresh cilantro
- 1/4 cup chopped green onions
- ¼ cup dried cranberries or raisins
- ¼ cup of roasted cashews coarsely chopped
- Salt and pepper, to taste

For the Lemon-Tahini Dressing:

- 1/4 cup tahini
- 2 tablespoons lemon juice
- 1 clove garlic, minced
- 2 tablespoons water
- Salt and black pepper, to your liking

Instructions:

For the Air Fryer Sweet Potatoes:

- Set your air fryer to preheat at 400°F (200°C).
- Toss the diced sweet potatoes in a bowl with a light coating of olive oil, salt, and black pepper to season them evenly.
- Arrange the seasoned sweet potatoes in a single layer in the air fryer basket so that they cook evenly.
- Air fry the sweet potatoes about 15-20 minutes, shaking the basket or stirring them halfway through, until they are tender with beautiful caramelized skin. Modify the cooking time according to your air fryer's wattage.

For the Quinoa Salad:

- As the sweet potatoes are air frying, we can prepare the quinoa. In a saucepan, mix the rinsed quinoa and water (vegetable broth). Boil it, lower the heat and cover, simmer for 15-20 minutes or until quinoa is light and fluffy with liquid absorbed. Take it off the heat and let it cool.

- Combine together in a large serving bowl the cooked quinoa, air-fried sweet potatoes, chopped cilantro, chopped green onions, dried cranberries (or raisins), and roughly chopped roasted cashews.

For the Lemon-Tahini Dressing:

- In another bowl, mix the tahini with the lemon juice, minced garlic, water, salt and pepper until you have a smooth dressing. Regulate the thickness by adding more or less water.
- Assembling the Salad:
- Sprinkle the Lemon-Tahini Dressing on top of the sweet potato and quinoa mixture.
- Toss all the ingredients lightly to make sure that everything is covered with the dressing.
- Taste and add more salt or black pepper if needed.
- Enjoy your Air Fryer Sweet Potato and Quinoa Salad with Crunchy Cashews as a healthy and filling dish for lunch or dinner.

Cooking Tips:

- The air fryer gives the sweet potatoes a lovely crunch, but note that cooking times may vary depending on your specific air fryer model.
- Alternatively, customize the salad by adding your favorite vegetables or greens to add some freshness and taste.

8.2.6 Air-fried halloumi and watermelon salad

Our Air Fried Halloumi and Watermelon Salad will make you gasp in amazement: a perfect match of salty halloumi cheese with the sweetness of watermelon, made even better by the air fryer. The salad is a delicious and unusual treat for your taste buds. Let's dive into creating this culinary masterpiece:

Ingredients for 4 Servings:

For the Air Fried Halloumi:

- 8 slices of halloumi cheese

- Olive oil, for brushing

For the Salad:

- 4 cups fresh watermelon cubes
- 4 cups of mixed greens (lettuce, arugula or spinach)
- ¼ cup chopped fresh mint
- 1/4 cup sliced red onion
- A quarter cup of pitted and sliced Kalamata olives

For the Balsamic Reduction:

- 1/2 cup balsamic vinegar
- 2 tablespoons honey (to taste)
- Salt and pepper, to taste

Instructions:

For the Air Fried Halloumi:

- Set your air fryer to 400°F (200°C) and preheat.
- Lightly coat both sides of the halloumi cheese slices with olive oil.
- Arrange the halloumi slices in a single layer on top of the air fryer basket.
- Air fry the halloumi slices for about two to three minutes per side until they turn golden brown and become crispy.

For the Balsamic Reduction:

- While the halloumi is air frying, we can make the balsamic reduction. In a small saucepan, mix the balsamic vinegar and honey together over medium heat.
- Simmer the mixture until it thickens after about 5-7 minutes of stirring occasionally. Add a pinch of salt and black pepper. Turn off heat and let it cool.

Assembling the Salad:

- In a large bowl, place the mixed greens as a foundation of your salad.
- Place the watermelon cubes, torn mint leaves, sliced red onion and Kalamata olives over the greens.
- After frying the halloumi in the air, put the crispy slices on top of the salad.

- Drizzle the balsamic reduction over the salad to achieve that ideal harmony of sweet and sour.
- Serve your Halloumi and Watermelon Salad Air Fried as an appetizer or a side dish that will blow the minds of your guests.

Cooking Tips:

- However, do not overcook the halloumi in the air fryer; it should be crispy on the outside but still have a creamy texture inside.
- Make the balsamic reduction sweeter or less sweet by adding more or less honey, to your liking.

8.2.7 Crispy Chickpea and Roasted Vegetable Salad

Air Fryer Crispy Chickpea and Roasted Vegetable Salad is a delicious combination of crispy chickpeas and flavorful roasted vegetables, all cooked to perfection in the air fryer. Let's dive into creating this scrumptious salad:

Ingredients for 4 Servings:

For the Air Fried Crispy Chickpeas:

- 2 cans (15 ounces each) chickpeas, rinsed and drained
- 2 tablespoons olive oil
- 1 teaspoon smoked paprika
- 1 teaspoon cumin
- Salt and pepper to taste

For the Air Fried Roasted Vegetables:

- 2 cups of your choice vegetables (bell peppers, zucchini, cherry tomatoes, red onion etc.) chopped.
- 2 tablespoons olive oil
- Salt and pepper to taste

For the Salad:

- Mixed greens (lettuce, arugula, spinach) – 4 cups
- 1/4 cup of feta cheese crumbled (optional).
- ¼ cup toasted pine nuts (optional)
- For the Air Fried Balsamic Vinaigrette:
- 1/4 cup balsamic vinegar
- 1/4 cup olive oil
- 1 tbsp honey (to taste)
- 1 teaspoon Dijon mustard
- Salt and pepper, to taste

Instructions:

- For the Air Fried Crispy Chickpeas:
- Set your air fryer to 400°F (200°C) and preheat it.
- In a bowl, combine the drained and dried chickpeas with olive oil, smoked paprika, cumin, salt and black pepper until evenly coated.
- The seasoned chickpeas should be arranged in the air fryer basket, all by themselves, so that they cook evenly.
- Cook the chickpeas in an air fryer for 15-20 minutes, shaking the basket or stirring them halfway through until they become crispy and golden brown.
- For the Air Fried Roasted Vegetables:
- As the chickpeas are air frying, you can combine a selection of chopped vegetables with olive oil, salt and black pepper.
- Set the air fryer basket with seasoned vegetables.
- At 375°F (190°C), cook the vegetables for about 10-15 minutes in an air fryer until they are tender and slightly caramelized.
- For the Air Fried Balsamic Vinaigrette:
- In a small bowl, whisk the balsamic vinegar, olive oil, honey, Dijon mustard, salt and black pepper until you have an emulsified dressing. Adjust the sweetness to taste by adding more or less honey.

Assembling the Salad:

- As the foundation of your salad, arrange the mixed greens in a large serving bowl.
- Serve the air fried roasted vegetables on top of the greens.
- Place the chickpeas on top of the ready salad for air frying.
- Alternatively, sprinkle the salad with feta cheese crumbles and roasted pine nuts to get more taste and texture.

- For a mild and tangy feel, sprinkle the slightly air-fried balsamic vinaigrette dressing on top.
- Prepare a delicious meal for lunch or supper with Air Fryer Crispy Chickpea and Roasted Vegetable Salad.

Cooking Tips:

- Include the vegetables of your choice in the salad or grill chicken or tofu for additional protein.
- Season the chickpeas and vegetables to your liking.

8.3 Grains and Legume Dishes

In this chapter, we are going to discuss the art of preparing tasty dishes that will reveal the variety and nutritional benefits of these components. Boring and dull meals are no more, enter the world of possibilities. We will demonstrate the grains like quinoa, rice and barley alongside protein-crammed legumes such as lentils and chickpeas. We are going to show you how to make delicious meals out of those vegetables which will not only be healthy but also very yummy.

8.3.1 Crunchy Air Fryer Risotto Balls

Just a few steps and we will be able to savor the delectable goodness of our Crispy Air Fryer Risotto Balls, an appetizer or snack that's bursting with flavor and crunch, all thanks to the air fryer.

For the Risotto:

- 1 cup Arborio rice
- 4 cups of chicken or vegetable stock
- Crusher 1-2 cups of dry white wine.
- 2 cloves garlic, minced
- 2 tablespoons unsalted butter
- 2 cups breadcrumbs
- 2 large eggs, beaten
- Olive oil spray

Instructions:

For the Risotto:

- Simmer the chicken or vegetable broth in a saucepan with low heat.
- In another large skillet or saucepan, melt the butter over medium heat. Sauté the diced onion and minced garlic until they turn translucent.
- Add the Arborio rice and cook for 2 minutes to coat the grains of rice with butter.
- Add the white wine (if using) and cook, stirring, until it evaporates.
- Start incorporating the warm broth, a ladleful at a time, while stirring it. Let each added broth be almost completely absorbed before adding more. This should be done repeatedly until the rice is creamy and cooked to your liking (around 18-20 minutes).

- Take the risotto off the heat, add the grated Parmesan cheese, and season with salt and black pepper. Let it cool.

For Assembling and Air Frying:

- When the risotto has cooled, take a small amount and form it into a round ball the size of a golf ball. Repeat until all the risotto is gone, making roughly twenty risotto balls.
- Dip each risotto ball in the beaten eggs, making sure it's coated all over.
- Coat the risotto ball in breadcrumbs, pressing on them to make sure it sticks.
- Set your air fryer to 370°F (190°C) and preheat.
- Spray some olive oil in the air fryer basket.
- Put the coated risotto balls in the air fryer basket, placing them in a single layer and ensuring they have space and are not overcrowded.
- Fry the risotto balls in air for about 10-12 minutes until they are golden brown and crisp on the outside.
- When completed, take out the risotto balls from the air fryer and let them cool down for a while.
- These delicious bites are great as a savory appetizer or snack to dip in marinara sauce or any dipping sauce of your choice.

Cooking Tips:

- Alter the risotto balls by incorporating ingredients such as chopped herbs, diced mozzarella, or cooked bacon pieces into the risotto before forming them into balls.
- Make sure you monitor the risotto balls as they air fry so that they do not get overcooked.

8.3.2 Fried Garlic Herb Couscous

Get ready for that divine aroma of Fried Garlic Herb Couscous, which is evenly cooked in an air fryer. With the help of the air fryer, this side dish is both flavorful and has a nice crunch texture to it.

Ingredients for 4 Servings:

- 1 cup couscous
- 2 measures of chicken or vegetable stock
- 2 tablespoons olive oil
- 4 cloves garlic, minced
- 1 teaspoon dried thyme
- 1 teaspoon dried rosemary

Instructions:

- In a saucepan, bring to the boil the chicken or vegetable broth. Once it begins to boil, remove from heat.
- In a different pan, add the olive oil and let it heat over medium heat. Now, introduce the minced garlic and sauté it for about 1-2 minutes until fragrant and starts to turn a little golden brown in color.
- Throw in the dried thyme and rosemary and cook for another minute to allow them to release their smells.
- Afterwards, add the hot broth into the skillet where garlic and herbs are placed.
- Into the skillet let in the couscous and mix thoroughly to distribute it evenly.
- Cover the skillet and remove it from heat. Leave it to rest for 5 minutes as the couscous picks up flavor from both the broth and steam.

For Air Frying:

- Preheat your air fryer at 375°F (190°C).
- After allowing the couscous to sit and absorb all of the liquid, use a fork to gently fluff it so that the grains separate.
- Put a layer of cooked couscous in the air fryer basket.
- Transfer couscous to an air fryer and cook for 6-8 minutes, then shake the basket or stir couscous halfway through until crispy and golden brown.
- Then, remove the Fried Garlic Herb Couscous from the air fryer.
- If desired, sprinkle with fresh parsley and salt and black pepper to taste.
- Present this crisp and tasty garnish as a great addition to your main course indulging the guests with delicious flavor.

Cooking Tips:

- You might also opt for your own herbs and spices or add-ins like some chopped fresh basil, parsley, or lemon zest to taste.
- Gear up to enjoy healthy lentil and vegetable patties that come with a crunchy exterior courtesy of the air fryer. These delicious cakes are filling and flavorful.

8.3.3 Lentil and Vegetable Patties

Get ready to savor the healthy goodness of Lentil and Vegetable Patties with a crispy outer layer, thanks to the air fryer. These savory patties are bursting with flavors and ideal for a hearty meal. Let's dive into creating this culinary masterpiece:

Ingredients for approximately 8 Patties:

- For the Lentil and Vegetable Patties:
- 1 cup of green or brown lentils, washed and drained
- 2 1/2 cups water
- Finely chopped 1 cup mixed vegetables (carrots, peas, corn etc.
- 1/2 cup breadcrumbs
- 2 cloves garlic, minced
- 1 teaspoon ground cumin
- 1/2 teaspoon paprika
- Salt and black pepper to taste
- Olive oil spray
- 1/2 cup Greek yogurt
- 1 tablespoon lemon juice
- One tablespoon of fresh dill, chopped or other herbs, if you prefer them.
- Salt and black pepper to taste

Instructions:

- Put the rinsed lentils in a saucepan together with water. Cook for about 20-25 minutes until the lentils are well cooked but not much.
- Take the cooked lentils into a large mixing bowl and mash it slightly with a fork or potato masher until it becomes coarse.
- Mash the lentils and add finely chopped mixed vegetables, breadcrumbs, minced onion, minced garlic, ground cumin, paprika salt and black pepper. Stir

everything together until well combined and incorporated into a homogeneous mass.
- The mixture should be separated into approximately eight even portions, shaped into patties.

For Air Frying:

- Preheat your air fryer to 375°F (190°C).
- Coat the air fryer basket with olive oil spray to avoid sticking.
- Place the lentil and vegetable patties one beside the other in a single layer on the air fryer basket, ensuring considerable space is left in between to prevent overcrowding.
- Fry the patties in an air fryer for 10-12 minutes, turning them over during this time until they become golden brown and crispy on both sides.
- While the patties are in the air frying process, prepare the dip by mixing together Greek yogurt, lemon juice, chopped fresh dill or herbs of your choice instead), salt and black pepper to taste. Season it to taste.
- The Lentil and Vegetable Patties should still be warm when serving them, with the creamy yogurt dipping sauce as a side.

Cooking Tips:

- Merge them with your personal flavor by introducing herbs or spices to the patties if you prefer.
- As a final product, you can eat these patties with your desired toppings in buns as a lentil and vegetable burger.

8.3.4 Black Bean and Corn Quinoa Salad

Prepare to relish the deliciousness of Black Bean & Corn Quinoa Salad that is not only healthy but also enhanced when you air fry it. It's an incredible melding of black beans that are full of protein, sweet summer corn and light-as-air quinoa all brought together with a touch of smokiness from the air fryer.

Ingredients for 4 Servings:

- 1 cup quinoa rinsed and drained.
- Water or vegetable stock 2 cups (to cook quinoa)
- 15-ounce can of black beans, rinsed and drained
- A cup of sweet corn kernels (fresh, frozen or canned)
- Juice of 2 limes
- 2 tablespoons olive oil
- 1 teaspoon ground cumin
- Salt and black pepper to taste.
- 2 ripe avocados, sliced
- Olive oil spray
- Salt and pepper, to taste

Instructions:

- For the Black Bean and Corn Quinoa Salad:
- In a saucepan, mix the rinsed quinoa and water (or vegetable broth). Boil, then reduce the heat; cover and simmer for 15-20 minutes or until quinoa is fluffy and liquid absorbed. Turn off the heat and let it cool.
- Combine the cooked and cooled quinoa, black beans, sweet corn kernels, diced red bell pepper, finely chopped red onion, and cilantro in a large mixing bowl.
- Meanwhile, in a small bowl, combine the lime juice, olive oil, ground cumin, salt and pepper to make a zesty dressing.
- Dress with the dressing and toss everything together until well combined. Add more salt and black pepper if needed.

For the Air Fryer Avocado Slices:

- Heat your air fryer to 375°F (190°C).
- Cut the avocados that are ripe and take out the seeds.
- Spritz the avocado slices with olive oil and add a pinch of salt and black pepper.
- The air fryer basket should have a single layer of the seasoned avocado slices.
- In about 5-6 minutes, air fry the slices of avocado until they are slightly crispy and golden on the outside.

Assembling the Salad:

- The Black Bean and Corn Quinoa Salad should be served in individual bowls or on a platter.
- To add texture and contrast, top the salad with crunchy air-fried avocado slices.
- If desired, garnish with more cilantro and lime wedges.
- Relish this healthy and tasty salad as a filling main course or an invigorating side dish.

Cooking Tips:

- Personalize the salad by mixing diced tomatoes, chopped jalapeños or any herb of your choice to spice it up.
- If desired, adjust the dressing by adding honey or maple syrup to add a little sweetness.

8.3.5 Spiced Lentil Stew with Tomatoes

The air fryer has taken our Sweet Potato and Chickpea Hash on a gastronomic adventure. This vibrant and nutritious meal includes sweetness from the potatoes, earthiness of the chickpeas fried to a crisp.

Ingredients for 4 Servings:

- 2 medium sweet potatoes, peeled and cubed.
- 15-ounce can of chickpeas, drained and rinsed
- 2 cloves garlic, minced
- 1 teaspoon smoked paprika
- 1/2 teaspoon ground cumin
- 1/2 teaspoon ground coriander
- ¼ teaspoon cayenne pepper to taste
- Olive oil for drizzling

Instructions:

- Preheat your air fryer to 375°F (190°C).

- Combine diced sweet potatoes, chickpeas and ~ of a red onion that has been finely chopped along with the previously minced garlic in a large bowl.
- Make sure to sprinkle the whole mixture with some olive oil so that everything is slightly greasy.
- Sprinkle the ingredients with smoked paprika, ground cumin, ground coriander, cayenne pepper, salt and black pepper all over.
- Combine all the ingredients in the bowl and ensure that seasonings are evenly distributed between sweet potatoes, chickpeas, and onions.
- Lay the sweet potato and chickpea mixture that has been seasoned on the air fryer basket.
- Air fry for 15 to 20 minutes, shaking the basket, stirring the mixture halfway through until sweet potatoes are tender and crisp.
- Then remove the Sweet Potato and Chickpea Hash from the air fryer.

Cooking Tips:

- Personalize the hash to your liking by including such favorite herbs as freshly chopped parsley or coriander that will provide extra freshness and flavor.
- Adjust the quantity of cayenne pepper as per your taste and level of spiciness.

8.3.6 Sweet Potato and Chickpea Hash

Let's go to the world of tastes with our Sweet Potato and Chickpea Hash,' you are going to receive a perfect healthy alternative as well. It is, therefore, a sweet potato recipe that capitalizes on the natural sweetness of this unique food and combines it with an earthy appetizing taste of chickpeas to create a complete meal.

Ingredients for 4 Servings:

- 2 medium sweet potatoes – peeled and cubed
- One (1) can of chickpeas, 15 ounces each and strained
- 2 cloves garlic, minced
- 1 teaspoon smoked paprika
- 1/2 teaspoon ground cumin
- 1/2 teaspoon ground coriander
- ¼ tsp of cayenne pepper (adjust to suit the taste).
- Salt and black peppers, to taste

- Olive oil for drizzling

Instructions:

- Set your air fryer to preheat at 375°F (190°C).
- In a large bowl, combine the sweet potatoes, chickpeas, finely chopped red onion and minced garlic.
- After this, the ingredients should be dusted evenly with the smoked paprika and the ground cumin and coriander followed by a sprinkling of cayenne pepper.
- Mix everything that is in the bowl, ensuring that all the spices have done a round of travel among sweet potatoes, chickpeas and onions.
- So, arrange the spiced sweet potato and chickpea batter in one layer on an air fryer drawer.
- Air fry until tender and crisp, for about 15-20 minutes – shake basket or stir halfway through time.
- After doing this, remove the Sweet Potato and Chickpea Hash from the air fryer.
- This colorful and flavorful hash may be served as a scrumptious accompaniment or main course.

Cooking Tips:

- You can also spice up the hash with your favorite herbs such as chopped fresh parsley or cilantro to give it a fresh taste.
- Adjust the quantity of cayenne pepper to taste fiery or mild.

8.3.7 Wild Rice with Cranberries and Pecans

Our Air Fryer Wild Rice with Cranberries and Pecans is a gastronomic journey that celebrates the air fried wild rice, nutty in flavor; sweet-tart cranberries, and delightful pecans. This nutritious and delicious side dish is a perfect companion to your dinner.

Ingredients for 4 Servings:

- 1 cup wild rice
- Approximately 2 1/2 cups of water or vegetable stock
- 1/2 cup dried cranberries
- 1/2 cup pecans, chopped

- 2 tablespoons olive oil
- 2 cloves garlic, minced
- 1 teaspoon fresh thyme leaves or ½ teaspoon dried thyme
- Salt and pepper as needed

Instructions:

- Preheat the air fryer to 375°F (190°C).
- Combine the wild rice and water (or vegetable broth) in a saucepan. Bring it to a boil then turn down the heat so that it simmers. Then, reduce the heat and cook for 40-45 minutes until the rice is done and all liquid has been absorbed. Remove it from the heat and let it cool.
- In a huge bowl, combine the cooled and cooked wild rice along with dried cranberries and pecans.
- Heat the olive oil in a small skillet over medium heat. Add the red onion and garlic, mixing everything well. Fry them to a golden brown color and transparency, cooking for an estimated 2-3 minutes.
- Sauté the onion and garlic mixture into the bowl having wild rice mixture.
- Add a few thyme leaves or dried thyme to the mixture and season with salt and pepper. Stir the ingredients properly to have them well combined.
- Transfer the blend into the air fryer basket.
- Air fry the mixture for approximately 10-15 minutes, ensuring to stir it every five or so minutes until hot and all flavors are combined.
- Then, remove the Air Fryer Wild Rice with Cranberries and Pecans from the air fryer.
- The tasty and healthy side dish recipe below, serve it with fresh parsley as garnish if desired.

Cooking Tips:

- If you want more variety, you can use other dried fruits, e.g.
- On the other hand, you may also experiment with almond or walnut for different variations in taste.

9. Breads and Pastries

9.1 Homemade Breads and Rolls

Say Bye to store-bought bread,So forget about buying bread at the store and say Hello to homemade deliciousness!We'll be discussing various recipes for different types of breads, starting with rustic artisanal loaves and ending with soft fluffy dinner rolls that will fill your home with the amazing aroma of freshly baked goods. Whether you are a novice baker or have mastered the art of bread, I may surprise you.

Now, if we go deeper into the world of dough, yeast and kneading. We are going to guide you through each step of the process, share some tips and tricks on how to get a perfect homemade bread or roll every time. Get ready to enjoy the happiness of eating together with relatives and friends, as you have prepared something really special from scratch.

9.1.1 Olive and Rosemary Focaccia

Get ready to embark on a culinary journey with our Air fryer Olive and Rosemary Focaccia. All made possible by an air fryer, this classic Italian dish is filled with the strong flavor of olives combined with the fragrant aroma of rosemary.

Ingredients for 6-8 Servings:

- 1 package active dry yeast (equivalent to 2 14 teaspoons)
- A cup of warm water should be about 110°F or 43°C
- 1 teaspoon sugar
- 2 tablespoons of olive oil and a little extra.
- 1 teaspoon salt
- ½ c. black olives, pitted and sliced

Instructions:

- Combine warm water, sugar, and active dry yeast in a small bowl. Let it stand for 5-10 minutes or until you see the froth and foam.
- In a big bowl, combine the flour and salt. Add yeast mixture and 2 tablespoons olive oil.

- Mix all the ingredients well and knead into dough. On a lightly floured surface knead dough for about 5 to 7 minutes until smooth and elastic.
- Place the dough in a greased bowl, and cover it with a damp cloth to idle at room temperature for an hour or more until doubled.
- Preheat the air fryer to 375°F (190°C).
- Knead the proofed dough and put it in the basket of an air fryer. If the texture is a bit rough, gently press it out to match with the basket evenly.
- The top of the dough should have a light splash of olive oil. Press the dough surface with your fingers to have indentations.
- Sprinkle the pieces of black olives and fresh rosemary leaves all over to decorate the dough. Finish it off by sprinkling the top with coarse sea salt to taste.
- Air fry the focaccia for 10-15 minutes, or until it becomes golden brown and crispy on top.
- When it is done, remove the Olive and Rosemary Focaccia gently from the air fryer.
- This aromatic and tasty focaccia can be sliced and eaten as an excellent snack or garnish for any dish according to your preference.

Cooking Tips:

- Add a personal touch to the focaccia by sprinkling grated Parmesan cheese, minced garlic, or other herbs on top for more flavor.
- Ensure that when it is frying in the air every few minutes, the focaccia does not turn too dark. Nevertheless, the time for cooking may vary with the model of air fryer you are using.

9.1.2 Whole Wheat Walnut Bread

Come, let us take a foodie trip with our Whole Wheat Walnut Bread air fryer recipe! This nutritious and nutty bread is whole wheat flour laced with the earthy flavor of walnuts.

Ingredients for 1 Loaf:

- 1 cup lukewarm water 43°C, or 110°F.
- 1 pkt active dry yeast or 2 14 teaspoon fulls.
- 1 tablespoon honey
- 1 teaspoon salt

- 1/2 cup chopped walnuts
- Olive oil for greasing

Instructions:

- In a small bowl, combine warm water, honey and active dry yeast. Allow it to still for 5-10 minutes until it becomes foamy.
- Take a large bowl and combine the wheat flour with salt in it. Incorporate the active yeast mixture.
- Mix all together to make a dough. Knead the dough on a floured surface for 5-7 minutes until it is smooth and elastic.
- Place the dough in a greased bowl and put a damp cloth over it – let rise for one hour or until doubled in a warm place.
- Deflate the dough when it has risen and gently work in the chopped walnuts.
- Form the dough into a loaf shape and put it in the greased fryer basket.
- If you have an air fryer, preheat it to 375°F.
- Fry the bread for approximately 25-30 minutes or until they become golden brown and when tapped at the bottom, sound hollow.
- Afterwards, take out Whole Wheat Walnut Bread from the air fryer and allow it to cool on a wire rack.
- When sliced, this fine and nutty bread is great with your favorite spreads or as a healthy snack.

Cooking Tips:

- To add more taste and texture to it as a whole, customized the bread by adding other types of seeds or dried fruits.
- Keep an eye on the breads while air frying them to avoid leaving them until they become too dark. It is however important to note that the cooking times may differ depending on your specific air fryer.

9.1.3 Cheddar and Chive Buttermilk Biscuits

Now, let us go on a cooking adventure with our Multigrain Seeded Dinner Rolls that have been air fryer to perfection. The yummy multigrain seeds in these filling dinner rolls lend each mouthful a very nice snap.

Ingredients for 6-8 Biscuits:

- ¼ cup of grain seed blend flaxseeds, sunflower seeds and sesame seeds.
- 1 package active dry yeast
- 1 tablespoon honey
- 1/2 teaspoon salt
- 1/2 cups of water at a temperature of 110°F or 43°C
- 2 tablespoons olive oil
- Optional-an additional multigrain seeds for garnishing

Instructions:

- In another bowl, stir dry yeast in warm water with honey. Let it stand for 5-10 minutes or until the mixture becomes frothy.
- In a large bowl, combine all-purpose flour, whole wheat flour, multigrain seed mix and salt.
- Pour in the yeast to create a mixture and also add two spoons of olive oil.
- Mix everything together to form the dough. Turn the dough out onto a lightly floured surface and knead for 5-7 minutes until smooth and elastic.
- Place the dough in a greased bowl, cover it with a moist cloth, and let it stand in a warm area for about 1 hour or until doubled in bulk.
- Roll the raised dough and divide it into 8 portions. Shape each part into a dinner roll.
- Before using your air fryer, preheat it at 375°F (190°C).
- Place the rolls in the basket of the air fryer, leaving a little bit of space around them.
- 12-15 minutes air frying the rolls until they are golden brown on the outside and sound hollow when tapped at their bottoms.
- Optionally, you can also decorate the rolls with more multigrain seeds to make them look and feel better.
- Remove the Multigrain Seeded Dinner Rolls slowly from the air fryer when ready.
- These dinner rolls make yummy side dishes to a meal or can even be eaten as a snack.

Cooking Tips:

- You can even choose your own combination of multigrain seeds for the rolls.

- Keep the rest of the rolls in an airtight container to maintain them fresh.

9.I.5 Garlic and Herb Tear Apart Bread

Let's start the food tour with a Garlic and Herb Pull-Apart Bread which I prepared in an air fryer to ensure that it came out perfect. This bread is a delight and highly flavored with garlic and fragrant herbs, it can be used as an accompaniment to any meal or eaten on its own.

Ingredients for 1 Loaf:

- For the Garlic and Herb Pull-Apart Bread:
- 1 loaf of bread (bakery or homemade, such as French or Italian).
- 1/2 cup (1 stick) melted unsalted butter
- 4 cloves garlic, minced
- 2 tbsp fresh parsley, finely chopped
- 1 teaspoon dried oregano
- 1/2 teaspoon dried thyme
- 1/2 teaspoon dried rosemary
- 1/2 teaspoon salt
- 1/4 teaspoon black pepper

Instructions:

For the Garlic and Herb Pull-Apart Bread:

- Melt the unsalted butter in a small saucepan or microwave-safe bowl. Stir in the minced garlic, fresh parsley, dried oregano, dried thyme, dried rosemary, salt and black pepper. Stir to incorporate, resulting in a tasty garlic and herb butter.
- With a serrated knife, score the bread loaf diagonally about 1 inch (2.5 cm) apart. However, be careful to not cut all the way through; you want the loaf to remain in one piece.
- Spoon the well-prepared garlic and herb butter carefully into the openings, making sure that it gets within the slices.
- Set your air fryer to 375°F (190°C) and preheat it.
- Cover the bread loaf with aluminum foil, but leave the top uncovered.

- The wrapped loaf should be air fried for about 10-15 minutes, or until the bread is warm and slightly crispy on the outside.
- Gently take the Garlic and Herb Pull-Apart Bread out of the air fryer.
- Serve this fragrant and tasty bread as a perfect side dish to your meal of choice or simply enjoy it as a delicious treat.

Cooking Tips:

- Adjust the herb and spice mixture to your preference by including or excluding ingredients as required.
- If you prefer stronger garlic flavor, the quantity of minced garlic in butter mixture can be raised.

9.1.6 Cranberry Orange Pecan Loaf

An air fryer would make our Cranberry Orange Pecan Loaf a culinary adventure. The cranberries' sweet-tart character, the orange zest's vibrant wake-up call, and the pecans' crunch all spring forth from an air fryer in this playful loaf.

Ingredients for 1 Loaf:

- 1 cup granulated sugar
- 1/2 cup buttermilk
- 2 large eggs
- 1 teaspoon vanilla extract
- 1 teaspoon baking powder
- 1/2 teaspoon baking soda
- 1/2 teaspoon salt
- 1 cup dried cranberries
- 1/2 cup chopped pecans

Instructions:

- In a large mixing bowl, cream the softened unsalted butter together with granulated sugar until light and fluffy.
- After adding eggs, mix thoroughly. Mix in orange zest, freshly squeezed orange juice and vanilla essence.

- In the meantime, in another bowl combine the all-purpose flour, baking powder, baking soda and salt.
- Sift the dry ingredients gradually into the wet ones, alternating with buttermilk. Begin and end with the dry components.
- Add the dried cranberries and chopped pecans to the batter and fold them in, but try not to mix unevenly.
- Preheat your air fryer to 325°F (160°C).
- Grease a loaf pan with oil and dust it before placing it in the air fryer basket.
- Transfer the batter into a greased loaf pan.
- Place the loaf pan into the basket of the air fryer, allowing some space around it so that there is proper ventilation.
- Air fry the Cranberry Orange Pecan Loaf for 40-45 minutes or until a toothpick inserted in the center comes out clean.
- When done, carefully remove the loaf pan from the air fryer and allow it to cool inside for a couple of minutes.
- Cool the loaf on a rack before cutting and consumption.

Cooking Tips:

- The loaf is able to have a light orange glaze drizzled over it or be lightly sprinkled with powdered sugar on top in order to add some extra flavor and appeal.
- The remaining loaf should be kept in an airtight container to maintain its freshness.

9.1.7 Sourdough Baguettes

So, let's go on a culinary journey with our Air Fryer Sourdough Baguettes – the final edition. Air fryer baguettes are a type of French bread and they have an outer texture that is crispy, while the middle part feels slightly chewy.

Ingredients for 2 Baguettes:

- For the Sourdough Baguettes:
- 1 cup active sourdough starter
- 1 1/2 cups lukewarm water
- 4 cups all-purpose flour
- 2 teaspoons salt

Instructions:

For the Sourdough Baguettes:

- In a large bowl, mix the sourdough starter and warm water.
- Add the all-purpose flour and salt to the mixture with a starter gradually. Stir until dough lumps up.
- Place dough on a floured board and knead for 5-7 minutes or until it is elastic in nature.
- Return the dough to the bowl, cover with a damp cloth and allow it to rise for 4-6 hours or until doubled in volume at a warm place.
- Punch down the dough and divide it into two equal parts.
- Develop each piece into a long, thin sausage shape to form the baguette. Line a baking tray with parchment paper and place the baguettes on top of it.
- Set your air fryer to 375°F (190°C) to preheat.
- Lightly spray or brush the air fryer basket tray with some oil.
- As you move the baguettes into the basket or tray where they will be air fried, ensure that you separate them a little bit so as to cook properly.
- Put the baguettes in an air fryer or oven and cook for 20-25 minutes, until they are golden brown in color and sound hollow when tapped.
- Then, remove the Sourdough Baguettes from the air fryer basket carefully.
- Allow the baguettes to cool a little before slicing and consuming. They are most tasty when eaten fresh while you can take them with your favorite spreads or even meals.

Cooking Tips:

- At the start of baking, steam can be generated in the air fryer to aid in crust development. To achieve this, place a small oven-safe dish with water in the air fryer during preheating and when you start baking.

9.2 Sweet Pastries and Desserts

From the delicate pastries that melt in your mouth to the decadent desserts that satisfy your sweet cravings, we'll uncover a plethora of recipes that will kindle your love for baking. From the professional pastry chef to the avid baker, there's something for everyone here.

Come along with us into the world of sugar, flour, and butter. We'll take you through each recipe, providing techniques and secrets to help you make your sweet creations just right. Prepare to make the moments delightful and share with family and friends the magic of homemade desserts. It's time to sweeten your life with one bite at a time.

9. 2.1 Raspberry Almond Frangipane Tart

Take us on a delicious gastronomic journey with our Raspberry Almond Frangipane Tart, made even more sublime using the air fryer. This delicious dessert consists of raspberries that are sweet and almond frangipane which is nutty, all covered by a tart crust made out of butter. Get ready to savor every delightful bite as we dive into creating this culinary masterpiece:

Ingredients for 1 Tart:

For the Tart Crust:

- 1 and 1/4 cups of all-purpose flour
- 1/4 cup granulated sugar
- 1/2 cup cold, cubed unsalted butter
- 1 egg yolk
- 2 tablespoons ice water
- For the Almond Frangipane Filling:
- 1/2 cup unsalted butter, softened
- 1/2 cup granulated sugar
- 1 cup almond flour

- 2 large eggs
- 1 teaspoon almond extract
- For the Raspberry Topping:
- 1 1/2 cups fresh raspberries
- Powdered sugar, for dusting (optional)

Instructions:

For the Tart Crust:

- In a food processor, blend the all-purpose flour and granulated sugar. Pulse a couple of times to combine.
- Add the cold, cubed unsalted butter and pulse until the mixture is crumbly.
- In a small bowl, mix the egg yolk with ice water. Add this mixture to the bowl of a food processor and pulse until the dough forms.
- Knead the dough briefly on a lightly floured surface to form a smooth ball.
- Wrap the dough in plastic and refrigerate it for at least 30 minutes.

For the Almond Frangipane Filling:

In a mixing bowl, beat together the softened unsalted butter and granulated sugar until pale and fluffy.

- Include the almond flour, eggs, and almond extract. Combine well to make the almond frangipane filling.
- Set your air fryer to 350°F (175°C) and preheat it.
- On a floured surface, roll out the cold tart dough into a circle big enough to cover your tart pan.
- With great care, place the rolled out dough in a greased tart pan and press evenly into the bottom and up the sides.
- The almond frangipane filling is then spread over the tart crust
- Top the filling with a decorative arrangement of fresh raspberries.
- In the air fryer basket, place the tart pan, leaving a little space around it for the circulation of air.
- It will take about 25-30 minutes to air fry the Raspberry Almond Frangipane Tart until the tart crust is golden and the filling is set.
- After that, carefully lift the tart out of the air fryer and allow it to rest.
- Dust with powdered sugar, if desired, before serving.

Cooking Tips:

- The tart can be personalized with other berries or fruits instead of raspberries.
- Allow the tart to cool before slicing and serving.

9.2.2 Chocolate Chip Brioche Rolls

Let us embark on a gastronomic journey with our Chocolate Chip Brioche Rolls, which we have perfected using the air fryer. These air fryer rolls are fluffy, rich and full of chocolate chips with a lovely golden-brown exterior. Get ready to savor every delightful bite as we dive into creating this culinary masterpiece:

Ingredients for 8 Brioche Rolls:

- 3 cups all-purpose flour
- 1/2 cup granulated sugar
- Two and a quarter teaspoons of active dry yeast
- 1/2 teaspoon salt
- 1/2 cup whole milk, lukewarm
- 3 large eggs
- 1/2 cup unsalted butter, softened
- 1/2 cup semi-sweet or milk chocolate chips

Instructions:

For the Chocolate Chip Brioche Rolls:

- In a small bowl, mix the lukewarm whole milk and active dry yeast. It should then be allowed to rest for about 5-10 minutes until it froths and foams.
- Whisk the all-purpose flour, granulated sugar and salt together in a large bowl.
- Make a well in the center of the dry ingredients and pour yeast mixture into it.
- Add a single egg at a time, stirring the mixture thoroughly every time you do so.
- Gradually incorporate softened unsalted butter and knead the dough for about 10-15 minutes until it becomes smooth and elastic. You may use a stand mixer fitted with the dough hook attachment.
- Gently mix in the chocolate chips into the dough so that they would be evenly distributed.

- Cover the bowl with a plastic wrap and let it rise for about 1-2 hours in a warm place until the dough doubles in size.
- When the dough has doubled in size, knock it down and cut into 8 pieces. Shape each piece into a round ball.
- Preheat your air fryer to 350°F (175 °C).
- You would also need to lightly oil the air fryer basket or tray.
- Arrange the brioche rolls in an air fryer basket or tray, so they are not too close to each other for uniform cooking.
- Air fry the rolls for approximately 12-15 minutes or until they turn golden brown in color and produce a hollow sound on tapping them from below.
- After a while, carefully remove the Chocolate Chip Brioche Rolls from the air fryer.
- Allow them to cool for several minutes before serving.

Cooking Tips:

- Customize the rolls to your liking by selecting your favorite type of chocolate chips or accentuating the decadence with a hint of chocolate glaze.
- If there are any rolls left over, they should be kept in an air tight container to prevent them from going stale.

9.2.3 Lemon Curd Danish Pastries

Let us set out on a gastronomic journey together with our Lemon Curd Danish Pastries which, thanks to the wonders of air frying, have been perfected. You can make that under the tangy lemon curd with a sweet ribbon of drizzle in this air fryer puff pastry.

Ingredients for 4 Danish Pastries:

- 1 puff pastry sheet (either bought or prepared at home)
- For the Lemon Curd Filling:
- Half a cup of lemon curd (store bought or homemade).
- For the Glaze:
- 1/2 cup powdered sugar
- 1 tablespoon fresh lemon juice
- 1-2 tbsp milk (adjust to desired thickness)

Instructions:

- If you are using already made puff pastry, let it thaw according to the package instructions. For homemade puff pastry, if using it, roll it into a thickness of the rectangle to approximately ¼".
- Using a knife, cut the puff pastry squares or rectangles that can be four depending on your preference.
- At the center of each pastry square put a teaspoonful of lemon curd.
- Afterwards, the pastry squares should be folded diagonally into triangles or rectangles while sealing the edges by pressing them using a fork.
- Preheat your air fryer to 375°F (190°C).
- Place the lemon curd filled pastries in the air fryer basket while leaving some space between them to allow for even cooking.
- Place the pastries in an air fryer and bake at 400°F for about 10-12 minutes or until golden brown and slightly puffy.
- While the pastries are air frying, make the glaze. In a medium sized bowl, mix the icing sugar, fresh lemon juice and milk together to create a smooth yet runny glaze.
- Once the pastries have cooked, remove them from an air fryer very carefully.
- Drizzle the warm pastries with lemon glaze.
- Serve the Lemon Curd Danish Pastries warm.

Cooking Tips:

- The glaze can be enhanced by dusting the surface with powdered sugar or grated lemon zest.
- The measure of the lemon juice and milk to be incorporated into the coat can similarly be adjusted depending on your sought consistency.

9.2.4 Apricot and Pistachio Pinwheels

Prepared in an air fryer, these nutty and sweet pinwheels are made with a flaky pastry, apricot jam, and pistachios. Get ready to savor every delightful bite as we dive into creating this culinary masterpiece:

Ingredients for 8 Pinwheels:

- 1 sheet of puff pastry (bought from the store or home-made)
- ¼ a cup of apricot jam or preserves
- 1/4 cup chopped pistachios

Instructions:

For the Apricot and Pistachio Pinwheels:

- If you decide to use a ready-made puff pastry, deferentially defrost it according to the package directions. If using puff pastry made at home, roll it out into the ¼-inch thick sheet.
- Apricot jam is applied as a thinly spread layer over the whole surface of puff pastry.
- Sprinkle the pistachios randomly over the apricot jam and press them slightly so that they can hold.
- From one side, tightly roll the puff pastry to a log.
- Set your air fryer to 375°F (190°C).
- Cut the rolled dough into 8 equal pinwheels.
- In the air fryer basket, place the pinwheels making space between them for even cooking.
- Cook the pinwheels in an air fryer for about 10-12 minutes until they are puffed and golden brown.
- After this, gently take out the Apricot and Pistachio Pinwheels from the air fryer.
- Let them cool a little before serving.

Cooking Tips:

- These pinwheels can be personalized with a sprinkle of powdered sugar on top to make them sweeter and more attractive.

9.2.5 Cinnamon Sugar Palmiers

Let's start a culinary journey with Cinnamon Sugar Palmiers air fryer recipe. These cinnamon-sugar palmiers are made with puff pastry and a generous coating of cinnamon sugar, easily cooked in the air fryer. Get ready to savor every delightful bite as we dive into creating this culinary masterpiece:

Ingredients for 12 Palmiers::

- 1 puff pastry sheet (store-bought or homemade)
- 1/2 cup granulated sugar
- 2 tablespoons ground cinnamon

Instructions:

- If you use frozen puff pastry, let it thaw as directed on the package. In the case of homemade puff pastry, roll it out into a rectangle about 1/4-inch thick.
- In a small bowl, combine the granulated sugar and ground cinnamon to make up the cinnamon sugar mixture.
- Sprinkle the cinnamon sugar mixture liberally to cover the entire surface of the puff pastry.
- From each side, roll up the puff pastry so that the rolls unite in the middle, creating two rolls which meet in the middle.
- Set your air fryer to 375°F (190°C), and preheat it.
- Cut the rolled pastry log into 12 palmiers of equal size.
- Put the palmiers in the air fryer basket so that they are not touching each other to ensure uniform cooking.
- Cook the palmiers in an air fryer for about 8-10 minutes until they are puffed and golden brown.
- When finished, gently take out the Cinnamon Sugar Palmiers from the air fryer.
- Let them cool down a bit before serving.

Cooking Tips:

- These palmiers can be personalized with a drizzle of icing or sprinkled powdered sugar for more sweetness and aesthetic appeal.

9.2.6 Blueberry Cream Cheese Strudel

Let's enjoy a wonderful culinary journey with our Blueberry Cream Cheese Strudel, made even better using the air fryer. This is a delicious and creamy strudel that has been filled with a luxurious blueberry and cream cheese filling, which can all be prepared in the air fryer. Get ready to savor every delightful bite as we dive into creating this culinary masterpiece:

Ingredients for 1 Strudel:

For the Blueberry Cream Cheese Strudel:

- One sheet of puff pastry, store-bought or homemade.
- half a cup of blueberry jam or preserves
- 4 ounces cream cheese, softened
- 1/4 cup granulated sugar
- 1/2 teaspoon vanilla extract
- 1 beaten egg (for egg wash)
- Powdered sugar, for dusting (optional)

Instructions:

For the Blueberry Cream Cheese Strudel:

- Should you prefer to use ready-made puff pastry, thaw it as directed on the package. For homemade puff pastry, roll it out into a 1/4-inch rectangle.
- In a large mixing bowl, mix the softened cream cheese with granulated sugar and vanilla extract. Mix until creamy and well blended.
- Cover the puff pastry with the cream cheese mixture uniformly.
- Spread the blueberry jam or preserves on top of the cream cheese layer.
- The puff pastry is rolled up starting from one edge into a log.
- Set your air fryer to 375°F (190°C) and preheat it.
- Brush the top surface of the strudel with beaten egg for a golden finish.
- Put the strudel in the air fryer basket with some space between it and all sides of the basket to allow for uniform cooking.
- Fry the strudel in air for about 15-18 minutes or until it is puffed and golden brown.
- After completion, gently take out the Blueberry Cream Cheese Strudel from the air fryer.
- Let it cool a little before serving.

Cooking Tips:

- You can make the strudel more personal by sprinkling a layer of powdered sugar over it for extra sweetness and beauty.
- It is best to serve the strudel warm or at room temperature.

9.2.7 Cherry and Almond Galette

And now, let's move to the heart of this dish. It is subtle in its rustic charm, like an old family jewel, simple but sophisticated. Just think of a crisp, flaky crust, golden on the edges and with magic inside. Every bite is a symphony not only of flavor but also of textures as they transport you amidst idyllic orchards and sun-kissed almond fields.

Ingredients for 1 Galette:

For the Cherry and Almond Galette:

- 1 (store-bought or homemade) refrigerated pie crust.
- Two cups of pitted and halved fresh or frozen cherries
- 1/4 cup granulated sugar
- 2 tablespoons almond flour
- 1/2 teaspoon almond extract
- 1 beaten egg (egg wash)
- Sliced almonds, for garnish (optional)
- Powdered sugar, for dusting (optional)

Instructions:

For the Cherry and Almond Galette:

- With store-bought pie crust, roll out the crust according to package directions. If you are using homemade pie crust, roll it out into a circle that is approximately 1/4-inch thick.
- In a mixing bowl, mix together the halved cherries, granulated sugar, almond flour and almond extract. Until the cherries are well coated, mix.
- To make it easier to transfer to the air fryer, place the prepared pie crust on a sheet of parchment paper.
- Using a spoon, place the cherry mixture in the center of the pie crust with about 2 inches of crust on each side.

- The pie crust edges are gently folded over the cherry filling to give it a rustic appearance.
- Heat your air fryer to 375°F (190°C).
- Apply the beaten egg over the pie crust edges to give a golden color.
- Place the galette on the parchment paper in the air fryer basket, leaving some space around it for even cooking.
- Air fry the galette at about 18 to 20 minutes or until the crust is golden brown and cherry filling starts bubbling.
- After that, gently lift the Cherry and Almond Galette from the air fryer.
- Let it cool slightly before serving.

Cooking Tips:

- Optionally, sprinkle the galette with some sliced almonds before air frying it for added flavor and visual interest.
- Before serving, lightly dust the galette with powdered sugar for a hint of sweetness.

9.3 Savory Pies and Quiches

The pie categories include a wide array of selections from the flaky golden crusts that are filled with savory fillings to the ultimate creamy custard quiches that will curb your hunger for rich, hearty flavors. No matter whether you are a professional cook or just an amateur, this menu will provide something special for everyone.

In each recipe, we will guide you tenderly and give some tricks and tips to ensure that your savory pies or quiches turn out successfully. Get ready for refreshing your cooking talents as well as the joy of sharing these wonderful dishes with family and friends. Now, it's time to relish in homemade pies and quiches.

9.3.1 Tart of Roasted Vegetable and Goat Cheese

So, come with us as we embark on a culinary adventure featuring our Roasted Vegetable and Goat Cheese Tart cooked to absolute perfection in the air fryer! The pastry in this case turns out to be an air-fried crust with roasted vegetables and goat cheese.

Ingredients for 1 Tart:

For the Roasted Vegetable and Goat Cheese Tart:

- 1 sheet of puff pastry, store-bought or homemade
- 1 small zucchini, thinly sliced
- One small yellow bell pepper thinly sliced
- 1 small red onion, cut into thin slices
- 1 cup cherry tomatoes, halved
- 2 tablespoons olive oil
- Salt and pepper, to taste
- 4 ounces goat cheese, crumbled
- Basil leaves, optional garnish
- Balsamic glaze, for drizzling (optional)

Instructions:

- For the Roasted Vegetable and Goat Cheese Tart:
- Ensure that your air fryer is preheated to 375°F (190°C).
- In a bowl, combine the thinly sliced zucchini, yellow bell pepper, red onion and halved cherry tomatoes with olive oil. Season with salt and freshly ground black pepper.
- Transfer the seasoned vegetables to the air fryer basket, leaving enough room between them for even cooking.
- Cook the vegetables in an air fryer for about 10-12 minutes until they are soft and slightly caramelized. Make sure to shake the basket or stir the vegetables once in a while for uniform cooking.
- As the vegetables are air frying, roll out the puff pastry to a rectangle about ¼ inch thick.
- Once you have finished cooking the vegetables, remove them from the air fryer.
- Evenly spread the crumbled goat cheese on the puff pastry, making sure to leave some room at the four sides of the pastry.
- Top the goat cheese with the roasted vegetables.
- Transfer the tart gently to the basket of an air fryer ensuring that there is some space around for uniform cooking.
- Air fry the prep for 12 to 15 minutes, until the pastry is golden and goat cheese has slightly melted.
- Following this step, remove the Roasted Vegetable and Goat Cheese Tart from the air fryer.
- If you'd like, you can also sprinkle fresh basil leaves and balsamic glaze.

Cooking Tips:

- Fillings of the tart can be personalized by choice of preferred roasted vegetable combination.
- You can also add even a more special flavor by shuddering some grated Parmesan cheese on the goat cheese before putting the roasted vegetables.

9.3.2 Spinach, Feta, and Pine Nut Phyllo Pie

So, let's embark on a gastronomic adventure with our Spinach, Feta and Pine Nut Phyllo Pie elevated to new heights through the air fryer. This pie is very delicious and multilayered as it consists of spinach, feta cheese, toasted pine nuts wrapped in phyllo pastry made from the air fryer.

Ingredients for 1 Phyllo Pie:

- Eight phyllo sheets, thawed if frozen
- 10 ounces fresh spinach leaves, chopped
- 1/2 cup crumbled feta cheese
- 1/4 cup toasted pine nuts
- 2 cloves garlic, minced
- 2 tablespoons olive oil
- Olive oil or cooking spray for basting

Instructions:

- In a large skillet, heat 2 tablespoons of olive oil on medium flame.
- Combine both the minced garlic and onion. Cook for 2-3 minutes until the onion becomes translucent.
- Place the spinach in the pan with 2 tablespoons of oil and cook it for about three minutes to wilt it down, this will drain all the water. Salt and pepper to taste. Remove it from the source of heat and let it cool.
- Preheat the air fryer to 375°F (190°C).
- In a clean countertop, put one sheet of phyllo pastry and spray it lightly with cooking oil or olive oil. Place another sheet on top and repeat the process until you have four sheets piled up, brush every other sheet with a little oil.
- Put a pile of sheets of phyllo in the basket for the air fryer, so that it entirely covers its bottom and sides with some excess.
- Using a spoon, the sautéed spinach mixture is to be placed in the basket of the air fryer after lining it with phyllo sheets.
- Top the spinach mixture with crumbled feta cheese and then sprinkle it with toasted pine nuts.
- Place another four phyllo sheets, each brushed with oil, one on top of the spinach mixture in the air fryer basket.
- Overhanging phyllo sheets should be pulled straight up and folded over the top, forming a closed pie.
- Lightly oil the top again.
- In an air fryer, cook the Spinach, Feta and Pine Nut Phyllo Pie for 15-18 minutes or until pastry turns crispy golden.
- Once done, carefully remove the pie from the air fryer.
- Allow some time to cool off before cutting it and serving.

Cooking Tips:

- You may also spice up the filling by incorporating some of your favorite herbs or spices.
- Phyllo pie should be served warm while still fresh and therefore can be an excellent appetizer or a side dish.

9.3.3 Caramelized Onion and Gruyere Quiche

This savory quiche is filled with sweet and caramelized onions, creamy Gruyere cheese and a perfectly set custard encased in butter pastry which can be easily baked in the air fryer. Get ready to savor every delightful bite as we dive into creating this culinary masterpiece:

Ingredients for 1 Quiche:

- One refrigerated pie crust (store bought or homemade).
- 2 large onions, thinly sliced
- 2 tablespoons butter
- 1 cup shredded Gruyere cheese
- 4 large eggs
- 1 cup of half-and-half (or milk and heavy cream mixture)
- Salt and ground black pepper, as desired
- Pinch of nutmeg (optional)

Instructions:

For the Caramelized Onion and Gruyere Quiche:

- If ready-made pie crust is used, proceed according to the package instructions for rolling out the crust. If the pie crust is homemade, roll it out to fit in the air fryer basket or tray.
- Melt the butter in a skillet over medium heat. Stir in the thinly sliced onions and cook until softened and caramelized, approximately 20-25 minutes. Season with salt and ground black pepper to taste. For more flavor, add a pinch of nutmeg.

- Preheat your air fryer to 375°F (190°C).
- Gently lay the pie crust dough that you rolled out over your air fryer basket or tray so that it lines both the bottom and sides.
- Spread the cooled caramelized onions on the pie crust.
- Distribute the grated Gruyere cheese over the onions that have been caramelized.
- In a bowl, combine the eggs and half-and-half. A pinch of salt and black pepper.
- Onions and cheese should be placed in a pie crust, after which one needs to pour the egg mixture over them.
- Place the quiche in the air fryer basket or on the tray.
- Air fry for 18-20 minutes until the Caramelized Onion and Gruyere Quiche sets, and the crust turns golden brown.
- When done, carefully remove the quiche from the air fryer.
- Allow it to cool a bit and then slice it for serving.

Cooking Tips:

- The quiche is also adaptable; one can use fresh herbs or opt to employ other types of cheese depending on higher taste.
- Enjoy it as a great meal or snack when served hot or at room temperature.

9.3.4 Broccoli and Cheddar Hand Pies

Our culinary journey is complete with the Broccoli and Cheddar Hand Pies that have been perfected in the air fryer. These savory pastries filled with creamy broccoli and melty cheddar cheese, wrapped in a buttery crust are easily and conveniently prepared using the air fryer.

Ingredients for 4 Hand Pies:

- A single sheet of puff pastry; this can either be bought from a store or homemade.
- 1 12 cups steamed broccoli florets, finely chopped
- 1/4 cup sour cream
- 1/2 teaspoon garlic powder
- Salt and black pepper, to taste
- Optional garnish sesame or poppy seeds

Instructions:

- If you are using store-bought puff pastry, defrost it according to the package guidelines. Roll it into a rectangle shape of about ¼-inch thickness.
- In a mixing bowl, combine the steamed broccoli that you have finely chopped, shredded cheddar cheese, sour cream, garlic powder and salt and black pepper.
- Preheat your air fryer to 375°F (190°C).
- Divide the rolled puff pastry into 4 equal squares.
- Use a tablespoon and place mounds of the broccoli and cheddar mixture in the center of each pastry square.
- Fold each square along the diagonal to form a triangle, going ahead and seal the edges by pressing them down using a fork.
- For a golden hue, brush the top of each hand pie with an egg wash.
- You can also sprinkle with sesame or poppy seeds if you want to add texture and flavor.
- Carefully arrange the hand pies in the air fryer basket so that they heat through well.
- Air fry the hand pies for 10-12 minutes until they are golden brown and puffed.
- Then remove the Broccoli and Cheddar Hand Pies from the air fryer.
- Serve them warm.

Cooking Tips:

- To make the pies personal, other vegetables, herbs or spices can be included in the filling to enrich it with more flavor.
- These hand pies should be served warm and can be enjoyed as an appetizer or a snack.

9.3.5 Prosciutto and Arugula Quiche

So, join us on a culinary journey with our Prosciutto and Arugula Quiche in the air fryer – just to make perfection even better. In this buttery crumbly pastry crust, air fryer is a delicious quiche with the tender flavors of prosciutto and spiky arugula leaves.

Ingredients for 1 Quiche:

- A store-bought or homemade refrigerated pie crust

- 4 large eggs
- 1 cup heavy cream
- 2 ounces prosciutto, chopped
- Pinch of nutmeg (optional)

Instructions:

- In case of using ready-made pie crust, the directions indicated on its package should be followed with regard to rolling out. If you made your own pie crust, roll it out to fit into the air fryer basket or tray.
- Preheat your air fryer to 375°F (190°C).
- Ensure that the pie crust rolled out covers all the bottom and sides of your air fryer basket or tray.
- In a large bowl, whisk together eggs and heavy cream; season with salt, black pepper, and nutmeg (if using).
- Spread the sliced prosciutto over the crust.
- At the top, put shredded Swiss cheese over the prosciutto.
- Distribute fresh arugula leaves on top of the cheese.
- Then pour the egg mixture over the cheese, prosciutto and arugula in the crust.
- The quiche is to be put into the air fryer basket or onto the tray.
- Air fry the Pie Floater on 180°C for 18-20 minutes or until pie set and crust is golden brown.
- Once ready, carefully remove the quiche from the air fryer.
- Allow it to cool slightly before you slice and serve.

Cooking Tips:

- To make the quiche taste better, one can use other ingredients like sautéed mushrooms, onions or herbs to personalize it.

9.3.6 Mushroom and Leek Galette

Let's explore the gastronomic world of our Mushroom and Leek Galette, cooked to unparalleled excellence with the help of an air fryer. This air fryer galette is a savory masterpiece, with earthy mushrooms and delicate leeks in a flaky pastry crust. Get ready to savor every delightful bite as we dive into creating this culinary masterpiece:

Ingredients for 1 Galette:

For the Mushroom and Leek Galette:

- 1 piece of puff pastry (store-bought or homemade).
- 8 ounces mushrooms, sliced
- 2 cleaned and thinly sliced leeks
- 2 tablespoons olive oil
- 2 cloves garlic, minced
- a quarter of a teaspoon dried thyme (or thyme leaves, fresh).
- Salt and pepper to taste
- 1 cup shredded Gruyere cheese
- 1 beaten egg (for egg wash)
- Fresh parsley, for garnish (optional)

Instructions:

For the Mushroom and Leek Galette:

- If the puff pastry is store-bought, defrost it following the instructions on its package. If you use homemade puff pastry, roll it out into a circle or rectangle, about 1/4-inch thick.
- In a skillet, heat the olive oil on medium heat. Incorporate the sliced mushrooms and continue cooking until their moisture is released and they become soft, around 5-7 minutes. Season with salt and pepper, as well as some dried thyme. Add the minced garlic and cook for one more minute. Take off heat and let it cool.
- Set your air fryer to 375°F (190°C) and preheat it.
- With great care, place the rolled-out puff pastry onto the air fryer basket so it covers both the bottom and sides.
- The shredded Gruyere cheese should be sprinkled over the pastry.
- It is the sautéed mushroom and leek mixture that should be spread on top of the cheese.
- To create a bumpy border, the sides of the dough should be added to this filling.
- Coat the upper side of the galette with an egg wash to achieve a nice, golden finish.
- Begin by placing the galette into the air fryer basket.
- Cook the Mushroom and Leek Galette for approximately 15 to 18 minutes in an air fryer, until the pastry has a golden brown color that is crisp.

- After it is done, remove the galette from your air fryer cautiously.
- You may garnish it with parsley.

Cooking Tips:

- The galette can be customized according to taste preference by using other cheeses or fresh herbs with different flavor combinations.
- Galette is best served warm as a great starter or main dish.

9.3.7 Tomato, Basil and Mozzarella Tart

So, let's cast off on a flavorsome journey of the palate with our air fryer version of Tomato, Basil and Mozzarella Tart. This luscious tomato basil tart with mozzarella has the beautiful flavors of ripe tomatoes, fresh basil and smooth creamy texture from the cheese all nestled in a homemade crust made effortless by an air fryer.

Ingredients for 1 Tart:

- 1 sheet of puff pastry (either store-bought or homemade).
- 1 ½ cup mozzarella cheese, shredded
- 2 cloves garlic, minced
- 2 tablespoons olive oil

Instructions:

- If you are using store-bought puff pastry dough, simply roll it out the way it says on the package. Roll the homemade puff pastry dough into a rectangle or round, using ¼ inch thick.
- Preheat the air fryer and set it to 375°F (190°C).
- Lay the rolled puff pastry in the air fryer basket, ensuring you line the bottom and sides.
- Place half of the shredded mozzarella cheese over the crust.
- Layer some fresh basil leaves over the cheese.
- Evenly distribute the tomato slices over the layer of basil.
- Spread the minced garlic evenly over the tomatoes.
- Salt and pepper to taste the tart.
- Drizzle the olive oil over the tomato and basil.

- Sprinkle the leftover shredded mozzarella over the tops of each tart.
- Place the tart in an air fryer basket.
- Then, air fry the Tomato, Basil and Mozzarella Tart at 180°C for roughly 15-18 minutes or until the pastry turns golden brown with a light bubble in cheese.
- When it is ready, carefully remove the tart from the air fryer.
- If desired, you may pour over the tart balsamic glaze just prior to serving.

Cooking Tips:

- In order to make the tart better, you can also sprinkle some grated Parmesan cheese onto it or just pour a little bit of the best olive oil.
- Serve the hot tart as either a delicious appetizer or an interesting entrée.

10 The 60-Day Meal Plan

10.1 Weekly Meal Planners

One of the critical measures to sustain a healthy, varied, and tasty menu is developing a weekly recipe plan. The trick here is that you only need to plan your meals in advance and get a balanced diet, including variety and convenience. In this chapter, I will guide you through the whole process of developing your meal plans for the week in a step-by-step manner in order to suit your special needs and dietary preferences.

Assessing Your Week:

Differentiate days that are busy and require quick meals from those that permit the luxury of cooking. This not only allows one to choose the appropriate recipes for each day but also helps in managing stress. On busy days, consider dishes that can be cooked ahead of time or require a short cooking time. If you have a day off, experiment with new recipes or methods of cooking. This equilibrium enables you to avoid being overwhelmed and savor cooking as well as eating. Remember that the goal is to synchronize your food time with your rhythm of life and make each meal a nourishment as well as enjoyment not another hedged activity.

Balancing Your Diet:

Healthy eating is the product of a good diet. Aim at having a variety of foods in your weekly meal plan. Use different types of proteins including vegetarian alternatives such as lentils and chickpeas in addition to animal products like chicken meat, fish, or beef. Also, do not forget to include other types of vegetables so as to acquire different minerals and vitamins. Also, one must take into account carbohydrates – whole grains as well – brown rice, quinoa or whole-wheat pasta. Include some meals while focusing on leafy greens for iron and fiber. The diversity does not only nourish the body, but also keeps tongues sharp.

Planning for Leftovers:

Leftover cooking is especially very practical since it saves time and money. Anticipate and cook a little more than the required amount of some meals so that you can have leftovers for lunch or supper the following day. Casseroles, stews and stir-fries are usually great the following day and can be easily warmed up. This also helps in reducing the loss of food. However, remember that your food safety leftovers should be kept and consumed while still fresh. This approach helps to cut down the amount of cooking that you need to do, especially those days when everything seems chaotic and offers convenience in meal planning.

Variety in Your Meals:

In order not to get bored with your meals it would be good to give different cuisines and dishes every week. Consider theme nights to make the dining more fun, such as 'Italian Night' or 'Taco Tuesday'. Therefore, do not be afraid to experiment with new recipes or modify old ones and discover them again. This trip not only adds thrill to your meal but also contributes to the creation of new culinary abilities and appreciation. Nevertheless, do not lie to yourself about cooking abilities and lack of time – find a golden mean between complex dishes and easy tested recipes.

Flexibility in Planning:

The future is unpredictable; it may turn out that plans change. A meal plan has to be flexible. Keep a few easy recipe or quality freezer options on hand for those surprise late nights or unexpected changes in schedule. These can be simple pasta dishes, fast stir-fries or even nutritious frozen meals. The secret is not to resort to unhealthier takeouts. Meal planning flexibility provides an opportunity to lead a liberated life without binding yourself on only one side of the healthy eating perspective.

Review and Adjust Your Plan:

Weekly, think about your diet plan at the end of every week. What did not occur as anticipated? Were there times when you wanted change or simplicity? Use these tips to make changes in your meal plan for the following week. This cycle of improvement ensures that your meal planning only gets better and more satisfying over time. It is also a great opportunity to celebrate success and gain lessons from the challenges.

10.2 Shopping Lists and Prep Guides

In this part we will cover the procedure of creating shopping lists and prep guides, which are very simple tools of efficient meal planning. It is a process that calls for good planning and a visionary eye to make sure you have everything in your hands for the weekly meals with minimal wastage. We will guide you on how to create a comprehensive shopping list and prepare ingredients in advance, which makes your cooking process more efficient. Let us now embark on the journey of ensuring that your weekly meal preparation is an enjoyable and stress free process.

Categorizing Your List:

To begin with, prioritize your shopping list in relation to the layout of a store that you usually shop. This makes it quicker and easier for shopping. Your main categories can include, but not limited to, produce, dairy, meat, pantry items and frozen foods. For each category, organize things according to your weekly meals. What is more, this strategy does not only help you make your shopping much faster but also saves you from the risk of missing some important ingredients. Additionally, it prevents undesirable unnecessary wandering throughout the store that eventually leads to impulse buying.

Inventory Check:

Before anything else, it is necessary to have a full inventory of what is in your pantry, refrigerator and freezer before going shopping. Be on the lookout for products such as oils, spices and grains. This is also a necessary step to ensure that you do not buy items which you already have, thereby minimizing wastage and saving your money. It also helps you to dispose of such ingredients that are on the verge of expiry. Have a list in your kitchen in which you write things as they get over. This addition to your plan will make the list of shopping more accurate and faster.

Seasonal Shopping:

Not only are these products fresher and more delicious, they also cost much less. This approach can also add a little change to your meals as various fruits and vegetables are harvested. Also, visit the farmers' markets which are nearby so that you can get the vegetables directly from them. With seasonal shopping, you can change around with the various ingredients and recipes; this way, your meal plan becomes enjoyable.

Bulk Buying Strategies:

For non-perishable goods or staples that you consume often, purchase in bulk. This can be more cost effective in the long term. But be careful to purchase only what you can actually use. Bulk purchasing is effective for such products as rice, pasta, canned goods and some spices. This approach also limits the number of shopping visits, thus saving time and energy.

Preparation Organization:

After you have gathered your ingredients, arrange them by the time of use. The perishables that you'll use during the early part of the week should be more accessible. Think about preparing vegetables, portioning meats and making any marinades or sauces ahead of time. This not only reduces the time required on a weekly basis, but it also increases your chances of adhering to your meal plan as much of the work is already completed.

Smart Storage:

It's important to store your ingredients properly to ensure their freshness. Find out how to store produce, meats, and pantry items most effectively. For instance, certain vegetables stay fresh longer in a cool, dark environment while others require the refrigerator. Clear containers for chopped and prepped ingredients make them easily recognizable while also helping to track their freshness. Correct storage preserves the freshness of your ingredients, which means less waste and better return on investment for your grocery purchases.

10.3 Balanced Meal Ideas

Every recommended recipe includes a proper proportion of protein, carbohydrates and healthy fats as well as different vegetables and fruits to ensure a balanced diet. The objective is to create meals that are filling, high in nutrients, and suitable for a variety of dietary habits, demonstrating the capability of the air fryer in preparing balanced meals.

Day 1 Meal Plan

Breakfast: Air Fryer Banana Oatmeal Muffins

These muffins blend the wholesomeness of oats and the natural sweetness of bananas, creating a high-fiber filled breakfast that is an excellent source of energy.

Lunch: Crispy Tofu and Veggie Stir Fry

This dish is a plant-based treat, providing the right amount of protein from tofu and a variety of nutrients from mixed veggies. The air fryer guarantees the tofu gets crispy without an overload of oil thus, making this a healthier alternative.

Dinner: Chicken Lemon Herbs with Roasted Potatoes

The lean protein from the chicken, seasoned with lemon and herbs, is complementary to the satisfying roasted potatoes that provide a healthy conclusion of the day's meals.

Snack: Cinnamon Apple Chips

A sweet, guilt-free snack. The air fryer crisps the apples perfectly, which are rich in fiber and antioxidants – with a flavor boost from cinnamon.

Day 2 Meal Plan

Breakfast: Spinach and Feta Omelet Air Fried.

A high-protein beginning with the benefit of spinach and the sour flavor of feta, containing important nutrients to initiate metabolism.

Lunch: Stuffed Peppers with Quinoa and Black Beans

By pairing the quinoa's complete protein with antioxidants-rich black beans stuffed into peppers that are rich in vitamin C, this lunch is both nutritious and filling.

Dinner: Salmon Air Fryer with Dill Yogurt Sauce and Asparagus

Omega-3 rich salmon with a light dill yogurt sauce and nutritional asparagus provides a healthy, tasty meal.

Snack: Zucchini Parmesan Crisps

A healthier option to the regular snacks, these crisps contain a nutritional value of zucchini with some savory flavor from Parmesan.

Day 3 Meal Plan

Breakfast: Berry Compote with Greek Yogurt

A healthy and antioxidant-filled beginning to the day, the berries pair well with the Greek yogurt rich in protein.

Lunch: Falafel in the Air Fryer with Tzatziki Sauce

A delightful vegetarian option, the falafel is a protein and fiber-packed dish made crispy in an air fryer and paired with cool tzatziki.

Dinner: Herbed Pork Tenderloin and Sweet Potato Fries

One of the lean protein choices, pork tenderloin is full of flavors and comes with guilt-free air-fried sweet potatoes.

Snack: Crunchy Chickpeas

It is a protein and fiber-packed snack, which is also crunchy in the air fryer.

Day 4 Meal Plan

Breakfast: Avocado Toast with Poached Eggs

A contemporary healthy breakfast choice, complemented with a combination of healthy fats from avocado and protein-rich poached eggs.

Lunch: Spicy Shrimp Tacos with Cabbage Slaw

A delicious and fulfilling meal for lunch, inclusive of high protein shrimp in a crunchy coleslaw.

Dinner: Balsamic Glazed Chicken Breasts with Steamed Broccoli

Chicken is a rich source of protein and when used as a dinner, it makes for healthier and tastier food than snacking on hamburgers or cold cuts; the broccoli only adds to its nutritional value.

Snack: Baked Apple with Cinnamon and Nuts

It is a satisfying and nourishing snack with apple sweetness, cinnamon spice, and nuts crunch.

Day 5 Meal Plan

Breakfast: Sweet Potato and Black Bean Breakfast Burritos

The burritos are a wholesome and healthy start, the fibrous nutrients of sweet potatoes mixing with protein filled black beans.

Lunch: Mediterranean Chickpea Salad

This salad has a plant protein, fiber, complemented by various vitamins and minerals.

Dinner: Glazed Salmon Teriyaki with Brown Rice and Broccoli

For instance, a tasty teriyaki-glazed salmon that is rich in omega-3s can be served with brown rice filled with fiber along with vitamin-rich broccoli to create a wholesome meal.

Snack: Air Fryer Kale Chips

Kale chips are low on calories but have high nutritional value as they contain vitamins A, C and K.

Day 6 Meal Plan

Breakfast: Blueberry Pancakes

Great for a breakfast, these pancakes are yummy and packed with some antioxidants.

Lunch: Grilled Chicken Caesar Salad

One of the traditional lunch offers that include lean protein obtained from chicken and a mix of greens to provide essential vitamins and fiber.

Dinner: Lemon Garlic Shrimp with Quinoa

A light, yet filling supper that has protein-packed shrimp and nutrient-rich quinoa with a hint of lemony garlic fragrance.

Snack: Stuffed Dates with Almond Butter

Dates are a healthy and delicious snack which is high in fiber and natural sugars, while almond butter gives a good portion of proteins and fats.

Day 7 Meal Plan

Breakfast: Chia Seed Pudding with Fresh Berries

Chia seeds are an excellent source of nutrients, containing omega-3 fatty acids, fiber and protein along with the vitamins and antioxidants found in fresh berries.

Lunch: Spiced Lentil Soup

The chia seeds are a great provider of nutrition as they contain omega-3, fiber and proteins just like the vitamins and antioxidants present in fresh berries.

Dinner: Beef and Vegetable Stir Fry

A healthy meal that includes beef, a source of protein, and vegetables providing vitamins, minerals and fiber.

Snack: Greek Yogurt with Honey and Nuts

A yogurt-based protein snack that contains natural sweetness from honey and healthy fats from nuts.

Nutritional Balance Summary – Week 1 (Days 1 to 7)

To ensure an appropriate balance of macronutrients (proteins, carbohydrates, and fats) as well as a variety of micronutrients (vitamins and minerals), the meal plans from Day 1 to Day 7 were constructed with precision. Each day features:

Protein sources: Ranged from plant-based (tocopherol, legumes) to animal-based (chicken, salmon), promoting enough and varied protein intake.

Healthy Carbohydrates: Options such as sweet potatoes, quinoa and whole grains provide long lasting energy and are high in fiber which helps digestion.

Healthy Fats: Some of the ingredients, such as avocado, nuts and seeds are rich in essential fatty acids which are vital for brain health and reduction of inflammation.

Fruits and Vegetables: Every day features different fruits and vegetables that provide a broad spectrum of vitamins, minerals, and antioxidants essential for good health.

Diversity in Cuisine: The menu plans provide a global variety, which not only makes the meals more exciting but also guarantees a diverse range of nutrients.

Portion Control: The dishes are prepared so that they remain filling and controlled, thus helping to keep one's weight in check.

Day 8 Meal Plan

Breakfast: Green Smoothie Bowl

This is a filling and nutritious breakfast, full of leafy greens, fruits and seeds.

Lunch: Air Fryer Veggie Burger

A hearty, healthy vegetarian choice that is high in protein and fiber while low in saturated fats.

Dinner: Garlic Butter Shrimp with Zucchini Noodles

The shrimp, a light yet protein-rich dish, is served with low-carb zucchini noodles and so forms a nutritious and substantial dinner.

Snack: Roasted Chickpeas

A protein-rich snack that is crunchy and can satisfy hunger when one needs to eat in between meals.

Day 9 Meal Plan

Breakfast: Avocado and Egg Toast

A balanced breakfast consisting of healthy fats from avocado and high-quality protein found in eggs on whole-grain toast.

Lunch: Quinoa Salad with Roasted Vegetables

Roasted Vegetables consist of a mixture of various roasted vegetables and it is full of fiber to help other nutrient movements in the body.

Dinner: Grilled Salmon with Asparagus

With serving asparagus which is filled with nutrients, this omega-3 salmon transforms into a beautiful and heart healthy meal.

Snack: Baked Pear with Cinnamon

When combined with cinnamon, a natural stimulant and digestive aid, pears are a sweet indulgence that is not only high in fiber and vitamins but also taste delicious.

Day 10 Meal Plan

Breakfast: Yogurt Parfait with Granola and Berries

Greek yogurt, granola and berries would therefore not only be a delicious but also a healthy breakfast.

Lunch: Tuna Salad Stuffed Avocado

A mixture of avocados which are high in protein and healthy vegetables compared to full nutrient value; this makes it a nourishing diet.

Dinner: Herb-Roasted Chicken with Sweet Potatoes

A well-rounded meal that provides proteins from the chicken and complex carbohydrates from sweet potatoes.

Snack: Air Fryer Apple Chips

Crispy apple chips with a hint of cinnamon for health-conscious chip lovers.

Day 11 Meal Plan

Breakfast: Oatmeal with Fresh Fruits and Nuts

A heart-friendly beginning with a fiber-rich oatmeal, topped with fresh fruits for vitamins and nuts for healthy fats and protein.

Lunch: Mediterranean Chickpea Wrap

A delicious lunch meal made of chickpeas, vegetables and Mediterranean spices that is rich in protein.

Dinner: Lemon Herb Tilapia with Quinoa

Light, protein-rich fish served with quinoa that is high in nutrients and flavored by lemon and herbs for a delicious evening meal.

Snack: Carrot Sticks with Hummus (8.11.4)

Carrots are a healthy, crunchy snack that is high in beta-carotene and fiber while the hummus provides protein and healthy fats.

Day 12 Meal Plan

Breakfast: Berry and Banana Smoothie

A healthy and delicious way to start your day, with berries and bananas combining antioxidants, vitamins, and natural sweetness.

Lunch: Air Fryer Cauliflower Tacos

A delicious and healthy alternative to tacos, using cauliflower as a nutritious fiber-rich filling, seasoned and cooked in the air fryer.

Dinner: Balsamic Glazed Chicken Breast with Roasted Vegetables

A balanced meal with lean protein provided by the chicken as well as a variety of nutrients from the roasted vegetables, all brought together beautifully in a delicious balsamic glaze.

Snack: Nut and Seed Trail Mix

A high-energy, nutrient-rich snack choice that uses various nuts and seeds to create a combination of healthy fats, protein, and fiber.

Day 13 Meal Plan

Breakfast: Spinach and Mushroom Omelet

A protein-based breakfast supplemented with vegetable additions such as spinach and mushrooms, containing vitamins, minerals, and antioxidants.

Lunch: Grilled Cheese and Tomato Soup

A delicious and filling meal, with the traditional combination of a hot tomato soup and a crunchy cheese sandwich made even more nutritious by using an air fryer.

Dinner: Lemon Pepper Cod with Brown Rice

A cod is a filling but light meal since it provides lean protein and is sprinkled with lemon pepper for taste and served with brown rice which is high in fiber.

Snack: Greek Yogurt with Honey and Nuts

A yogurt-based protein snack that contains natural sweetness from honey and healthy

fats from nuts.

Day 14 Meal Plan

Breakfast: Peanut Butter and Jelly Oatmeal

A nutritive breakfast that contains the fiber in oatmeal, proteins from peanut butter and the sweetness of jelly.

Lunch: Avocado Chicken Salad

It is a healthy and hearty lunch that is rich in lean protein from the chicken, fats availed by avocado as well as crunchy vegetables.

Dinner: Black Bean and Corn Stuffed Peppers

The vegetarian delight of these stuffed peppers filled with muscle-building black beans and corn is a smorgasbord of nutrients and flavors.

Snack: Air Fryer Zucchini Fries

These zucchini fries are low in calorie content as compared to ordinary fries, but they contain essential nutrients.

Nutritional Balance Summary – Week 2 (Days 8 to 14)

Diverse Protein Sources: The menu plans contain both plant-based protein sources (e.g., chickpeas and lentils) and animal-based proteins (such as chicken, fish, and eggs), providing a well rounded profile of essential amino acids.

Complex Carbohydrates: Consumption of whole grains such as brown rice and quinoa together with fiber vegetables and legumes maintain energy levels over a period of time while keeping the digestive system healthy.

Healthy Fats: The frequent consumption of ingredients rich in healthy fats, such as avocado, nuts, seeds and olive oil helps the absorption of nutrients and promotes brain health.

Fruits and Vegetables: Every day includes multiple different kinds of fruits and vegetables to provide a wide range of vitamins, minerals, and antioxidants that are essential for general health.

Global Flavors and Textures: The meal plans show variety in cuisines and flavors that the air fryer can produce.

Mindful Snacking: Snack selections are always healthy because they emphasize fruits, nuts and air-fried versions of the usual snacks that provide a healthier alternative without sacrificing taste.

Balanced Meals: The meals are meticulously created to ensure proper macronutrient (proteins, fats, carbohydrates) balance and provide a wide range of micronutrients which reflects an integrated healthy eating plan.

Day 15 Meal Plan

Breakfast: Cinnamon Apple Quinoa Bowl

In this case, a warm and nourishing beginning provided by the combination of quinoa protein and fiber with apple natural sweetness and vitamins as well as cinnamon for taste.

Lunch: Thai Inspired Peanut Chicken Wraps

A healthy lunch choice with chicken that has protein and a tasty peanut sauce, wrapped in a wholesome whole grain tortilla.

Dinner: Lemon-Dill Salmon with Asparagus

A healthy heart meal, consisting of salmon rich in omega-3s and nutrient-dense asparagus seasoned with lemon and dill for a fresh taste.

Snack: Mixed Berries and Honey Greek Yogurt

A creamy sweet treat that brings the protein of Greek yogurt, the antioxidants of berries and natural sweetness from honey.

Day 16 Meal Plan

Breakfast: Banana Nut Muffins

These muffins are a healthy and tasty breakfast that offers energy, fiber, and vital nutrients through whole grains and ripe bananas.

Lunch: Caprese Salad with Balsamic Reduction

A light yet filling dish with ripe tomatoes, fresh mozzarella, and basil topped with balsamic reduction for a taste explosion.

Dinner: Spicy Black Bean Burgers

These burgers are a plant-based dinner choice and contain protein and fiber with some spice for flavor.

Snack: Air Fryer Sweet Potato Chips

Sweet potatoes are a healthier alternative to snacking, rich in vitamins and fiber while air frying provides crunch without the added oil.

Day 17 Meal Plan

Breakfast: Veggie and Cheese Frittata

This frittata is one of the protein-rich and vegetable-full ways to start the day, which is not only delicious but also healthy.

Lunch: Grilled Chicken Caesar Wrap

A simple lunch option consisting of lean protein from the chicken along with a healthy Caesar salad in an easy-to-carry wrap.

Dinner: Air Fryer Shrimp Scampi with Zucchini Noodles

A light and flavorful dinner dish, with protein-rich shrimp and low-carb zucchini noodles cooked to perfection in the air fryer.

Snack: Fruit and Nut Energy Balls

These energy balls are a quick and healthy snack; they contain nuts, dried fruits, and seeds that supply energy and nutrients.

Day 18 Meal Plan

Breakfast: Berry Protein Smoothie

This smoothie is a convenient and healthy breakfast, which combines berries with protein powder and milk or yogurt for a filling morning drink.

Lunch: The Quinoa and Roasted Vegetable Bowl

A healthy and satisfying lunch option, consisting of nutritionally dense quinoa and roasted vegetables, containing a mix of protein, fiber, and vitamins.

Dinner: Apple Slaw with Herbed Pork Chops

A dinner that is savory and well-balanced; lean protein from the pork chops and a crunchy apple slaw for side.

Snack: Air Fryer Baked Apples

This baked apple snack is very warm, sweet and comforting, it is a healthier version of the traditional desserts made easy in the air fryer.

Day 19 Meal Plan

Breakfast: Avocado and Salmon Bagel

A balanced and filling beginning, combining the healthy fats of avocado with protein-rich smoked salmon on a whole grain bagel.

Lunch: The Roasted Veggie and Hummus Wrap

A healthy and fiber-filled lunch with roasted vegetables, hummus, and a whole grain wrap.

Dinner: Air Fryer Lemon Garlic Chicken Thighs with Quinoa Salad

It was a delicious and well-rounded meal, featuring chicken thighs that are high in protein as well as quinoa salad that is rich in nutrients.

Snack: Baked Banana Chips

These banana chips are a healthy, sweet alternative to regular crisps that can be prepared easily in the air fryer.

Day 20 Meal Plan

Breakfast: Greek Yogurt with Granola and Honey

A healthy breakfast, consisting of the protein of Greek yogurt, crunchy granola and natural sweetness of honey.

Lunch: Spicy Tuna Salad on Rye Bread

A fiery lunch that contains protein-rich tuna and lots of fiber in the bread.

Dinner: Air Fryer BBQ Ribs with Coleslaw

A hearty meal, including succulent ribs dripping with a tasty BBQ sauce and crisp coleslaw.

Snack: Air Fryer Popcorn

Popcorn made in the air fryer is a delicious and healthy alternative to the traditional way of cooking popcorn.

Day 21 Meal Plan

Breakfast: Spinach and Tomatoes Omelet

This omelet is a protein-rich breakfast that contains vitamins and minerals through the spinach and tomatoes.

Lunch: Quinoa and Black Bean Salad

This salad is the ideal blend of plant-based protein and fiber, which makes it both satisfying and healthy.

Dinner: Pork Tenderloin with Roasted Brussels Sprouts Air

Pork tenderloin is a great lean protein choice and when served with Brussels sprouts, the combination makes for a healthy dinner.

Snack: Cucumber and Carrot Sticks with Yogurt Dip

These vegetable sticks with a yogurt dip are tasty and healthy, and they make an excellent source of vegetables.

Nutritional Balance Summary – Week 3 (Days 15 to 21)

Protein Variety: This week includes a great variety of protein sources. Animal proteins such as chicken, salmon and pork tenderloin are combined with plant-based sources of amino acids including quinoa, black beans and chickpeas to ensure a high availability of essential amino acids.

Complex Carbohydrates and Fiber: Meals contain the complex carbs, quinoa, whole grain bread and brown rice; these provide slow-releasing energy that supports digestion. Fiber-rich vegetables and fruits also contribute to digestive health.

Healthy Fats: The meal plans include healthy fats such as avocados, nuts, and seeds, along with olive oil that are essential for brain health and reducing inflammation.

Fruits and Vegetables: Variety of fruits and vegetables prevent deficit in vitamins, minerals, and antioxidants. This type does not only increase the nutritional value of meals but also provides color and taste.

Global Cuisine and Flavors: The meals serve as examples of different cuisines and tastes, including spicy tuna salad, lemon garlic chicken, to show how the air fryer can produce various dishes that are also healthy.

Mindful Snacking: Weekly snack options are healthy and whole foods oriented. Options such as baked banana chips, cucumber and carrot sticks, and roasted almonds give necessary nutrients and sustain energy levels during intervals.

Balanced Meals: Each meal is carefully designed to ensure macronutrient harmony and a broad spectrum of micronutrients for optimal health.

Day 22 Meal Plan

Breakfast: Berry and Banana Oatmeal

A healthy heart begins with fiber-packed oats, balanced by the natural sweetness and vitamins of berries and bananas.

Lunch: Chicken and Avocado Salad

A balanced mixture of protein from chicken and healthy fats from avocado, thus nutritious and fulfilling.

Dinner: Air Fryer Shrimp Tacos with Mango Salsa,

A delicious combination of shrimp, which is a source of protein, and fresh mango salsa that gives both sweetness and savory in the light taco.

Snack: Roasted Almonds

A healthy snack with fats, protein and fiber.

Day 23 Meal Plan

Breakfast: Toasted Whole Grain Bread with Avocado and Eggs

A well-rounded morning meal that includes good fats from the avocado, protein in the egg, and fiber offered by whole grain bread.

Lunch: Falafel Bowl Air Fryer with Tzatziki Sauce

A healthy plant-based meal consisting of falafel, which is high in protein and served with a tzatziki sauce for a flavorful and enjoyable lunch.

Dinner: Garlic Butter Cod with Steamed Vegetables.

A balanced yet light dinner with lean protein in the form of cod, and a wide array of steamed vegetables for essential nutrients.

Snack: Fresh Fruit Salad

A healthy and vitamin-rich snack consisting of a wide range of fresh fruits to provide natural sweetness combined with nutrients.

Day 24 Meal Plan

Breakfast: Mixed Nuts and Honey Greek Yogurt

A combination of Greek yogurt, a source of protein and the crunch nuts with natural sweetness from honey is an ideal breakfast

Lunch: Turkey and Cheese Lettuce Wraps

A satisfying and nourishing lunch option of a turkey sandwich with cheese on lean, wrapped in crunchy iceberg lettuce.

Dinner: Spicy Air Fryer Chicken Wings with Celery Sticks

Served with refreshing celery sticks, these spicy chicken wings are a great dinner choice.

Snack: Baked Apple Slices with Cinnamon

A sweet snack, made of apples with a cinnamon touch.

Day 25 Meal Plan

Breakfast: Smoothie Bowl with Spinach, Banana and Berries

This smoothie bowl made from leafy greens and fruits is a nutrient-rich beginning to the day.

Lunch: Air Fryer Veggie Quesadilla

A delicious lunch, a combination of vegetables and cheese cooked to perfection in the air fryer.

Dinner: Lemon Herb Roasted Chicken and Quinoa

A nutritious and tasty dinner including chicken as a protein source, quinoa full of vitamins.

Snack: Carrot and Cucumber Sticks with Hummus

A healthy, crunchy snack ideal for dipping in protein-loaded hummus.

Day 25 Meal Plan

Breakfast: Smoothie Bowl with Spinach, Banana, and Berries

A lively and enriching beginning, full of vitamins from the spinach and berries, as well as natural power from the banana.

Lunch: Air Fryer Veggie Quesadilla

A good source of fiber and protein is a delicious union of vegetables and cheese wrapped in crispy tortilla.

Dinner: Lemon Herb Roasted Chicken with Quinoa

A nutritious and delicious chicken dish that provides the body with essential amino acids from chicken which is a protein source, fiber as well as nutrients such as iron.

Snack: Carrot and Cucumber Sticks with Hummus

A healthy, crunchy snack – great for an energy boost with a combination of vegetables and protein-rich hummus.

Day 26 Meal Plan

Breakfast: Almond Butter and Banana Toast

A delightful and filling breakfast option is to spread almond butter rich in healthy fats on whole-grain bread with the natural sweetness of banana.

Lunch: Mediterranean Chickpea Salad

A filling and protein-rich lunch that includes chickpeas, fresh vegetables and a tasty dressing.

Dinner: Air Fryer Salmon with Roasted Brussels Sprouts

Heart-healthy dinner with omega-3 rich salmon and sprout of nutrients.

Snack: Mixed Berries Greek Yogurt

A creamy and antioxidant-filled snack that combines the protein in Greek yogurt with the vitamin content of mixed berries.

Day 27 Meal Plan

Breakfast: The Oatmeal with Chopped Nuts and Dried Fruit

A good start to the day in a very healthy way, full of fiber from oats, fat from nuts and sweetness straight from nature comes the dried fruit.

Lunch: Grilled Chicken and Avocado Wrap

A chicken and avocado sandwich, made with whole grain tortilla.

Dinner: Tilapia with Garlic Roasted Potatoes made in an Air Fryer

Light and delicious dinner with garlic roasted potatoes rich in fiber and tilapia fish high in protein.

Snack: Air Fryer Kale Chips

Kale chips are a nutritious and crispy snack that is low in calories but high in vitamins A, C, and K.

Day 28 Meal Plan

Breakfast: Berry and Yogurt Parfait

Yogurt worked as probiotics and fresh berries added antioxidants, all together turned into a pleasing breakfast that looked perfect in layers.

Lunch: Turkey and Spinach Salad with Balsamic Vinaigrette.

A light and nutritious lunch containing turkey breast, spinach which is a good source of iron and balsamic dressing.

Dinner: Air Fryer BBQ Chicken with Corn on the Cob

A cozy and delicious dinner, with protein-rich chicken and a side of succulent corn which is rich in fiber.

Snack: Roasted Pumpkin Seeds

Pumpkin seeds are a healthy and delightful snack; they contain magnesium, zinc, and good fats.

Nutritional Balance Summary – Week 4 (Days 25 to 28)

Varied Protein Sources: This period is characterized by both animal and plant proteins, providing a wide range of essential amino acids for overall well being.

Complex Carbohydrates and Fiber: Whole grains, legumes and vegetables rich in fiber ensure continuous energy levels along with proper functioning of the digestive system.

Healthy Fats: Meals and snacks contain monounsaturated and polyunsaturated fats from nuts, seeds, and avocados that improve heart health and satiety.

Fruits and Vegetables Diversity: A variety of fruits and vegetables offer vitamins, minerals, and antioxidants necessary for a strong immune system as well as overall health.

Balanced Snacking: The snack options remain health-oriented, incorporating the air fryer for healthier versions of classic snacks and highlighting whole, nutrient-rich foods.

Culinary Variety: The meal plans feature various types of cuisines and cooking styles to illustrate the versatility of the air fryer and make healthy eating fun.

Day 29 Meal Plan

Breakfast: Spinach and Feta Scrambled Eggs

A protein-rich breakfast that pairs the benefits of eggs with iron spinach and feta cheese.

Lunch: Stuffed Bell Peppers with Air Fryer

A satisfying and healthy lunch option, bell peppers stuffed with a combination of protein and vegetables cooked just right in the air fryer.

Dinner: Baked Cod with Lemon Butter Sauce and Steamed Asparagus

A light and healthy dinner, consisting of a cod fish with lean meat and an asparagus side dish enhanced by a lemon butter sauce.

Snack: Homemade Nuts and Dried Fruit Trail Mix

A blend of healthy fats, protein, and natural sugars from nuts and dried fruit to make a customizable snack that will provide an energy boost.

Day 30 Meal Plan

Breakfast: Mixed Berry Yogurt Smoothie

A vitamin-rich and refreshing beginning to the day, blending mixed berries with yogurt for a creamy and healthy smoothie.

Lunch: Quinoa Salad with Roasted Vegetables

A nutritious and filling lunch with quinoa, which is rich in nutrients, combined with roasted vegetables that provide a balance of protein, fiber, and vitamins.

Dinner: Pork Chops Air Fryer with AppleSauce

A delicious and filling dinner, consisting of tender pork chops accompanied by the homemade apple sauce that provides protein and natural sweetness.

Snack: Carrot and Cucumber Sticks with Guacamole

A crispy and nourishing snack, ideal for dipping into healthy guacamole.

Day 31 Meal Plan

Breakfast: The Oatmeal with Fresh Berries and Almond Butter

A filling and heart-healthy breakfast, a combination of the fiber in oatmeal with the antioxidants from fresh berries and the healthy fats of almond butter.

Lunch: Chicken Caesar Salad

A timeless and protein-packed lunch choice, with grilled chicken, crisp romaine lettuce, and a light Caesar dressing.

Dinner: Air Fryer Teriyaki Salmon and Brown Rice

A teriyaki-glazed dinner with omega-3-rich salmon and fiber-filled brown rice.

Snack: Greek Yogurt and Honey with Walnuts

A high-protein snack that includes the richness of Greek yogurt, the natural sweetness of honey and the crunchiness of walnuts.

Day 32 Meal Plan

Breakfast: Avocado Toast with Cherry Tomatoes

A delicious and nutritious breakfast, with healthy fats from avocado and the freshness of cherry tomatoes on whole grain toast.

Lunch: Mediterranean Tuna Wrap

A light, healthy lunch with tuna full of protein, fresh vegetables and Mediterranean spices in a whole wheat tortilla.

Dinner: Air Fryer Lemon Pepper Chicken and Green Beans

A simple yet tasty dinner using chicken as the lean protein with a side of green beans, adding lemon pepper for added zest.

Snack: Air Fryer Plantain Chips

These air fryer plantain chips are a healthier option to the usual chips and provide a unique taste while also offering vitamins and fiber.

Day 33 Meal Plan

Breakfast: Pancakes with Maple Syrup Protein

As a delicious and energy-giving breakfast, these protein pancakes are great for starting the day with natural maple syrup.

Lunch: Shrimp and Avocado Grilled Salad

A light and nutritious lunch that includes grilled shrimp with creamy avocado over a bed of mixed greens.

Dinner: Air Fryer Beef and Broccoli Stir-Fry

A typical stir-fry, which provides good protein by using the beef and healthy nutrients from broccoli cooked efficiently in the air fryer.

Snack: Pear Baked with Cinnamon and Nutmeg

Baked with cinnamon and nutmeg, the baked pear is a cozy treat that is also healthful.

Day 34 Meal Plan

Breakfast: Mango Chia Seed Pudding

Chia seeds are a healthy base as they contain omega-3 fatty acids and fiber, while mango adds a tropical sweetness that is rich in vitamins.

Lunch: Air Fryer Falafel with Greek Salad

A protein-rich and nutritious lunch, with falafel as the main course and a Greek salad on the side.

Dinner: Air Fryer Glazed Ham with Roasted Sweet Potatoes

A delicious and flavourful meal, comprising lean ham glazed in the air fryer with nutritious sweet potatoes.

Snack: Celery Sticks with Almond Butter

A tasty, healthy snack made from the freshness of celery and the protein and healthy fats of almond butter.

Day 35 Meal Plan

Breakfast: Blueberry Oatmeal with Flax Seeds

The oats are a good source of fiber and the blueberries provide antioxidants along with omega-3s from flaxseeds.

Lunch: Air Fryer Chicken Tenders with Honey Mustard Dip

These chicken tenders are served as an appetizing and protein-rich lunch, with a healthier version in the air fryer, accompanied by honey mustard dip.

Dinner: Grilled Salmon Quinoa and Steamed Broccoli

A healthy and balanced meal, consisting of salmon rich in omega-3, quinoa filled with fiber, and broccoli packed with vitamins.

Snack: Baked Cinnamon Apple Slices

These apple slices are a simple and sweet snack that is baked with cinnamon, making it a nutritious and tasty option.

Nutritional Balance Summary – Week 5 (Days 29 to 35)

Protein Diversity: The meals for this week feature a variety of protein sources, ranging from plant-based options like falafel and quinoa to animal proteins including salmon and chicken, providing all the necessary amino acids.

Healthy Carbohydrates: Complex carbohydrates such as sweet potatoes, quinoa, and oats are included in the diet which provides sustained energy and helps to maintain digestive health.

Essential Fatty Acids: Brain health and inflammation reduction with the help of chia seeds, flaxseeds, and salmon as foods rich in omega-3s and healthy fats are featured.

Fruits and Vegetables: The varied nature of the fruits and vegetables guarantees a substantial supply of vital vitamins, minerals as well as antioxidants that support both overall health and immune function.

Flavorful and Varied Cuisine: The meal plans represent a variety of flavors and cooking methods, indicating the air fryer's potential to produce pleasurable and nutritional meals.

Nutrient-Dense Snacks: Snack options are mainly nutrient-dense foods such as fruits, nuts and vegetables that provide energy and essential nutrients between meals.

Balanced Meals: Every meal is carefully crafted to have a balance of macronutrients and includes various micronutrients, promoting an integrative approach to nutrition.

Day 36 Meal Plan

Breakfast: Protein-Rich Greek Yogurt with Mixed Nuts

A healthy and easy to make beginning, combining the high protein Greek yogurt with a range of nuts for good fats and texture.

Lunch: Air Fryer Veggie Burger with Whole Grain Rolls

An enjoyable plant-based lunch with a nutritious veggie burger on top of a fiber rich whole grain bun.

Dinner: Chicken Breast with Balsamic Glaze and Steamed Vegetables.

A nutritionally balanced and delicious meal, consisting of lean chicken breast accompanied by a selection of healthy steamed vegetables that have been jazzed up with a balsamic glaze.

Snack: Fresh Fruit Skewers

These skewers are a fun and fresh snack with different fruits that provide natural sweetness and vitamins.

Day 37 Meal Plan

Breakfast: Oatmeal with Peanut Butter and Banana

A nutritious and filling breakfast, combining the fibre in oatmeal with peanut butter, for protein and healthy fat content, topped with banana slices for natural sweetness.

Lunch: Quinoa Stuffed Peppers

A healthy lunch choice, comprising stuffed bell peppers filled with high-protein quinoa and a combination of vegetables.

Dinner: Air-fried Lemon Herb Fish filets with Quinoa Salad

A light, healthy meal consisting of omega-3 rich fish fillet and quinoa salad garnished with lemon and herbs.

Snack: Roasted Chickpeas

These roasted chickpeas are a perfect snack, high in protein and crunchy.

Day 38 Meal Plan

Breakfast: Berry Smoothie containing Spinach and Protein Powder

A healthy smoothie for the day's beginning, combining antioxidant-rich berries with spinach and protein powder to create a balanced drink.

Lunch: Air Fried Chicken Caesar Salad Wrap

An easy eating, protein-based lunch with a classic Caesar salad and chicken.

Dinner: Pork Loin with Roasted Root Vegetables

A substantial and satisfying meal consisting of air-fried lean pork loin and a selection of nutrient-dense root vegetables.

Snack: Greek Yogurt Honey and Berries

A creamy and sweet snack that combines the protein of Greek yogurt, the natural sweetness of honey with antioxidant properties of berries.

Day 39 Meal Plan

Breakfast: Avocado and Egg Breakfast Sandwich

A hearty breakfast, consisting of a fat-rich avocado and an egg which is full of proteins in the whole grain sandwich.

Lunch: Mixed Green Tuna Salad

A healthy and protein-rich lunch, tuna salad being served with a bed of mixed greens, providing an ideal balance of nutrients.

Dinner: Air Fryer Beef Steak and Asparagus

A delicious dinner full of protein from the beef steak and nutrients in asparagus made simple with an air fryer.

Snack: Baked Cinnamon Apples

These cinnamon apples are a tasty treat that is healthy compared to other desserts, but they provide natural sweetness with a little kick of spice.

Day 40 Meal Plan

Breakfast: Almond Milk and Berry Smoothie,

A healthy and tasty breakfast, combining almond milk with a range of berries for a vitamin-rich smoothie.

Lunch: Spicy Black Bean Soup

This soup is a hearty and warming lunch, which contains plant-based protein and fiber from black beans with a spicy kick for more flavor.

Dinner: Air Fried Garlic Shrimp with Zucchini Noodles

A light and healthy dinner, with protein-rich shrimp accompanied by zucchini noodles that are low in carbs, seasoned with garlic and cooked in the air fryer.

Snack: Mixed nuts and dried fruit

This combination of nuts and dried fruits is a great snack that provides energy, as it contains healthy fats, proteins and natural sugars.

Day 41 Meal Plan

Breakfast: Greek Yogurt Granola and Fruit

A healthy and satisfying breakfast, blending the protein of greek yogurt with granola for texture and a selection of fresh fruits for natural sweetness.

Lunch: Air Fryer Veggie and Hummus Pita Pocket

This is a delectable and fiber-enriched lunch consisting of air-fried veggies with creamy hummus in a whole grain pita pocket.

Dinner: Lemon Pepper Tilapia with Steamed Broccoli

A simple but healthy dinner, with omega 3-rich tilapia and vitamin-containing steamed broccoli seasoned with lemon pepper for a tangy taste.

Snack: Carrot Sticks with Almond Butter.

Carrots are a healthy and crispy snack that contains important nutrients and fiber, while almond butter has protein and beneficial fats.

Day 42 Meal Plan

Breakfast: Spinach and Mushroom Omelette

Packed with protein and vegetables, this omelet is filled with healthy spinach and mushrooms.

Lunch: Quinoa Tabbouleh Salad

A healthy and nutritional lunch consisting of quinoa, herbs, and vegetables in a light lemon dressing.

Dinner: Air Fryer BBQ Chicken Drumsticks with Corn Salad

An enjoyable dinner, consisting of succulent chicken drumsticks and a vibrant corn salad both prepared in an air fryer.

Snack: Baked Peach Slices

These peach slices are baked to accentuate their sweetness as a healthy snack, which is delicious.

Nutritional Balance Summary – Week 6 (Days 36 to 42)

Diverse Protein Sources: The ratio of amino acids, which were obtained from plant and animal protein sources, is balanced in the meal plans.

Complex Carbohydrates and Fiber: The foods include whole grains, beans and vegetables high in fiber which ensures a sustained release of energy and aids digestion. Fruits and vegetables with high fiber content also promote the digestive system.

Healthy Fats: Inclusion of healthy fats rich sources like nuts, seeds and avocados enhances absorption of nutrients and proper functioning of the brain.

Fruits and Vegetables: The consumption of a broad range of fruits and vegetables delivers the required vitamins, minerals, and antioxidants that are vital for healthy living.

Flavor and Culinary Variety: The versatility of the air fryer is demonstrated by the meal plans, which include Mediterranean salads and Asian stir-fries; these are healthy recipes of many cuisines and flavors.

Mindful Snacking: Some of the healthy snack options that are available for customers throughout the week include whole foods such as fruits and nuts along with air-fried versions of regular snacks; in this manner, they are able to create healthier alternatives that do not compromise on taste.

Balanced Meals: All the meals are carefully designed to achieve a perfect balance in macronutrients and a wide-ranging selection of micronutrients, which reinforces the general healthy eating strategy.

Day 43 Meal Plan

Breakfast: Toasted Whole Grain Bread with Avocado-Tomato

A delicious and healthy breakfast with the combination of avocado's healthy fats and tomato freshness on fiber-rich whole grain bread.

Lunch: Air Fryer Turkey and Cheese Sandwich

A healthy air fryer version of a classic lunch, with lean turkey and cheese to provide balanced protein and calcium.

Dinner: Baked Salmon with Lemon and Dill, Accompanied by Quinoa

A hearty dinner, made with fatty omega-3 salmon and a side of protein quinoa with lemon dill for a light and refreshing taste.

Snack: Greek yogurt with almonds and honey

A protein-based snack, which combines the creamy texture of Greek yogurt with almonds and honey.

Day 44 Meal Plan

Breakfast: Blueberry Banana Protein Shake

A speedy and revitalizing breakfast alternative, blending blueberries, banana and protein powder for a healthy start of the day.

Lunch: Grilled Vegetable Salad with Feta

A light but filling lunch, comprising different grilled vegetables and feta cheese that gives a good combination of vitamins, minerals, and protein.

Dinner: Air Fryer Lemon Garlic Chicken Thighs with Steamed Green Beans

A flavorful and well-balanced dinner, featuring protein-rich chicken thighs with a side of nutrient-dense green beans seasoned with lemon and garlic.

Snack: Apples with Peanut Butter

A delicious and nutritious snack that combines the natural sweetness of apples with protein and healthy fats from peanut butter.

Day 45 Meal Plan

Breakfast: Spinach and Goat Cheese Frittata

This frittata is a protein-rich and vegetable-heavy dish to start your day on the right note.

Lunch: Chickpea and Avocado Salad

A nutritious and filling plant-based lunch, combining protein and fiber from chickpeas with creamy avocado.

Dinner: Air Fryer Pork Tenderloin with Roasted Sweet Potatoes

The pork tenderloin is a lean protein option that complements the nutritious sweet potatoes for a balanced and filling meal.

Snack: Baked Sweet Potato Fries

These are sweet potato fries, which is a healthier alternative to conventional fries because they contain vitamins and fiber.

Day 46 Meal Plan

Breakfast: Cottage Cheese and Fresh Pineapple

A delicious and protein-based breakfast, combining cottage cheese with the natural sweetness and vitamins of fresh pineapple.

Lunch: Tuna salad on whole wheat bread

A typical and protein-based lunch meal consisting of tuna salad on whole wheat bread to provide an appropriate balance of nutrients.

Dinner: Beef Stir-Fry with Mixed Vegetables using Air Fryer

A delicious and healthy dinner, full of proteins from beef and an array of vegetables, all cooked fast and lightly in the air fryer.

Snack: Homemade Granola Bars

These granola bars are a healthy and energizing snack that contains oats, nuts, and dried fruit.

Day 47 Meal Plan

Breakfast: Scrambled Eggs With Sautéed Spinach and Mushrooms

A protein-based breakfast that includes the goodness of spinach and mushrooms, which makes it a healthy and satisfying meal for the day.

Lunch: Air fried chicken caesar pita pocket

A good lunch option that is easy to eat in a pita pocket of chicken and caesar salad.

Dinner: Grilled shrimp skewers with quinoa salad.

A light and proteinous dinner, composed of grilled shrimp skewers with a quinoa salad for an optimal balance between essential nutrients.

Snack: Roasted Pumpkin Seeds

Pumpkin seeds are an excellent source of magnesium, zinc and healthy fats for a healthy snack.

Day 48 Meal Plan

Breakfast: Chia and Berry Yogurt Parfait

A tasty and healthy breakfast, layering chia seeds with Greek yogurt and fresh berries, providing a mix of omega-3 fatty acids, protein and antioxidants.

Lunch: Air Fryer Vegetable Quesadilla

A delicious and fulfilling lunch, consisting of a wholegrain tortilla stuffed with an assortment of vegetables and cheese, cooked to perfection in the air fryer.

Dinner: Baked Salmon with Avocado Salsa and Quinoa

A nutritional dinner with omega-3 containing salmon topped by a fresh avocado salsa and accompanied by protein rich quinoa.

Snack: Fresh carrot and celery sticks with hummus.

It is a healthy and crunchy snack that can be dipped in hummus protein-rich, which provides essential nutrients and fiber.

Day 49 Meal Plan

Breakfast: Oatmeal, Sliced Almonds and Honey

A healthy way to start the morning, a combination of oatmeal with the texture of almonds and the sweetness of honey.

Lunch: Tuna Salad with Mixed Greens

A balanced, protein-rich lunch with tuna salad on a bed of mixed greens for vitamins and minerals.

Dinner: Air Fryer Chicken Parmesan with Steamed Broccoli

A flavorful and balanced dinner featuring a healthy chicken breast coated in crispy Parmesan crust served with broccoli that is highly nutritious.

Snack: Baked Apple Chips

A healthy but simple snack, these apple chips are a perfect substitute for crisps that provide natural sugars and fiber.

Nutritional Balance Summary – Week 7 (Days 43 to 49)

Varied Protein Sources: This week still provides an assortment of protein sources, both animal-based (chicken , salmon, tuna) and plant-based (beans, nuts, seeds), resulting in a full range of nutrients.

Complex Carbohydrates and Fiber: Whole grains, legumes, and vegetables and fruits rich in fiber promote energy levels that last a long time as well as the health of the digestive system.

Healthy Fats: Meals provide monounsaturated and polyunsaturated fats as well as avocado, nuts and seeds for heart health and satiety.

Fruits and Vegetables: A variety of fruits and vegetables offer an array of vitamins, minerals, and antioxidants that lead to a strong immune system as well as the overall healthiness.

Culinary Diversity: The air fryer is a versatile appliance that can produce different cuisines and flavors, as shown in the meal plans above.

Mindful Snacking: The snack offerings remain health oriented, using the air fryer to prepare healthier versions of traditional snacks and focusing on whole nutrient-dense foods.

Balanced Meals: Each meal is carefully constructed to balance macronutrients and offer a variety of micronutrients, promoting a comprehensive view on nutrition.

Day 50 Meal Plan

Breakfast: Protein-Packed Smoothie Bowl

This smoothie bowl provides an enriching and stimulating breakfast that combines protein powder with different fruits and nuts to create a nutritional dish.

Lunch: Air Fryer Caprese Sandwich

A beautiful lunch with fresh mozzarella, tomato and basil in a whole grain sandwich that is toasted crispy in the air fryer.

Dinner: Lemon-Garlic Shrimp with Asparagus and Quinoa

A light, healthy dinner that includes protein-rich shrimp and asparagus with vitamin-dense quinoa seasoned with lemon and garlic.

Snack: Sliced Cucumbers and Carrots with Greek Yogurt Dip

A healthy and delicious snack, mixing crunchy veggies with the protein-loaded Greek yogurt dip.

Day 51 Meal Plan

Breakfast: Avocado and Egg Toast

A filling and healthy breakfast, with a creamy avocado and an egg full of protein on whole grain bread.

Lunch: Quinoa Salad with Roasted Vegetables

A nutritious and filling lunch of protein-rich quinoa with a variety of roasted vegetables, providing a good balance between fiber and nutrients.

Dinner: In Air Fryer Teriyaki Chicken with Steamed Broccoli

A delicious and well-balanced meal with tender chicken cooked in a mouthwatering teriyaki sauce accompanied by steamed broccoli rich in vitamins.

Snack: Fresh Fruit Salad

A quick and vitamin packed snack, which combines a wide array of fresh fruits for a sweet but nutritious treat.

Day 52 Meal Plan

Breakfast: Greek Yogurt with Honey and Mixed Berries

A creamy and antioxidant breakfast, where Greek yogurt meets the natural sweetness of honey and a variety of berries.

Lunch: Air Fryer Fish Taco with Mango Salsa

A light and zesty lunch choice, which includes the preparation of fish tacos with a mango salsa full of freshness and fruitiness cooked in an air fryer.

Dinner: Balsamic Glazed Beef Skewers with Quinoa Salad

A tasty and healthy dinner, with balsamic glazed beef skewers accompanied by a side of quinoa salad rich in protein.

Snack: Roasted Almonds and Dried Cranberries

A delicious and healthy snack, with the good fats of almonds that are combined with the natural sweetness of dried cranberries.

Day 53 Meal Plan

Breakfast: Oatmeal with Almond Butter and Banana

An enriching and satisfying breakfast, where the fiber of oatmeal is complemented by the healthy fats from almond butter and natural sweetness of banana.

Lunch: Grilled Chicken Salad With Avocado Dressing

A light and healthy lunch, consisting of grilled chicken on a bed of greens with an avocado dressing.

Dinner: Air Fryer Pork Chops with Roasted Sweet Potatoes

A filling dinner of lean pork chops and vitamin-rich sweet potatoes, both made quickly in the air fryer.

Snack: Greek Yogurt Granola and Fresh Fruit

A high-protein snack, with a combination of Greek yogurt, granola and several fresh fruits.

Day 54 Meal Plan

Breakfast: Berry Parfait with Chia Seeds and Yogurt

A colorful and tasty breakfast that provides the probiotics of yogurt, as well as antioxidants from berries, along with omega-3s found in chia seeds.

Lunch: Air Fryer Veggie Wrap with Hummus

A delicious and fiber-filled lunch, comprising a multitude of vegetables with creamy hummus wrapped in a whole grain tortilla.

Dinner: Lemon Herb Chicken and Roasted Vegetables

A nutritious and tasty dinner comprising herbed chicken and a combination of roasted vegetables, providing adequate protein, vitamins and minerals.

Snack: Sliced Apples and Peanut Butter (8.54.47)

The classic healthy snack that provides the sweetness of apples combined with peanut butter protein and healthy fats.

Day 55 Meal Plan

Breakfast: Spinach and Mushroom Egg Muffins

These egg muffins are an easy and healthy breakfast that is rich in protein and vegetables. It is a quick option for the morning meal.

Lunch: Air Fryer Turkey Burger with Sweet Potato Fries

A healthier version of a classic with protein and fiber from the lean turkey burger as well as air-fried sweet potato fries.

Dinner: The grilled shrimp and vegetable skewers

These skewers make an excellent light and flavourful dinner, as they feature protein-rich shrimp with a variety of grilled vegetables.

Snack: Cottage Cheese with Pineapple Chunks

As a snack that is rich in protein, cottage cheese complements the sweetness of pineapple to provide a healthy and satisfying treat.

Day 56 Meal Plan

Breakfast: Banana and Blueberry Oatmeal

A healthy and satisfying morning meal that unites the fiber of oatmeal with natural sweetness from bananas, antioxidants in blueberries.

Lunch: Quinoa and Black Bean Salad

A healthy and satisfying lunch that included protein-packed quinoa, fiber-filled black beans, and vegetables with a variety of vitamins and minerals.

Dinner: Air Fryer Salmon with Asparagus and Lemon Butter

A healthy dinner choice, salmon with omega-3 and asparagus full of nutrients enriched by a light lemon butter sauce.

Snack: Homemade Granola with Yogurt

A delicious and healthy snack, consisting of homemade granola mixed with yogurt rich in proteins for a filling and nutritious bite.

Nutritional Balance Summary – Week 8 (Days 50 to 56)

Diverse Protein Sources: The week combines animal and plant proteins, so it includes a wide range of necessary amino acids.

Complex Carbohydrates and Fiber: The main staple is wholegrain which includes quinoa and oats, coupled with high fiber fruits and vegetables that provide a constant source of energy while ensuring the digestion process is carried out effectively.

Healthy Fats: Consuming good fats including avocados, nuts and fish contributes to cardiovascular health among other general benefits.

Rich in Fruits and Vegetables: A wide selection of fresh fruits and vegetables offers enough essential vitamins, minerals, and antioxidants.

Balanced Snacking: The range of snacks is healthy in nature, focusing on a mix of proteins, good fats and carbohydrates to provide an even energy boost.

Culinary Diversity: The meal plans provide different flavors and cooking styles, which serve to demonstrate the multi-functionality of the air fryer in delivering delicious and healthy meals.

Well-Rounded Meals: All meals are artfully crafted acing ratios of macronutrients and an impressive array of micronutrients.

Day 57 Meal Plan

Breakfast: Mixed Berry Compote and Greek Yogurt

A great way to start the morning, combining antioxidant-rich berries and protein-packed Greek yogurt for a healthy breakfast.

Lunch: Air Fryer Chicken and Vegetable Stir-Fry

A fast and healthy lunch menu that includes tasty tender chicken served with different vegetables, which are all prepared to perfection in the air fryer.

Dinner: Lemon-Herb Baked Cod with Steamed Green Beans

Light and healthy dinner with cod rich in omega-3 along with nutrient dense green beans flavored with lemon and herbs for a refreshing taste.

Snack: Apple Slices and Almond Butter

A quick and easy snack in which apple's natural sweetness is complemented by almond butter, a source of protein and healthy fats.

Day 58 Meal Plan

Breakfast: Scrambled Eggs with Spinach and Feta

A protein-based and vegetables laden breakfast providing a healthy and tasty morning meal.

Lunch: Roasted Chickpea Quinoa Salad

A satisfying and healthy lunch, with protein-heavy quinoa and fiber filled roasted chickpeas as well as a combination of vegetables.

Dinner: Air Fryer Pork Tenderloin and Roasted Brussels Sprouts

This is a satisfying dinner offering, composed of pork tenderloin and nutrient-rich Brussels sprouts prepared with ease in the air fryer.

Snack: Greek Yogurt and Fresh Berries.

A healthy and protein-packed snack, that combines Greek yogurt with an array of fresh antioxidant berries.

Day 59 Meal Plan

Breakfast: Toast with Banana and Nut Butter

A healthy and satisfying breakfast, including whole grain toast with nut butter and slices of banana for natural energy.

Lunch: Air Fryer Veggie Pizza

This is a healthier version of the usual favorite, which is made in an air fryer to get a crispy crust and with various vegetables on top.

Dinner: Grilled Shrimp over Quinoa and Asparagus

A healthy and protein-rich dinner with grilled shrimp accompanied by quinoa dishes and asparagus for a balanced meal.

Snack: Baked Sweet Potato Chips

Sweet potato chips provide a healthy alternative to regular chips, which are baked to crispy perfection for an enjoyable and nutritious snack.

Day 60 Meal Plan

Breakfast: Tomatoes, Peppers and Onions Omelette

This omelette is a protein-rich and colorful breakfast filled with different vegetables to add flavor and nutritional value.

Lunch: Tuna Salad and Mixed Greens

A light and protein-packed lunch, with tuna salad on a bed of mixed greens for a range of vitamins and minerals.

Dinner: Air Fryer Beef Steak with Roasted Root Vegetables

A delicious and filling dinner with a seasoned beef steak served alongside root vegetables that are rich in nutrients.

Snack: Carrot Sticks with Hummus

A healthy and crunchy snack, great for dipping in protein-laden hummus to provide a nutritious and satisfying treat.

Day 61 Meal Plan

Breakfast: Greek Yogurt and Honey with Granola

A simple yet protein-rich breakfast, with the crunch of granola and natural sweetness of honey.

Lunch: Air Fryer Turkey Wrap Avocado and Tomato

An appealing and filling lunch choice of a lean turkey, creamy avocado, and fresh tomato in a whole grain wrap.

Dinner: Lemon-Dill Salmon with Steamed Broccoli

A healthy and delicious dinner, which included omega-3 rich salmon with vitamin enriched broccoli flavored with lemon and dill for a light and refreshing meal.

Snack: Mixed Nuts and Dried Fruits

This mixture is a nutritionally balanced snack that can provide an energy boost, as it contains several different types of nuts and dried fruits with healthy fats, proteins, and natural sugars.

Day 62 Meal Plan

Breakfast: Banana Nut Porridge

A tasty and satisfying breakfast, which mixes the natural sweetness of banana with the nutritious porridge enriched with nuts.

Lunch: Quinoa and Roasted Vegetable Bowl

A fiber-filled and nutrient-loaded lunch with roasted vegetables and protein-rich quinoa.

Dinner: Air Fryer Garlic-Parmesan Chicken Wings.

These chicken wings are flavored with garlic and Parmesan, making them a delicious and satisfying dinner that is reminiscent of the original but with a twist.

Snack: Cucumber and Hummus

Cucumber slices are a light and crisp snack, providing hydration and crunch which is then balanced by the protein-rich hummus.

Day 63 Meal Plan

Breakfast: Scrambled Eggs with Spinach and Whole Grain Toast.

This breakfast is protein-rich and vegetable-laden, as the nutritional qualities of eggs and spinach are complemented by whole grain toast.

Lunch: Air Fryer Vegetable and Cheese Quesadilla.

A delicious and filling lunch consisting of assorted vegetables combined with melted cheese in a crispy quesadilla, was prepared quickly using an air fryer.

Dinner: Baked cod with lemon butter and asparagus.

A healthy and low-calorie dinner with omega-3 rich cod and asparagus served with a delicate lemon butter sauce.

Snack: Fresh Berry Salad

A sweet and antioxidants-rich snack, using a mixture of fresh berries for healthy and tasty snacks.

Nutritional Balance Summary – Week 9 (Days 57 to 63)

Diverse Protein Sources: The nutritional value of proteins is also enhanced by combining animal and vegetable sources in the meals for this week to ensure maximum consumption of critical amino acids.

Complex Carbohydrates and Fiber: The introduction of whole grains such as quinoa, along with fruit and vegetable containing fiber helps to provide sustained energy and encourage digestion.

Healthy Fats: The introduction of healthy fats from nuts, seeds, and avocados also falls within the scope of the promotion of heart health and overall well-being.

Fruits and Vegetables Variety: It is rich in vitamins, minerals and antioxidants that the diversity of fruits and vegetables provides.

Balanced Snacking: The snack options revolve around nutrient-dense foods that provide the needed energy and nutrients between various meals.

Culinary Diversity: Various types of flavors and cooking cultures are shown in the meal plans, which is a clear indication that the air fryer can deliver delicious as well as healthy meals.

Well-Rounded Meals: The nutrition support packages are designed in carefully to have balanced macronutrients and varied micronutrients, thus creating an encompassing attitude towards the issue of nutrition.

11. Troubleshooting and FAQs

11.1 Common Air Fryer Issues

In this section, we are going to address common issues like unbalanced cooking results, food not crispy enough, the air fryer shutting down without any reason or smoking. Also, we will cover the topics of food sticking to the basket, strange smells and overheating of an outer surface. This is precisely the objective of this section to give practical resolutions to these urban challenges, enabling users to have a peaceful time doing their cooking using an air fryer. Each problem will be solved using simple, practical measures that will improve the overall use of the air fryer in a satisfying manner.

Uneven Cooking: To make sure cooking is well-balanced, do not over-crowd the basket. Lay food in a single layer and shake or turn halfway through cooking. This ensures that hot air circulates uniformly around each of the pieces.

Food Not Getting Crispy: To make the food crispier, it is advisable to either use a spray or brush, by brushing oil on the surfaces of the food just before placing it in the oven. Additionally, the preheating of the Air Fryer in two or three minutes can improve texture. The essential things are cooking at the required temperature and not putting much food in the basket.

Air Fryer Turning Off Unexpectedly: In case the air fryer stops working while cooking, make sure it is not overheated. Ensure that it is placed on a surface that can withstand high temperatures and should be kept away from the wall or other devices. In addition, air vents should be inspected and cleaned at regular intervals.

Smoke Production: In order to minimize such smoke, especially when cooking fatty foods, you should put some water or bread at the bottom of the drawer so that they will absorb dripping fats. Make sure the appliance is clean to avoid production of smoke due to residue when heated.

Food Sticking to the Basket: Despite having non-stick baskets, some types of food may still stick. This can be prevented with the use of parchment paper or by adding a slight amount of oil to the basket before placing your food. Take note that you should not use metal spoons or ladles because these will ruin the nonstick coating.

Unusual Odors: When buying new appliances, there may be an odor at first. The smell can be removed by running the air fryer empty for a few minutes before the first use. This will also help in reducing the accumulation of odors from any food remains.

Outer Surface Getting Too Hot: Make sure to have enough clearance space around the air fryer for heat release. Do not put it under the cabinets or nearby other sensitive subjects to heat.

Using these simple tips, you will be able to address most of the common problems and make your air frying fun and successful.

11.2 Maintenance and Cleaning Tips

Taking care of your air fryer, and cleaning it, is not something you do because you have to; that's a practice meant to guarantee the durability and productivity of this hi-tech kitchen tool.

Initial Cooling: After cooking, it is important to allow the air fryer to cool. This eliminates any risks of accidents and simplifies the process of cleaning.

Cleaning Removable Parts: The basket and tray which are often removable ought to be cleaned between the uses. If a dishwasher is safe to use, they can be put into it. In cases where that is not possible, hand washing using warm water and mild detergent also works. Take care when using material that is not sticky to avoid destroying it.

Attending to the Heating Element: With time, the heating element can collect grease or food particles. When it's cool, use a soft bristle broom or cloth to remove any dirt left on the coal.

Exterior Maintenance: Wipe the outside of the air fryer using a clean, damp cloth. Do not use any abrasive cleaning products or scourers that would mar the finish.

Air Intake Vents: Make sure the air intake vents are checked periodically. When any blockage is formed, then it can compromise the efficiency of an air fryer. Clean the vents carefully so that there are no blockages when air circulates.

Interior Cleaning: To clean the inside, you should wipe with a wet cloth. Make sure water does not access the electric parts.

Removing Tough Residues: For stubborn stains, submerge the basket or tray in a bath of hot soapy water. Scrub with materials that do not abrasive.

Odor Management: In order to get rid of the persistent odors, apply a cleaning paste made from baking soda and water on the basket.

Proper Storage: Keep the air fryer safely in a dry and clean place. It should be covered to avoid dust.

Routine Check-Ups: Check your air fryer occasionally for any damage; especially the electrical cord and plug.

Avoid Overfilling: Avoid filling the basket too much to prevent buildup of residue and for even cooking.

Use of Accessories: In the case of foil or parchment paper, make sure that they do not involve the entire basket so that there is proper airflow.

If you embrace these maintenance and cleaning hacks in your schedule, the air fryer will continue to be a productive part of your kitchen armory, maintaining its effectiveness and cleanliness.

13. Conclusion

This cookbook is just another sign of the transformative path that the people go through in their attempt to discover new cooking styles and embrace healthier lifestyles. Every recipe created in the confines of these pages embodies something more than a simple direction; they embody a promise to live better. The air fryer, an uncomplicated yet groundbreaking invention in the world of kitchen appliances, has been our loyal friend and guide through countless cooking terrains. Starting from crispy hors d'oeuvres and moving to delicious entrees and sweet desserts, we have come a long way in terms of flavors and textures that defy traditional cooking methods.

This air fryer journey has so much been a voyage of revelation – about nourishment, regarding wellbeing and about the delight in cooking. It's been a journey of forgetting and learning anew – that oil reduction does not equal taste, and 'fried' is synonymous with 'healthy'. It has created a universe in which cooking is faster, cleaner and more sustainable but still generates meals that are at least as tasty if not better.

In addition, this book has been designed to give you – the home cook – the means and confidence to be creative. These recipes we have given here are only the beginning of your cooking journey. The fact that the air fryer is a gadget of unlimited possibilities, means you can play with these recipes, tweaking them here and there to turn out your own unique creations. The variations are endless, whether you want the spices to fit your taste buds, change them for dietary reasons or create brand new recipes.

Let your air fryer continue to encourage you on the type of choices that are healthy for you and the taste buds as well as the planet. Take advantage of being able to cook oils less, have less wasted energy and a cleaner workspace. Consider each and every meal as an opportunity to feast on good health and flavor. The End of this book is not the end of the journey in Our Mutual Friend, it is just its beginning. Therefore, your air fryer which is a representation of contemporary and healthy cooking actually represents the world of culinary that has remained hidden to be explored.

So, continue discovering more, continue preparing more and better meals, and most importantly, keep relishing every bite of air fried foods that you make. So there are too many, many more dinners when joy fills your face and warmth fills your heart.

Printed in Great Britain
by Amazon